D1291838

# EUROPEAN POLITICAL FACTS
## 1789–1848

# EUROPEAN
# POLITICAL FACTS
# 1789–1848

Chris Cook and John Paxton

*First published 1981 by*
**THE MACMILLAN PRESS LTD**
*London and Basingstoke*
*Companies and representatives*
*throughout*
*the world*

*Printed in Hong Kong*

British Library Cataloguing in Publication Data

Cook, Chris
European political facts, 1789–1848
1. Europe – Social conditions
2. Europe – History – 1789–1815
3. Europe – History – 1815–1848
I. Title    II. Paxton, John
309.1′4′027        HN373

ISBN 0–333–21697–0

# CONTENTS

CONTENTS

# PREFACE

This is the third volume to appear in the *European Political Facts* series published by Macmillan. Hence this book has been designed to be a companion to the existing *European Political Facts 1848–1918* and *European Political Facts 1918–1973*. As with those volumes, the editors have aimed to gather together, in one volume, as many of the important political facts as possible for one of the most crucial and formative periods of modern history. Once again, all the countries of Europe have been included, from the Iberian kingdoms in the west to the Tsarist and Ottoman empires of the east.

Inevitably, for a period as far back as 1789 to 1848, reliable sources become ever more scarce. Dates are often difficult to give with absolute precision. Reliable economic or social statistics are even more difficult to find. As more and more doctoral research is completed, some of these gaps will perhaps be filled. The editors would like to be informed of error or inconsistency so that these may be taken into account in planning future editions of this book. Suggestions for additional chapters will also be welcome.

Our thanks for help and research in the preparation of this volume go to Stephen Brooks and Sheila Fairfield. For secretarial help, we are indebted once again to Jean Ali and Penny White. The late Anthony Bax provided much of the material on religion. It is a cause of sadness to both editors that they could not have presented this book to him.

*London and Bruton*  Chris Cook
*February 1980*  John Paxton

# 1 THE ERA OF REVOLUTION

## CHRONOLOGY OF PRINCIPAL EVENTS DURING THE FRENCH REVOLUTION, 1789–95

| | |
|---|---|
| 5 May 89 | States-General opened. |
| 17 June 89 | Title of 'The National Assembly' assumed by the Third Estate. |
| 20 June 89 | Tennis Court Oath. |
| 27 June 89 | Clergy and nobility ordered by the King to join the Commons. |
| 11 July 89 | Dismissal of Necker. |
| 14 July 89 | Fall of the Bastille. |
| 16 July 89 | Necker recalled. |
| 22 July 89 | Fouillon and Berthier murdered. |
| Aug 89 | Beginning of 'The Great Fear'. |
| 4–11 Aug 89 | Decrees abolishing feudal privileges. |
| 26 Aug 89 | Declaration of Rights. |
| 11 Sep 89 | Suspensive veto for the King accepted by the Assembly. |
| 5–6 Oct 89 | March of the women to Versailles; return of Louis XVI to Paris. |
| 19 Oct 89 | National Assembly meets. |
| 31 Oct 89 | Decree establishing uniform tariff throughout France. |
| 2 Nov 89 | Nationalization of the property of the Church. |
| 12 Dec 89 | First issue of *assignats*. |
| 14–22 Dec 89 | Decrees reorganized system of local government. |
| 21 May 90 | Paris reorganized into 'Sections'. |
| 22 May 90 | Wars of conquest renounced. |
| 19 Jun 90 | Abolition of the nobility. |
| 12 July 90 | Civil Constitution of the Clergy. |
| 14 July 90 | First *Fête de la Fédération*. |
| 27 Nov 90 | Decree enforcing the clerical oath. |
| 2 Apr 91 | Death of Mirabeau. |

| | |
|---|---|
| 13 Apr 91 | Civil Constitution condemned by Papal Bull *Caritas*. |
| 16 May 91 | 'Self-Denying Ordinance' passed. |
| 14 Jun 91 | *Loi Chapelier*. |
| 20 Jun 91 | Louis XVI's flight to Varennes. |
| 17 July 91 | Massacre of the *Champ de Mars*. |
| 27 Aug 91 | Declaration of Pilnitz. |
| 14 Sep 91 | Constitution accepted by the King. |
| 30 Sep 91 | Dissolution of National Assembly. |
| 1 Oct 91 | First meeting of Legislative Assembly. |
| 9 Nov 91 | Decree against *émigrés*. |
| 12 Nov 91 | King vetoes decree against *émigrés*. |
| 29 Nov 91 | Decree against non-juring priests. |
| 19 Dec 91 | King vetoes decree against non-juring priests. |
| 10 Mar 92 | 'Patriot Ministry' formed by Dumouriez. |
| 20 Apr 92 | War declared on Austria. |
| 27 May 92 | Decree against non-juring priests. |
| 13 June 92 | 'Patriot' ministers dismissed. |
| 19 Jun 92 | Decree against non-juring priests vetoed. |
| 20 Jun 92 | First invasion of the Tuileries. |
| 29 Jun 92 | Attempt by Lafayette to close Jacobin Club. |
| 22 July 92 | Proclamation '*La Patrie en danger*'. |
| 28 July 92 | Brunswick Manifesto reaches Paris. |
| 30 July 92 | Marseillais reach Paris. |
| 3 Aug 92 | Petition of the Sections demands deposition of the King. |
| 10 Aug 92 | Revolution of 10 August; suspension of the King; reinstatement of 'patriot' ministers. |
| 19 Aug 92 | Prussian Army crosses frontier. |
| 20 Aug 92 | Longwy fortress falls. |
| 2 Sep 92 | Fall of Verdun. |
| 2–6 Sep 92 | 'September Massacres'. |
| 20 Sep 92 | Prussian forces in retreat after Battle of Valmy. |
| 21 Sep 92 | First Session of Convention; monarchy abolished; beginning of Year I. |
| 24 Sep 92 | Power of Paris attacked by the Brissotins. |
| 10 Oct 92 | Jacobin Club expels Brissot. |
| 11 Oct 92 | Formation of Constitutional Committee. |
| 19 Oct 92 | Sections protest against attacks on Paris. |
| 29 Oct 92 | Brissotins' second attack on the capital. |
| 5 Nov 92 | Robespierre defends Paris and the Montagnards. |
| 6 Nov 92 | Battle of Jemappes; French invade Belgium. |
| 19 Nov 92 | French offer aid to all peoples striving to recover their liberty. |

| | |
|---|---|
| 3 Dec 92 | Convention decides to try the King. |
| 11 Dec 92 | Interrogation of Louis XVI by Convention. |
| 27 Dec 92 | Buzot and Salle call for a referendum on King's fate. |
| 14–17 Jan 93 | Convention votes on King's position. |
| 21 Jan 93 | Execution of Louis XVI. |
| 22 Jan 93 | Resignation of Roland. |
| 1 Feb 93 | Declaration of war on England. |
| 15 Feb 93 | Condorçet's constitutional proposals. |
| 25 Feb 93 | Food rioting in Paris. |
| 1–7 Mar 93 | Revolt against French in Belgium. |
| 7 Mar 93 | Declaration of war against Spain. |
| 10 Mar 93 | Creation of the Revolutionary Tribunal. |
| 16 Mar 93 | Beginning of revolt in the Vendée. |
| 18 Mar 93 | Battle of Neerwinden; Dumouriez evacuates the Netherlands. |
| 21 Mar 93 | Creation of local revolutionary committees. |
| 5 Apr 93 | Defection of Dumouriez. |
| 6 Apr 93 | Creation of the Committee of Public Safety. |
| 13 Apr 93 | Impeachment of Marat. |
| 4 May 93 | First 'Maximum' decreed. |
| 10 May 93 | Convention moves to the Tuileries. |
| 20 May 93 | Commission of Twelve appointed to investigate plots against Convention of Paris. |
| 30 May 93 | Conservative coup in Lyons. |
| 31 May 93 | Unsuccessful rising in Paris. |
| 2 June 93 | Revolution; Convention purged by Montagnards and Sections of Paris; arrest of Brissot and others. |
| 6–19 June 93 | Protest of the 75. |
| 9 June 93 | Vendéens take Saumur. |
| 24 June 93 | Convention accepts Constitution of 1793. |
| 10 July 93 | Fall of fortress of Condé; Danton no longer a member of Committee of Public Safety. |
| 13 July 93 | Murder of Marat. |
| 23 July 93 | Fall of fortress of Mayence. |
| 27 July 93 | Robespierre enters Committee of Public Safety. |
| 28 July 93 | Fall of fortress of Valenciennes. Eighteen Brissotin deputies outlawed. |
| 10 Aug 93 | Festival of Unity in honour of 1793 Constitution. |
| 23 Aug 93 | *Levée en masse* declared. |
| 27 Aug 93 | Surrender of Toulon to British. |
| 5 Sep 93 | Hébertist rising in Paris; beginning of the Terror. |

| | |
|---|---|
| 8 Sep 93 | Battle of Hondschoote; British forced to retire from Dunkirk. |
| 11 Sep 93 | Fall of fortress of Lequesnoy. |
| 17 Sep 93 | Law of Suspects declared. |
| 22 Sep 93 | Beginning of Year II. |
| 29 Sep 93 | General 'Maximum' in restraint of prices and wages. |
| 3 Oct 93 | Impeachment of Brissot and 44 other deputies. |
| 5 Oct 93 | Revolutionary calendar established. |
| 10 Oct 93 | Decree sanctioning revolutionary government for duration of the war. |
| 16 Oct 93 | Battle of Wattignies relieves Maubeuge; execution of Marie-Antoinette. |
| 17 Oct 93 | Vendéens defeated by Cholet. |
| 22 Oct 93 | Creation of Central Food Commission. |
| 24–30 Oct 93 | Trial of Brissot and 20 other deputies. |
| 31 Oct 93 | Execution of the Brissotins. |
| 10 Nov 93 | Festival of Reason in Notre Dame. |
| 21 Nov 93 | Robespierre denounces atheism as aristocratic. |
| 22 Nov 93 | Closure of churches in Paris. |
| 4 Dec 93 | Law of the Revolutionary Government; massacres at Lyons. |
| 5 Dec 93 | First issue of *Vieux Cordelier* initiates campaign against Hébetists. |
| 15 Dec 93 | Third issue of *Vieux Cordelier* challenges the Terror. |
| 19 Dec 93 | British evacuate Toulon. |
| 23 Dec 93 | Defeat of Vendéens at Savenay. |
| 25 Dec 93 | Robespierre's speech on principles of revolutionary government. |
| 26 Dec 93 | Recapture of Landau by French. |
| 30 Dec 93 | Festival of Victory. |
| 12 Jan 94 | Arrest of Fabre d'Eglantine. |
| 5 Feb 94 | Robespierre speaks on principles of political morality. |
| 21 Feb 94 | Revision of policy of price controls. |
| 26 Feb–3 Mar 94 | Laws of the Ventôse. |
| 4 Mar 94 | Attempted insurrection at Cordeliers Club. |
| 14 Mar 94 | Arrest of the Hébertists. |
| 24 Mar 94 | Execution of the Hébertists. |
| 30 Mar 94 | Arrest of Danton. |
| 5 Apr 94 | Execution of Dantonists. |
| 27 Apr 94 | Police Law of 27 Germinal. |
| 7 May 94 | Robespierre introduces worship of the Supreme Being. |
| 18 May 94 | Battle of Tourcoing; rout of the British in Belgium. |

| | |
|---|---|
| 23–4 May 94 | Attempts to assassinate Robespierre. |
| 1 June 94 | Battle of Glorious 1st June, British naval victory. |
| 8 June 94 | Festival of the Supreme Being. |
| 26 June 94 | Battle of Fleurus; French reconquer Belgium. |
| 23 July 94 | Introduction of wage regulation in Paris. |
| 27 July 94 | Proscription of Robespierrists. |
| 28 July 94 | Execution of Robespierre. |
| 30 July 94 | Reorganization of Committee of Public Safety. |
| 12 Nov 94 | Closure of Jacobin Club. |
| 24 Dec 94 | Abolition of the 'Maximum'. |
| 1 Apr 95 | Day of 12 Germinal. |
| 5 Apr 95 | Peace of Basle with Prussia. |
| 16 May 95 | Peace with Holland. |
| 20 May 95 | Day of 1st Prairial. |
| 8 June 95 | Death of Louis XVII. |
| 22 July 95 | Peace with Spain. |
| 22 Aug 95 | Constitution of Year III, and the two-thirds decree. |
| 5 Oct 95 | Revolt of 13 Vendémiaire. |
| 26 Oct 95 | Dissolution of the Convention; rule of the Directory. |

## CHRONOLOGY OF PRINCIPAL EVENTS UNDER NAPOLEON, 1796–1805

| | |
|---|---|
| 11 Mar 96 | Napoleon leaves Paris to take control in Italy. |
| 11–14 Apr 96 | Napoleon breaks through Austrian front to Italy. |
| 10 May 96 | Battle of Lodi; Napoleon crosses R. Adda. Arrest of Babeuf and the 'Equals' in Paris. |
| 20 June 96 | Moreau crosses Rhine into Germany. |
| 5 Aug 96 | French alliance with Spain at San Ildefonso. |
| 4 Sep 96 | Battle of Roverto, near Mantua. |
| 22 Sep 96 | Beginning of Year IV. |
| 15–18 Nov 96 | French victory at Battle of Arcola, near Mantua. |
| 14 Jan 97 | French victory at Rivoli. |
| 14 Feb 97 | British naval victory at Cape St Vincent. |
| 19 Feb 97 | Trial of Babeuvists begins at Vendôme. |
| 12 Apr 97 | Napoleon renews his offensive in Italy. |
| 18 Apr 97 | Napoleon agrees to Preliminaries of Peace at Leoben. |
| 27 May 97 | Conviction and execution of Babeuf at Vendôme. |
| 9 June 97 | Repeal of Law of 3 Brumaire. |
| 25 July 97 | Closure of all political clubs. |

| | |
|---|---|
| 4 Sep 97 | *Coup d'état* of 18 Fructidor. |
| 19 Sep 97 | Napoleon's letter of representative government. |
| 11 Oct 97 | British naval victory at Camperdown. |
| 18 Oct 97 | Peace of Campo Formio with Austria. |
| 22 Jan 98 | Purge of Dutch Convention. |
| 25 Feb 98 | Merlin de Douai becomes President of the Directory. |
| 11 May 98 | *Coup d'état* of 22 Floréal. |
| 16 May 98 | Treilhard becomes a Director. |
| 21 July 98 | Napoleon wins Battle of the Pyramids. |
| 31 July 98 | Nelson destroys French fleet at Battle of the Nile. |
| 5 Sep 98 | Jourdan's Conscription Law. |
| 9 Sep 98 | Turkey declares war on France. |
| Nov 98 | Renewal of war in Italy. |
| 15 Dec 98 | French forces re-occupy Rome. |
| 23–9 Dec 98 | Russia allies with Turkey and Britain. |
| 23 Jan 99 | Napoleon advances into Syria. |
| 12 Mar 99 | Renewal of war against Austria. |
| 5 Apr 99 | Partial elections of Year VII; substantial Jacobin gains. |
| 18 June 99 | 30 Prairial VII; fall of Lepeaux and Merlin de Douai. |
| 27 June 99 | Emergency legislation: forced loan, *levée en masse*. |
| 14 July 99 | Sieyès' anti-Jacobin speech. |
| 25 July 99 | Napoleon defeats Turks at Aboukir. |
| 22 Aug 99 | Napoleon leaves Egypt for France. |
| 27 Aug 99 | Anglo-Russian invasion of Holland begins. |
| 23 Sep 99 | Beginning of Year VIII. |
| 25–7 Sep 99 | Masséna victorious at Second Battle of Zurich. |
| 16 Oct 99 | Napoleon arrives in Paris. |
| 9–10 Nov 99 | *Coup d'état* of 18–19 Brumaire. |
| 25 Dec 99 | Constitution of Year VIII in effect. |
| 26 Dec 99 | Emancipation of relatives of *émigrés*. |
| 13 Jan 1800 | Establishment of Bank of France. |
| 17 Feb 00 | Law of 28 Pluviôse establishes prefectorial system. |
| 19 Feb 00 | Napoleon moves to the Tuileries. |
| 18 Mar 00 | Law of 27 Ventôse establishes new judicial system. |
| 14 June 00 | Battle of Marengo. |
| 23 Sep 00 | Beginning of the Year IX. Malta falls to the British. |
| 19 Nov 00 | Moreau resumes hostilities against Austria. |
| 3 Dec 00 | Battle of Hohenlinden. |
| 16 Dec 00 | Formation of the Armed Neutrality against Britain. |
| 24 Dec 00 | Crime of 3 Nivôse: attempted assassination of Napoleon. |
| 5 Jan 01 | Proscription of Jacobins approved by Senate. |
| 9 Jan 01 | Treaty of Lunéville with Austria. |

| | |
|---|---|
| 2 April 01 | Battle of Copenhagen; British victory and disruption of Armed Neutrality. |
| 16 July 01 | Concordat of 1801 between France and the Papacy. |
| 23 Sep 01 | Beginning of Year X. |
| 1 Oct 01 | Preliminary Peace of London with Britain. |
| 8 Oct 01 | Peace between France and Russia. |
| 11 Jan 02 | Napoleon goes to Lyons to become President of Italian Republic. |
| 27 Mar 02 | Treaty of Amiens concluded with Britain. |
| 1 Apr 02 | Purge of Tribunate and Legislative Body by Senate. |
| 18 Apr 02 | Promulgation of the Concordat: Easter Mass at Notre Dame. |
| 12 May 02 | Assemblies approve the Life Consulate. |
| 19 May 02 | Establishment of the Legion of Honour. |
| 4 Aug 02 | Constitution of the Year X; Napoleon becomes Consul for life. |
| 23 Sep 02 | Beginning of Year XI. |
| 19 Feb 03 | Act of Mediation for Switzerland. |
| 26 Apr 03 | Ultimatum to France from Britain. |
| 24 Sep 03 | Beginning of Year XII; last festival of the Republic. |
| 21 Mar 04 | Execution of d'Enghien; promulgation of Civil Code. |
| 18 May 04 | Constitution of Year XII; Napoleon made Emperor. |
| 24 June 04 | Moreau exiled. |
| 28 June 04 | Cadoudal executed. |
| 2 Dec 04 | Napoleon's coronation in Notre Dame. |

# GLOSSARY OF PEOPLE AND TERMS OF THE REVOLUTION

*Ancien régime.* Literally, the 'old order'. It describes the social and political order existing throughout Europe at the time of the Revolution. With a monarch at the head, societies could be divided into 3 'estates'. The first estate consisted of the ruling aristocracy, the second the senior prelates and clergy, together with the mercantile and administrative classes, and the third contained the many poor farm and town workers. The *ancien régime* in France ended with the Revolution.

*Bourgeois.* Translated this meant 'pertaining to the town'. Originally, the term referred simply to those who lived in towns and were prosperous enough to pay municipal taxes. However, with industrialization and the growth of

7

towns, it came to mean the citizen class, and included merchants, businessmen, professional people and men with a concern of their own. Even in the eighteenth century the word also implied a certain attitude, as well as a social and economic position.

*Cahiers de doléances.* Translated this means 'lists of grievances'. These were lists of complaints drawn up by each of the orders or estates for presentation at the meeting of the States-General.

*Citoyen, Citoyenne* (fem.). Both meaning 'citizen', a title signifying loyalty to the Republican or Revolutionary cause. Many who refused to be called by the title were executed in the course of the Revolution.

*Committee of General Security.* The Committee worked alongside the Committee of Public Safety, and was the chief instrument of the secret police. During 1793–4 all effective political power was concentrated in these two bodies, although the Committee of General Security gradually lost influence to the Committee of Public Safety.

*Committee of Public Safety.* Originally called the Committee of General defence, the Committee acted as the executive body of the Revolutionary Tribunal. Re-organized in April 1793 and renamed by Danton, it was composed of 9 members, of whom Danton soon established himself as the most effective. He ousted the Girondins, replacing them with his own associates. The Committee concentrated power in the hands of a few able men for the first time during the Revolution. When Robespierre replaced Danton, he increased the Committee's powers and functions. Foreign policy and the administration of France fell under its control. Its repressive measures, which ignored established legal safeguards, resulted in the Reign of Terror. After Robespierre fell from power, the Committee was run by more moderate men.

*The Commune.* The smallest of the Paris administrative districts. After the storming of the Tuileries in August 1792, its members, together with the Jacobins, established a provisional ministry under the Legislative Assembly. After the execution of Louis XVI, the Commune re-organized itself on the basis of manhood suffrage. The 20 who were so elected then sat in the National Convention under the leadership of Hébert and Chaumette. Later the Commune dominated Robespierre and had the moderate Girondins removed. In its turn, however, it was overcome by the powerful Montagne Committees (of Public Safety and General Security), and its leaders were guillotined in March 1794. The Commune's influence thenceforth dwindled.

*Condorçet.* Jean Antoine, Marquis de Caritat, 1743–94. A liberal aristocrat who became a brilliant mathematician and philosopher. During the Revolution he sat in the Legislative Assembly, becoming its President in 1792. He was a deputy in the National Convention, and in 1793 sided with the Girondins. As the principal author of the constitutional proposals condemned by the Montagnards he was forced into hiding. He then wrote his famous *Esquisse d'un tableau historique des progrès de l'esprit humain*, a work which traces 9 epochs of human development, predicting the perfectability of man in the tenth. After being forced from Paris in March 1794, he was arrested and committed suicide.

*Contrôleur Général des finances.* The most important position in Louis XVI's government. Its holder was in command of the country's finances as well as its agriculture, trade, industry and communications. Turgot, and then the dishonest Necker, both held the post before the Revolution, and it was largely their respective successes and failures that led to its outbreak. The position was the French equivalent of the English office of Prime Minister.

*Corvée.* The compulsory labour demanded of the *roturiers* of the third estate by the local lord. It was defended on the grounds that the work was limited and consisted only of casual farm labour. The frequent commandeering, however, of animals, and implements by landlords at short notice resulted in inconvenience and grievances. An alternative to direct taxation, the *corvée* was the most hard-felt of the peasants' burdens.

*Danton.* George Jacques, 1759–94. One of the leaders of the Revolutionary Left, Danton was a powerful speaker who came to dominate the Jacobin Club and the National Convention. Earlier he had been associated with the Tuileries Riots and the September Massacres of 1792. His position was usurped by Robespierre, who had him imprisoned and then guillotined.

*Dixième. Dîme.* Tenth. The tithe or tenth part of the harvest demanded as of right by the Church from farmers and peasantry, and for which no payment was made. The practice dated back to medieval times.

*Émigrés.* Literally 'emigrants', but came to mean those members of the French nobility who fled the country to escape the Revolution. The first group, headed by the Comte d'Artois, left France immediately after the fall of the Bastille in July 1789. When the Terror ended, and when Louis XVIII was established on the throne after Napoleon's exile, many émigrés returned to France. They were variously known as Les Chouans, Les Vendéens or the Paris Royalists.

9

*États Généraux* (States-General). The French National Assembly. It included representatives from each state or province in the country. These were classed as either *pays d'état* or *pays d'election*. Regular sessions were ended in 1614. The membership was heavily biased in favour of the aristocracy, which removed any peasant grievances from its agenda. It was after a 2-month session in 1789 of the States-General that the third estate proclaimed itself the National Assembly (*q.v.*).

*Fouché,* Joseph, Duc d'Otrante, 1759–1820. The son of a merchant from Nantes, Fouché was educated by the Oratorians and took minor orders. In 1789 he became their principal in his home town. After renouncing his orders, he became a Jacobin and was elected in 1792 as a deputy to the Convention. He encouraged attacks on Christianity and was associated with the Thermidor plot to overthrow Robespierre. Impeached in 1795, he lived in poverty until he was entrusted with diplomatic missions in 1797. In 1799 he became chief of police, and as such worked for Napoleon, rising to be Governor of the Illyrian Provinces. Returning to Paris after the fall of the Empire, he was banished in 1816 and died a naturalized Austrian.

*Girondins.* A middle-class Republican party founded in 1791 and so named because many of its members came from the *département* of the Gironde in Guyenne, south-west France. They were led by Jacques Brissot, Vergniaud, Gaudet and Pétion, and were strong advocates of the abolition of the monarchy. In 1792 they formed a ministry under the Legislative Assembly pursuing aggressive foreign and anti-clerical policies. They were gradually forced to the right to oppose the fanaticism of the Montagne group. By October 1793 almost all the Girondins had been either imprisoned or executed. The survivors formed the Council of Five Hundred under the Directory between 1795 and 1799.

*Intendant.* The *Intendants* were the main instruments of Louis XVI's government. There was one *Intendant* to every *département*, and he was responsible for the administration, both social and economic, of the area. They were carefully selected men of ability and sound training, and in theory possessed great powers. In reality their ability to act was hampered by the entrenched power and privileges of the nobility. *Intendants* were abolished by the Revolution, although Napoleon later copied this system of adminis-tration for the Empire, re-naming his officials 'prefects'.

*Jacobins.* The members of a political club founded in 1789, and named after its first meeting place in the Rue St Jacques. Originally moderately demo-cratic, the club later became more radical when its leadership fell into the hands of Robespierre, Danton and Murat. The Jacobins became the driving force of the Revolution, dominating the Committee of Public Safety, and establishing the Reign of Terror. Branches of the club were opened throughout the country. The Jacobins fell from power with the death of Robespierre, but remained a vocal force under the Directory.

*Lafayette*, Marie Joseph, Marquis de, 1757–1834. Lafayette rose to prominence by organizing and leading a French force to fight with the Americans for their independence. A moderate Jacobin, he became a member of the Legislative Assembly, but broke with the club to form a group called the 'Feuillants'. He was largely responsible for the adoption of the tricolour as the flag for the National Guard in 1789. When France became involved in war with Austria in 1792, Lafayette was given command of a third of her armies, but after being defeated he was banished and fled to Flanders. Imprisoned by the Austrians at Olmütz until 1796, he returned to France in 1799 but took no further part in politics.

*Legislative Assembly.* Formed in 1791, the Legislative Assembly reflected the growing Republican spirit of the country. It consisted of a moderate middle-class group, the Plain, together with the Girondins who formed a moderate Left. The rule of the mob and the rise of the Jacobins, following the storming of the Tuileries and the September Massacres of 1792, rendered its authority ineffectual. It was superseded by the National Convention.

*Lettre de Cachet.* An order signed by the King under which anyone could be arrested and held without trial indefinitely without any reason given. The practice corresponded with the suspension of *habeas corpus* in England, which usually occurred only in wartime. It was one of the more repressive features of the *ancien régime*.

*Marat*, Jean Paul, 1744–93. Marat was one of the most vicious and extreme of the Revolutionary leaders. His paper *L'Ami du Peuple*, published in 1789, openly called for mob violence; its ferocious articles were partly responsible for the fall of the monarchy in 1792. Marat was the leader of the extreme group called the 'Cordeliers', and was later elected to the National Convention. Arrested and tried by the Girondins, he escaped execution and joined Robespierre in plotting the overthrow of the Girondins. He was assassinated by Charlotte Corday, who was horrified by the excesses of the Revolution. She stabbed him in July 1793 while he was taking a bath, and was guillotined 4 days later.

*Métayage.* The system of agriculture called 'share cropping' (a *métayer* is a

11

farmer). Under the system peasants either owned or rented strips of land in a field and worked their own section. Clearly it did not permit the introduction of new methods and meant that some good land was poorly farmed. It was another inheritance from the Middle Ages.

*Mirabeau*, Honoré, Comte de, 1749–91. Throughout the Revolution Mirabeau exercised a moderating influence. He was a third-estate deputy for Aix and Marseilles, and from June 1789 was a leading figure in the National Assembly. A fine speaker and a strong personality, he favoured a constitutional monarchy.

*Montagne*. An extreme political party in the Legislative Assembly and National Convention. The word literally means 'a mountain', and the party was given this name because the seats it occupied in the Legislative Assembly were on the highest part of the left-hand side. Composed of two groups, the Cordeliers and the Jacobins, the Montagne was the most revolutionary of the parties.

*National or Constituent Assembly*, 1789–91. The first Revolutionary government, most of whose members were from the middle or upper middle class. The first spokesmen were Mirabeau and Sieyès, who wanted a constitutional monarchy with restricted powers. A minority group were the future leaders of the Girondins, Jacobins and Cordeliers. True to its original oath, the Assembly dissolved itself when Louis XVI accepted the revised version of its Constitution of 1790.

*The National Convention*, 1791–5. The most long-lasting of the 3 Revolutionary assemblies. It was more democratic than its predecessor and consisted of 749 members elected by male suffrage, all of whom were Republicans. The Girondins developed as the party of the Right, while Robespierre and his Jacobins grew in strength on the Left and eventually came to dominate the Convention. During the period of its control Louis XVI and Marie Antoinette were guillotined, and the Reign of Terror was instituted. In October 1795, after the worst of the excesses, the Convention dissolved itself and was succeeded by the Directory.

*Necker*, Jacques, 1732–1804. Of Swiss birth, Necker succeeded Turgot as *Contrôleur Général* in 1776, remaining in power for another 5 years. His success was based on a falsification of the nation's economic situation: the deficit was understated, and large loans were raised to tide the country over for short periods, resulting in bankruptcy. In spite of this, confidence in Necker's ability continued, and he was summoned to the States-General in May 1789.

However his suggestions were not adopted, and his dismissal led to the storming of the Bastille. He finally gave up public life in 1790 and retired to his estate in Switzerland.

*Orders or Estates.* Society under the *ancien régime* was divided into 3 groups, whose rights, privileges and obligations were defined by law. These were the first, second and third estates. These restrictions and duties were not simply legal matters but affected people's daily lives. Peasants were forced to work on the lord's land, to give him a portion of their crops and were not permitted to take any part in local or national government. Estates were defined according to economic, social and political considerations.

*Parlements.* The provincial assemblies which represented the various *pays* throughout France. De Tocqueville, in his study *The Ancien Régime and the French Revolution*, argued that only two *parlements* were properly representative and independent, those of Brittany and the Languedoc. Otherwise these bodies were controlled by the Crown. Often the King's representative, the *Intendant*, carried out their traditional functions.

*Pays d'état.* Navarre, Brittany, Béarn and the Languedoc were the *pays d'état*, and enjoyed more administrative and political freedom than the *pays d'election*. In the first, the 3 estates sat to determine the level of taxation and its collection; in the others, this was done directly by the Crown. This distinction, despite royal pressure, was maintained until the Revolution.

*Philosophes.* The name given to a group of great 18th-century French thinkers. They included mathematicians, logicians, philosophers, jurists and constitutional writers, of whom the best known were Voltaire, Montesquieu, Diderot and Rousseau. They believed that they had a role to play in moulding public opinion, and so were responsible for publicizing and developing revolutionary ideas. They fostered a spirit of inquiry and suggested alternative systems of government and different views of human nature. Diderot's *Encyclopaedia* was the principal vehicle for their criticism of established views.

*Physiocrats.* A group of *philosophes* who concerned themselves with economic problems. They included Quesnay, their founder, Mirabeau and Gournay. They were concerned with problems of taxation, the development of trade, and the organization of labour on the land; accordingly they were often critical of the existing feudal arrangements.

*Republican Calendar.* The names for the Republican Calendar were invented by Fabre d'Eglantine and arranged in order by Gilbert Romme. Year I began with the autumnal equinox of 1793, and the system continued to operate until January 1806. The months were arranged as follows: Vendémiaire (grape harvest), Brumaire (mist), Frimaire (frosts), Nivôse (snows), Pluviôse (rains), Ventôse (winds), Germinal (sowing), Floréal (blossoms), Prairial (hay-making), Messidor (harvesting), Thermidor (heat), Fructidor (fruit-picking).

*Robespierre*, Maximilien de, 1758–94. A lawyer who sat in the Legislative Assembly, Robespierre became a leader of the Jacobin Club in 1791. Nicknamed the 'Incorruptible Patriot', he soon gained a reputation for violence and cruelty. He gained overwhelming power in the Committee for Public Safety and deposed his rivals, Hébert and Danton; he was responsible for the Reign of Terror. In 1794 he was arrested and guillotined.

*Sans-culottes*. Literally, 'those without breeches'. Breeches were the mark of the aristocracy and upper members of the third estate, who were described as *culottes dorées*, 'fancy breeches'. Hence the masses who formed the revolutionary mobs were called the *sans-culottes*, as they wore simple trousers. Their views were most consistently represented in the period of the Committees of 1793.

*Seigneurie*. Under the *ancien régime, seigneurie* consisted of two types of property-holding. First, there was *domaine proche* where the lord owned the land and let it out to tenant farmers. Secondly, there was *domaine utile*, which was land wholly cultivated by peasant farmers who had to render feudal dues to the lord for their use of the soil.

*Taille*. A tax which fell most heavily on the peasants. It was levied on their possessions and on the land they cultivated, but did not own. Because of various exemptions, members of the first and second estates were not affected by it.

*Thermidoreans*. The politicians who finally broke the power of Robespierre and the Jacobins. They arrested him and had him executed, and thereby ended the Reign of Terror. They were moderate leaders opposed to the violence, motivated largely by a desire to oust Robespierre.

*The Terror*. Lasting from 1793 to 1794, the Terror corresponded with Robespierre's period of leadership. Thousands who were opposed to his régime or who would not publicly offer their support were guillotined. The purge continued until Robespierre's own death, when public opinion, disgusted by the violence, compelled more moderate policies.

14

*Tu and Toi*. In French there are two ways of saying 'you'. *Vous*, the plural form, is for formal use, while *tu* is used to denote strong friendship. During the Revolution *tu* (emphatic, *toi*) was generally used in place of *vous* to demonstrate that the formality of the old order had gone. It suggested Republican solidarity and comradeship. Towards the end of the Terror the old form of *vous* returned, as *tu* was felt to detract from the dignity of the Revolutionary achievements.

*Turgot*; Anne Robert Jacques, 1727–81. *Contrôleur Général* from 1774 to 1776, Turgot was one of the few really able and far-sighted ministers appointed by Louis XVI. He did his utmost to cure France's bankruptcy without resorting to loans. He believed in changing the tax system to strike at the rich, relieve the peasantry, and to encourage industrial and commercial expansion. Opposition by the nobility to his policies, and a weak king, ensured that his political reign was a short one.

*Vingtième*. A tax introduced in 1749 by Machault d'Arounville, the *Contrôleur Général*. It was a general tax on all incomes at the rate of one-twentieth of their value. There were no exceptions, and it was designed to restore France's economic fortunes after the War of the Austrian Succession. The nobility, long accustomed to tax privileges, refused to pay, and were backed by the clergy. The King was not able to overcome this entrenched opposition, and the scheme was abandoned in December 1751.

*Voltaire*, François Marie Arouet, 1694–1778. One of the leading *philosophes*, now best known for his satirical novel *Candide*. His prodigious output of pamphlets, plays, tracts and over 12,000 letters was characterized by his disrespect for authority, established tradition and the Church. He suffered persecution and imprisonment, but in the end was able to retire to Paris.

# NAPOLEON BONAPARTE: CHRONOLOGY OF EARLY LIFE

| | |
|---|---|
| 15 Aug 69 | Napoleon Bonaparte born. |
| 15 Dec 78 | Leaves Corsica for France. |
| 1 Jan 79 | Together with his older brother, Guiseppe, enters religious school at Autun. |
| 15 May 79 | Enters cadet school at Brienne. |
| 30 Oct 84 | Enters École Militaire, Paris, as *cadet-gentilhomme*. |
| 24 Feb 85 | Death of Napoleon's father, Carlo Bonaparte. |

| | |
|---|---|
| 1 Sep 85 | Passes out of École Militaire as *lieutenant en second d'artillerie*. |
| 30 Oct 85 | Leaves Paris to join La Fère Artillery Regiment at Valence-sur-Rhone. |
| 1 Sep 86 | Goes to Corsica on long furlough until June 1788. |
| June 88 | Rejoins his regiment at Auxonne, attached to School of Artillery. |
| 15 Sep 89 | Goes on leave to Corsica. |
| 14 July 90 | Paoli returns from exile to Corsica; Bonaparte adheres to him. |
| 10 Feb 91 | Returns from Corsica to regimental duty at Auxonne. |
| 1 Apr 91 | Promoted *premier lieutenant*. |

# THE NAPOLEONIC DYNASTY

### THE BONAPARTE FAMILY

Napoleon I (15 Aug 1769–5 May 1821). First Consul of the Republic, 9 Nov 1799. Consul for Life, 2 Aug 1802. Emperor of the French: proclaimed 18 May 1804; crowned 2 Dec 1804. King of Italy: proclaimed 18 Mar 1805; crowned 26 May 1805.

Napoleon II, Francis-Charles-Joseph (20 Mar 1811–22 July 1832). King of Rome, 1811. Duke of Reichstadt, 1817.

Bonaparte, Jérôme (19 Nov 1784–24 Jun 1860). Prince of France, 1804. King of Westphalia, 1807–13.

Bonaparte, Joseph (7 Jan 1768–28 Jul 1844). First Prince of the Blood, 1804. King of Naples, 1806. King of Spain, 1808–13.

Bonaparte, Louis (5 Sep 1778–25 July 1846). King of Holland, 1806–10.

Bonaparte, Lucien (21 May 1775–29 Jun 1840). Prince of Canino, 1807.

Beauharnais, Eugène de (3 Sep 1781–21 Feb 1824). Prince, 1805. Viceroy of Italy, 1806–14. Duke of Leuchtenberg, 1814.

Murat, Joachim (25 Mar 1767–13 Oct 1815). Grand Duke of Berg and Clèves. 1806. King of Naples, 1808–15. First served: 23 Feb 1787; Marshal, 19 May 1804.

*'Les Grandes Dames'*

Beauharnais, Josephine de (1763–1814). Empress, 1804–10.

Marie-Louise, of Austria (1791–1847). Empress, 1810–15.

Bonaparte, Caroline (1782–1839). Grand Duchess of Berg and Clèves, 1806. Queen of Naples, 1808.

Bonaparte, Élisa (1777–1820). Princess of Lucca. Grand Duchess of Tuscany, 1808.

Bonaparte, Marie-Letizia (1750–1836). *Madame Mère* and Dowager Empress, 1804.

Bonaparte, Pauline (1780–1825). Duchess of Guastalla and Princess Borghèse, 1803.

Beauharnais, Hortense de (1783–1837). Queen of Holland, 1806.

PRINCES OF THE EMPIRE

Bernadotte, Jean B. J. de (26 Jan 1763–8 Mar 1844). Prince of Ponte-Corvo, 1805. Crown Prince of Sweden, 1810. King of Sweden, 1818. Appointed Marshal of the Empire, 19 May 1804.

Berthier, Louis-Alexandre (20 Nov 1753–1 Jun 1815). Prince of Neuchâtel, 1806. Prince of Wagram, 1809. Appointed Marshal of the Empire, 19 May 1804.

Davout, Louis-Nicolas (10 May 1770–1 Jun 1823). Duke of Auerstadt, 1808. Prince of Eckmühl, 1809. Appointed Marshal of the Empire, 19 May 1804.

Masséna, André (6 May 1758–4 Apr 1817). Duke of Rivoli, 1808. Prince of Essling, 1810. Appointed Marshal of the Empire, 19 May 1804.

Ney, Michel (10 Jan 1769–7 Dec 1815). Duke of Elchingen, 1808. Prince of the Moskowa, 1813. Appointed Marshal of the Empire, 19 May 1804.

Poniatowski, Joseph A. (7 May 1763–19 Oct 1813). Polish prince. Appointed Marshal of the Empire, 18 Oct 1813.

Talleyrand-Périgord, Charles-Maurice de (12 Feb 1754–17 May 1838). Bishop of Autun, 1789. Prince of Benevento, 1806. Special posts: Minister of Foreign Affairs, 1797–1807; Grand Chamberlain of the Empire, 1804.

DUKES

Augereau, Charles-Pierre-François (21 Oct 1757–12 Jun 1816). Duke of Castiglione, 1808. Appointed Marshal of the Empire, 19 May 1804.

Bessières, Jean-Baptiste (6 Aug 1768–1 May 1813). Duke of Istria, 1809. Appointed Marshal of the Empire, 19 May 1804.

Cambacérès, Jean-Jacques (18 Oct 1753–8 Mar 1824). Duke of Parma, 1808. Special posts: Minister of Justice, 1799; Arch-Chancellor of the Empire, 1804; President of the Senate.

Caulaincourt, Armand-Augustin-Louis (9 Dec 1773–19 Feb 1827). Duke of Vicenza, 1808. Highest military rank: General of Division, 1805. Special posts: Grand Equerry, 1804; Foreign Minister, 1813.

Clarke, Henri-Jacques-Guillaume (17 Oct 1765–28 Oct 1818). Duke of Feltre, 1809. Highest military rank: General of Brigade, 1793 (later Marshal of France, 1816). Special posts: Diplomatic envoy; Minister of War, 1807–14.

Duroc, Géraud-Christophe-Michel (25 Oct 1772–23 May 1813). Duke of Frioul, 1808. Highest military rank: General of Division, 1803. Special posts: Grand Marshal (or Lord High Steward) of the Empire, 1804.

Fouché, Joseph (21 May 1759–25 Dec 1820). Duke of Otranto, 1808. Special posts: Diplomatic appointments and Minister of Police, 1804–10.

Gaudin, Martin-Michel-Charles (1756–1841). Duke of Gaèta, 1809. Special post: Minister of Finance, 1799–1814.

Junot, Andoche (25 Sep 1771–29 July 1813). Duke of Abrantès, 1808. Highest military rank: General of Division, 1803.

Kellermann, François-Étienne-Christophe (28 May 1735–13 Sep 1820). Duke of Valmy, 1808. Appointed Marshal of the Empire, 19 May, 1804.

Lannes, Jean (10 Apr 1759–31 May 1809). Duke of Montebello, 1808. Appointed Marshal of the Empire, 19 May 1804.

Lefebvre, François-Joseph (25 Oct 1755–14 Sep 1820). Duke of Danzig, 1807. Appointed Marshal of the Empire, 19 May 1804.

MacDonald, Étienne-Jacques-Joseph-Alexandre (17 Nov 1765–25 Sep 1840). Duke of Tarentum, 1809. Appointed Marshal of the Empire, 12 July 1809.

Maret, Hughes-Bernard (1763–1839). Duke of Bassano, 1809. Special posts: Diplomatic appointments; Minister of Foreign Affairs, 1811–13.

Marmont, Auguste-Frédéric-Louis-Viesse de (20 July 1774–3 Mar 1852). Duke of Ragusa, 1808. Marshal of the Empire, 12 July 1809.

Moncey (Jeannot de Moncey), Bon-Adrien (31 July 1754–20 Apr 1842). Duke of Conegliano, 1808. Appointed Marshal of the Empire, 19 May 1804.

Mortier, Adolphe-Édouard-Casimir-Joseph (13 Feb 1768–28 Jul 1835). Duke of Treviso, 1808. Appointed Marshal of the Empire, 19 May 1804.

Oudinot, Nicolas-Charles (25 Apr 1767–13 Sep 1847). Duke of Reggio, 1810. Appointed Marshal of the Empire, 12 July 1809.

Savary, Anne-Jean-Marie René (26 Apr 1774–2 Jun 1833). Duke of Rovigo, 1808. Highest military rank: General of Division, 1805. Special post: Minister of Police, 1810–14.

Soult, Nicalas-Jean de Dieu (29 Mar 1769–26 Nov 1851). Duke of Dalmatia, 1808. Appointed Marshal of the Empire, 19 May 1804.

Suchet, Louis-Gabriel (2 Mar 1770–3 Jan 1826). Duke of Albufera, 1813. Appointed Marshal of the Empire, 1 July 1811.

Victor (Claude-Victor), Perrin (7 Dec 1764–1 Mar 1841). Duke of Belluno. Appointed Marshal of the Empire, 13 Jul 1807.


THE REMAINING MARSHALS OF THE EMPIRE

Brune, Guillaume-Marie-Anne (13 May 1763–2 Aug 1815). No title. Appointed Marshal of the Empire, 19 May 1804.

Gouvion-Saint-Cyr, Laurent (13 Apr 1764–17 Mar 1830). Count, 1808, later Marquis. Appointed Marshal of the Empire, 27 Aug 1812.

Grouchy, Emmanuel de (23 Oct 1766–29 May 1847). Hereditary Marquis. Appointed Marshal of the Empire, 3 Jun 1815.

Jourdan, Jean-Baptiste (29 Apr 1762–23 Nov 1833). Count, 1814. Appointed Marshal of the Empire, 19 May 1804.

Pérignon, Catherine-Dominique de (31 May 1754–25 Dec 1818). Count, 1811. Appointed Marshal of the Empire, 19 May 1804.

Sérurier, Jean-Mathieu-Philibert (8 Dec 1742–21 Dec 1819). Count, 1808. Appointed Marshal of the Empire, 19 May 1804.

## THE FRENCH REVOLUTIONARY CALENDAR

| | | |
|---|---|---|
| 22 Sep to 21 Oct | Vendémiaire | |
| 22 Oct to 20 Nov | Brumaire | Autumn |
| 21 Nov to 20 Dec | Frimaire | |
| | | |
| 21 Dec to 19 Jan | Nivôse | |
| 20 Jan to 18 Feb | Pluviôse | Winter |
| 19 Feb to 20 Mar | Ventôse | |
| | | |
| 21 Mar to 19 Apr | Germinal | |
| 20 Apr to 19 May | Floréal | Spring |
| 20 May to 18 June | Prairial | |
| | | |
| 19 June to 18 July | Messidor | |
| 19 July to 17 Aug | Thermidor | Summer |
| 18 Aug to 16 Sep | Fructidor | |

The year was divided into twelve months, each month having 30 days; the 5 additional days necessary to complete a common year were placed at the end of the last month, and were called 'Jours complémentaires'. They were celebrated as festivals, and became known as 'Sansculottides'.

| | | | | |
|---|---|---|---|---|
| Primidi | dedicated to | | Virtue | Sep 17 |
| Duodi | " | " | Genius | Sep 18 |
| Tridi | " | " | Labour | Sep 19 |
| Quartidi | " | " | Opinion | Sep 20 |
| Quintidi | " | " | Rewards | Sep 21 |

In Olympic, or Leap Years, a sixth additional day was to be observed, terminating the first 'Franciade'.

The Olympic year was to take place every 4 years, and mark the close of each Franciade; and of the hundredth years, only 4th hundredth years of the Republic were to be Olympic or Leap Years, until the 40th hundredth year, which was to terminate with a common year.

Instead of the months being divided into weeks, they were divided into 'Decades', consisting of 10 days each; and 9 days between, being called 1st, 2nd, 3rd and 4th, etc., before or after 'Decadi'.

# 2 HEADS OF STATE AND KEY MINISTERS

## HEADS OF STATE

### AUSTRIA

| | |
|---|---|
| Joseph II, m. (i) Isabella of Parma (ii) Josepha, succeeded his mother as King of Austria | 29 Oct 80 |
| having succeeded his father as Holy Roman Emperor (by election) | 18 Aug 65 |
| Leopold II, m. Maria-Louisa of Spain, succeeded his brother | 20 Feb 90 |
| and was made Holy Roman Emperor | 30 Sep 90 |
| Francis II, m. Maria Theresa of Naples, succeeded his father | 1 Mar 92 |
| and was created Holy Roman Emperor | 5 July 92 |
| the title of Holy Roman Emperor becoming extinct | 6 Aug 06 |
| Ferdinand I, succeeded his father | 2 Mar 35 |
| abdicated | 2 Dec 48 |

### BELGIUM

| | |
|---|---|
| Belgium declared itself independent of Holland on 18 Nov 30. | |
| Regent, Baron van Surlet van Chokier | 25 Feb 31–21 July 31 |
| Leopold I (formerly Leopold of Saxe-Coburg), m. (i) Charlotte of Great Britain (ii) Louise of Orleans, took oath as King | 21 July 31 |

## DENMARK

| | |
|---|---|
| Christian VII, m. Caroline Matilda of Hanover, succeeded his father | 14 Jan 66 |
| Frederick VI, m. Marie of Hesse-Cassel, succeeded his father, having been his regent since 1784 | 13 Mar 08 |
| Christian VIII, m. (i) Charlotte of Mecklenburg-Schwerin (ii) Caroline of Schleswig-Holstein-Sonderburg-Augustenburg, succeeded his cousin | 8 Dec 39 |
| died | 20 Jan 48 |

## FRANCE

| | |
|---|---|
| Louis XVI, m. Maria Antoinette of Austria, succeeded his uncle | 10 May 74 |
| deposed | 21 Sep 92 |
| executed | 11 Jan 93 |
| Louis XVII, recognized by the Royalist but not by the Republican cause as King from the death of his father to his own death in 1795 | |
| Government of the National Convention | 21 Sep 92 |
| Government of the Directory | 26 Oct 95 |
| Government of the Consulate | 11 Nov 99 |
| Napoleon Bonaparte, Consul for Life | 4 Aug 02 |
| Emperor | 18 May 04 |
| abdicated | 6 Apr 14 |
| Louis XVIII, brother of Louis XVI, returned as King | 6 Apr 14 |
| Napoleon Bonaparte returned as Emperor | 10 Mar 15 |
| abdicated | 22 June 15 |

Between 22 June and 7 July an executive committee held office; during this period the Emperor's son was recognized by some as Napoleon II.

| | |
|---|---|
| Louis XVIII returned as King again | 8 July 15 |
| Charles X, succeeded his brother | 16 Sep 24 |
| abdicated | 2 Aug 30 |
| Provisional government | 30 July 30–9 Aug 30 |
| Louis-Philippe of Orleans, m. Marie-Amelie of Sicily, elected King | 9 Aug 30 |
| abdicated | 24 Feb 48 |

## GERMAN STATES

In 1789 there were over 300 territorial units which regarded themselves as belonging to a Germanic political system in that their rulers were all vassals of the Holy Roman Emperor. About 100 were sovereign states with full sovereign rights; of these, many were very small. The re-organization of Germany by Napoleon produced a confederation of 39 states which was formed in 1815 and included, besides Austria and Prussia, 13 states considered sufficiently important to be given one place each in the Federal Diet.

1. *Prussia*

| | |
|---|---|
| Frederick William II, m. Frederika-Louise of Hesse-Darmstadt, succeeded his uncle | 17 Aug 86 |
| Frederick William III, m. Louise of Mecklenburg-Strelitz, succeeded his father | 16 Nov 97 |
| Frederick William IV, m. Elisabeth Louise of Bavaria, succeeded his father | 7 June 40 |

2. *Bavaria*

| | |
|---|---|
| Carl Theodore, Elector of the Palatinate, elected ruler | 30 Dec 77 |
| Maximilian I Joseph, m. (i) Wilhelmine of Hesse-Darmstadt (ii) Caroline of Baden, Elector | 16 Feb 99 |
| became King | 1 Jan 06 |
| Ludwig I, m. Therese of Saxe-Hildburghausen, succeeded his father | 13 Oct 25 |
| abdicated | 20 Mar 48 |

3. *Saxony*

| | |
|---|---|
| Frederick Augustus III, m. Marie Amelie of the Palatinate, succeeded his father as Elector | 17 Dec 63 |
| King (as Frederick Augustus I) | 11 Dec 06 |
| The Kingdom was ruled by Prussia, and then Russia, between Oct 13 and Jan 15 | |
| Frederick Augustus I returned as king | Jan 15 |
| Anton Clement, succeeded his brother | 5 May 27 |
| Frederick Augustus II, m. Caroline of Austria, shared the throne from 1830 and then succeeded his uncle | 6 June 36 |

4. *Hanover*

Ruled by the Sovereign of Great Britain until the accession of Queen Victoria

23

who, as a woman, was prevented by the Salic Law from succeeding to the throne of Hanover.

| | |
|---|---|
| Ernest Augustus, m. Frederika of Mecklenburg-Strelitz, succeeded his brother, William IV of Great Britain, as King | 6 June 37 |

### 5. *Württemberg*

| | |
|---|---|
| Carl Eugene, m. Francesca von Hohenheim, succeeded his father | 12 Mar 37 |
| Louis Eugene, m. Sophie von Beichlingen, succeeded his brother | 24 Oct 93 |
| Frederic Eugene, succeeded his brother | 20 May 95 |
| Frederic II, m. Augusta Caroline of Brunswick-Wolfenbüttel, succeeded his father as Duke | 23 Dec 97 |
| Elector | 27 Apr 03 |
| King | 1 Jan 06 |
| Wilhelm I, m. (i) Caroline Augusta of Bavaria (ii) Catherine Pavlovna of Russia (iii) Pauline of Württemberg, succeeded his father | 30 Oct 16 |

### 6. *Baden*

| | |
|---|---|
| Charles Frederic, m. (i) Caroline of Hesse-Darmstadt (ii) Louise von Hochberg, Margrave | 1738 |
| Grand Duke | 13 Aug 06 |
| Charles Ludwig Frederic, m. Stephanie Beauharnais, succeeded his grandfather | 10 June 11 |
| Ludwig, succeeded his nephew | 8 Dec 18 |
| Leopold I, m. Sophia of Sweden, succeeded his half-brother | 30 Mar 30 |

### 7. *Hesse-Cassel*

| | |
|---|---|
| William IX, Landgrave | 1785 |
| Elector | 1805 |
| William II, m. Augusta of Prussia, succeeded his father | 27 Feb 21 |
| Frederic William, m. Gertrude Lehmann (created Princess of Hanau), succeeded his father | 20 Nov 47 |

### 8. *Hesse-Darmstadt*

| | |
|---|---|
| Louis X, Landgrave | 1790 |
| Grand Duke (as Louis I) | 1806 |

| | |
|---|---|
| Louis II, m. Wilhelmine of Baden, succeeded his father | 6 Apr 30 |
| Insurrection, followed by a co-regency of Louis II and his son | 5 Mar 48 |
| Louis III, m. Mathilde of Bavaria, succeeded his father | 16 June 48 |

### 9. *Holstein and Lauenberg*
Ruled by the Sovereign of Denmark until 1863.

### 10. *Brunswick*

| | |
|---|---|
| Charles William Ferdinand, m. Augusta of England, Duke | 1780 |
| Frederick William, Duke | 1806 |

Charles William Ferdinand was mortally wounded at the battle of Auerstädt in Oct 06 and was, as part of the resulting Napoleonic victory, deposed. Frederick William succeeded his father in name only, m. Caroline of Nassau-Saarbrucken. Killed at Quatre Bras, 1815.

| | |
|---|---|
| Charles, succeeded his father, Duke | 16 June 15 |
| fled after rioting | 8 Sep 30 |
| declared unfit to govern | 2 Dec 30 |
| William I, head of provisional government | 2 Dec 30 |
| succeeded his brother | 25 Apr 31 |

### 11. *Nassau*

| | |
|---|---|
| William V, m. Frederika of Prussia, succeeded his father as Prince | 1751 |
| His son William Frederick, m. Wilhelmina of Prussia, became King William I of the Netherlands | 16 Mar 15 |

Nassau became a possession of the ruler of the Netherlands

### 12. *Mecklenburg-Schwerin*

| | |
|---|---|
| Frederick Francis I, m. Louise of Saxe-Gotha, succeeded his father | 1785 |
| Grand Duke | 9 June 15 |
| Paul Frederick, m. Alexandrine of Prussia, Grand Duke, succeeded his grandfather | 1 Feb 37 |

25

Frederick Francis II, m. (i) Augusta of Reuss-
Schleiz (ii) Anne of Hesse (iii) Marie of
Schwarzburg-Rudolstadt, succeeded his
father                                                    7 Mar 42

### 13. *Mecklenburg-Strelitz*
Charles Frederick, m. (i) Frederika of Hesse-
Darmstadt (ii) Charlotte of Hesse-Darmstadt,
Grand Duke
George, m. Marie of Hesse-Cassel, succeeded his
father                                                    6 Nov 16

### 14. *Luxembourg*
Ruled by the Sovereign of Holland until 1890.

The other, smaller, states were:
Hesse-Homburg (joined in 1817), Liechtenstein, Lippe-Detmold, Reuss-
Greiz, Reuss-Schleiz, Schaumberg-Lippe, Waldeck (all sharing one place in
the Federal Diet); Anhalt-Bernburg, Anhalt-Dessau, Anhalt-Kothen,
Oldenburg, Schwarzburg-Rudolstadt, Schwarzburg-Sondershausen (all sharing one place); Hohenzollern-Hechingen, Hohenzollern-Sigmaringen; the free
towns of Hamburg, Bremen, Frankfurt and Lübeck (all sharing one place);
Saxe-Coburg, Saxe-Gotha, Saxe-Meiningen, Saxe-Weimar, Saxe-Altenburg
(all sharing one place; Saxe-Gotha became extinct in 1826 and its territory was
divided between Saxe-Coburg and Saxe-Meiningen, the former then being
known as Saxe-Coburg-Gotha).

## GREAT BRITAIN

George III, m. Charlotte of Mecklenburg-
Strelitz, King                                            1760
George IV, m. Caroline of Brunswick, succeeded
his father                                                29 Jan 20
having been Regent since 1811
William IV, m. Adelaide of Saxe-Meiningen,
succeeded his brother                                     26 June 30
Victoria, m. Albert of Saxe-Coburg-Gotha, suc-
ceeded her uncle                                          20 June 37

## GREECE

Independence from Turkey was proclaimed and a provisional government set up 21 Mar 29. Turkey recognized Greek independence 14 Sep 29.

| | |
|---|---|
| John Capodistria, President at | 14 Sep 29 |
| Augustin Capodistria, President | 20 Dec 31 |
| Otto of Bavaria elected King | 7 May 32 |
| acceded under a regency (as a minor) | 5 Oct 32 |

## ITALIAN STATES

In 1789 there were 11 political units in Italy. Milan (including Mantua), Tuscany and Modena were ruled by Austrian Hapsburgs or rulers under their influence; Parma and the Kingdom of the Two Sicilies were ruled by Spanish Bourbons; Sardinia-Piedmont-Savoy, Lucca and San Marino were independent kingdoms; Venice and Genoa were republics; the other unit was the Papal States. These states were regrouped as republics by Napoleon between 1797 and 1804. They were then redistributed between 1805 and 1815 when, after the Congress of Vienna, 10 states were established and remained in being until re-unification in 1861.

1. *Kingdom of Sardinia* (Sardinia-Piedmont-Savoy)

| | |
|---|---|
| Victor Amadeus III, m. Maria Antonia of Spain, King | 1773 |
| Charles Emanuel IV, m. Marie Anne Clotilde of France, succeeded his father | 16 Oct 96 |
| The kingdom was annexed to France | 9 Dec 98 |
| The kingdom was occupied by Russian and Austrian forces | 22 June 99 |
| French rule restored | 25 June 1800 |
| Charles Emanuel IV abdicated in favour of his brother | 4 June 02 |
| Victor Emanuel I, succeeded his brother | 20 May 14 |
| abdicated in favour of a third brother | 13 Mar 19 |
| Charles Felix, m. Christina of Naples, succeeded his brother | 13 Mar 21 |
| (his cousin Charles Albert had ruled as Regent in his absence between the abdication in Mar 19 and his own return to the country in Mar 21) | |
| Revolutionary provisional government | 23 Mar 21 |

27

| | |
|---|---|
| Charles Felix as head of a military government | 10 Apr 21 |
| Charles Felix reinstated as King | 18 Oct 21 |
| Charles Albert, m. Teresa of Austria, succeeded his cousin | 27 Apr 31 |

## 2. *Republic of Genoa*

### *Doges*

| | |
|---|---|
| Aleramo Pallavicini | 30 July 89 |
| Michelangelo Cambiaso | 3 Sep 91 |
| Giuseppe Doria | 16 Sep 93 |
| Giacomo Brignole | 17 Nov 93 |
| Genoa became part of the Ligurian Republic | May 97 |
| Provisional government under Giacomo Brignole | 14 June 97 |
| Ligurian Republic government under a directory | 17 Jan 98 |
| Austrian occupation | 4 June 180C |
| French occupation | 24 June 00 |
| Ligurian Republic re-established, restoration of the title of Doge of Genoa: Doge, Girolamo Durazzo | 10 Aug 02 |
| Genoa annexed to France | 6 June 05 |
| Independent republic re-established | 18 Apr 14 |
| Girolamo Serra, President of the provisional government | 26 Apr 14 |
| Genoa became part of the Kingdom of Sardinia | 7 Jan 15 |

## 3. *Milan*

Ruled by Austria from 1765 until 9 May 96.

| | |
|---|---|
| Rule by an executive committee after the deposition of the Emperor Francis II as ruler | 9 May 96 |
| Union with France | 15 May 96 |
| Cisalpine Republic (including Milan) established under a directory | 9 July 97 |
| Austrian/Russian occupation | 28 Apr 99 |
| Civil government; President, Luigi Coccastelli | 29 Apr 1800 |
| Cisalpine Republic reinstated under a directory | 4 June 00 |
| Milan became part of the Italian Republic under Napoleon Bonaparte | 26 Jan 02 |
| Napoleon became King | 19 Mar 05 |
| Government by Council | 21 Apr 14 |
| Austrian occupation | 28 Apr 14 |

Kingdom of Lombardy-Venetia established under Francis I of Austria (formerly the Emperor Francis II) 7 Apr 15

The Austrian rulers held the territory until 1859.

## 4. *Republic of Venice*

| | |
|---|---|
| Lodovico Manin, Doge | 9 Mar 89 |
| abdicated | 12 May 97 |
| became President of a provisional government | 16 May 97 |
| Austrian rule established | 17 Oct 97 |
| Territory united to the Kingdom of Italy under Napoleon | 26 Dec 05 |
| Territory placed again under Austrian rule | 30 May 14 |
| Kingdom of Lombardy-Venetia established under Francis I of Austria (formerly the Emperor Francis II) | 7 Apr 15 |

The Austrian rulers held the territory until 1848.

## 5. *Parma*

| | |
|---|---|
| Ferdinand, m. Maria Amalia of Austria, Duke | 1765 |
| The territory was ceded to France | 21 Mar 01 |
| Austrian occupation | 14 Feb 14 |
| French government re-established | 2 Mar 14 |
| Austrian re-occupation | 9 Mar 14 |
| Marie Louise of Austria established as Duchess m. (i) Napoleon Bonaparte (ii) Adam von Neipperg (iii) Carlo Renato di Bombelles | 11 Apr 14 |
| Revolutionary provisional government | 11 Feb 31 |
| Marie Louise renounced the throne | 14 Feb 31 |
| was restored | 13 Mar 31 |
| Charles Louis of Bourbon, m. Maria Theresa of Savoy, Duke | 18 Dec 47 |
| (grandson of Philip of Bourbon, Duke of Parma 1749–65), deposed | 20 Mar 48 |

## 6. *Modena*

| | |
|---|---|
| Francis III d'Este, m. Charlotte of Orleans, Duke | 1748 |
| Ercole III, succeeded his father | 22 Apr 80 |
| deposed | 6 Oct 96 |
| Establishment by Napoleon of the Cispadane Republic, including Modena | Oct 96 |

Cispadane and Transpadane Republics united as
the Cisalpine Republic 1797
Austrian occupation 4 May 99
French occupation 12 June 99
Austrian occupation 20 June 99
Republic re-established 9 July 1800
Republic became part of the Italian Republic,
under Napoleon 19 Feb 02
The Italian Republic became the Kingdom of
Italy under Napoleon 17 Mar 05
Occupation by Joachim Murat, King of Naples 21 Jan 14
Francis IV of Austria d'Este, m. Maria Beatrice
of Savoy (son of Archduke Ferdinand of
Austria) proclaimed Duke 7 Feb 14
deposed 4 Apr 15
Renewed occupation under Joachim Murat 4 Apr 15
Francis IV re-established 13 Apr 15
Provisional revolutionary government 6 Feb 31
Francis IV re-established 9 Mar 31
Francis V, m. Adelgonda of Bavaria, succeeded
his father 21 Jan 46
deposed 21 Mar 48

7. *Tuscany*
Peter Leopold I (later Holy Roman Emperor
Leopold II), m. Maria Louisa of Spain, Grand
Duke 18 Aug 65
Government by Regency Council 20 Feb 90
Ferdinand III of Lorraine, succeeded his father 21 July 90
French occupation, provisional government 25 Mar 99
Ferdinand III restored by the Austrians 17 July 99
deposed 15 Oct 1800
Government by quadrumvirate 15 Oct 00
Government by triumvirate 27 Nov 00
Provisional government 21 Mar 01
Louis I de Bourbon, hereditary prince of Parma,
elected King of Etruria (but did not take
possession) 21 Mar 01
took possession 2 Aug 01
Charles Louis de Bourbon (later Duke of Lucca),
King of Etruria under the regency of his
mother Marie-Louise de Bourbon 27 May 03

30

| | |
|---|---|
| renounced the throne | 10 Dec 07 |
| French occupation | 10 Dec 07 |
| Government by council established by Napoleon | 12 May 08 |
| Tuscany joined to France | 24 May 08 |
| Occupation under Joachim Murat, King of Naples | 3 Feb 14 |
| Ferdinand III of Lorraine reinstated as Grand Duke | 15 Sep 14 |
| Leopold II, m. (i) Maria Anna of Saxony (ii) Marie Antoinette de Bourbon, succeeded his father | 13 June 24 |

## 8. *Lucca*

Government by a general council lasted from the fifteenth century until Jan 99.

| | |
|---|---|
| Republic established under a Senate | 15 Jan 99 |
| French occupation | 4 Feb 99 |
| Austrian occupation | 24 July 99 |
| French occupation | 9 July 1800 |
| Austrian occupation | 15 Sep 00 |
| French occupation | 9 Oct 00 |
| Restoration of the Republic of Lucca under a council | 26 Dec 01 |
| Felice Baciocchi, brother-in-law of Napoleon Bonaparte, made Governor | 24 June 05 |
| Austrian and Neapolitan occupation | 18 Mar 14 |
| Marie Louise de Bourbon, m. Louis I de Bourbon, King of Etruria, hereditary prince of Parma, created Duchess of Lucca | 7 Dec 17 |
| Charles Louis of Bourbon, m. Maria Teresa of Savoy, succeeded his mother | 13 Mar 24 |
| renounced the throne | 5 Oct 47 |

Lucca was then united with Tuscany.

## 9. *Papal States*

Popes ruled the states (*see* The Papacy) apart from the following periods of war (between 1798 and 1815) and uprising (1831–2):

| | |
|---|---|
| Pope overthrown by Napoleonic forces; establishment of the Republic of Rome and the end of the Pope's authority in the other Papal States | Feb 98 |

31

| | |
|---|---|
| Neapolitan occupation and a provisional government | 27 Nov 98 |
| Re-establishment of the Republic (ruled by consulate) | 12 Dec 98 |
| Re-occupation by Neapolitan forces | 30 Sep 99 |
| Re-establishment of the Pope | July 1800 |
| French occupation, and the Pope once more overthrown | Feb-July 08 |
| The Pope restored | 24 May 14 |
| Occupation under Joachim Murat, King of Naples | 22 Mar 15 |
| Austrian occupation | 22 May 15 |
| The Pope restored | 7 June 15 |

In Rome there was no further disturbance of the Papal power until 1849. The same continuous Papal rule applies to Benevento, Camerino, Perugia, Pesare, Spoleto, Urbino and Viterbo.

In the other Papal States there were risings in 1831 which temporarily replaced Papal rule with provisional governments:

| | |
|---|---|
| Ancona | 4 Feb–27 Mar |
| Bologna | 4 Feb–20 Mar |
| Cesena | 5 Feb–24 Mar |
| Faenza | 5 Feb–22 Mar |
| Ferrara | 7 Feb–15 Mar |
| Forli | 5 Feb–24 Mar |
| Imola | 5 Feb–21 Mar |
| Ravenna | 6 Feb–23 Mar |
| Rimini | 6 Feb–25 Mar |

10. *Kingdom of the Two Sicilies* (Naples and Sicily)

| | |
|---|---|
| Ferdinand IV, m. Marie Caroline of Austria, King | 1759 |
| deposed | 23 Jan 99 |
| French occupation | 23 Jan 99 |
| Ferdinand IV re-established | 23 June 99 |
| Joseph Bonaparte, commander-in-chief of the territory under Napoleon Bonaparte | 15 Feb 06 |
| Joseph Bonaparte declared King | 30 Mar 06 |
| renounced the throne | 2 July 08 |
| Joachim Murat declared King | 2 July 08 |
| deposed | 19 May 15 |
| Occupation under Leopold de Bourbon in the name of his father Ferdinand IV | 22 May 15 |

| | |
|---|---|
| Ferdinand IV restored (as Ferdinand I from Dec 16) | 2 June 15 |
| Provisional government | 15 Mar 21 |
| Ferdinand restored | 15 May 21 |
| Francis I, m. Maria Clementina of Austria, succeeded his father | 4 Jan 25 |
| Ferdinand II, m. Maria Christina of Savoy, succeeded his father | 8 Nov 30 |

## MONACO

| | |
|---|---|
| Onorato III, m. Maria Christina Brignole, Prince | 1731 |
| French occupation, Onorato III deposed | 15 Feb 93 |
| Onorato IV, succeeded his father on the latter's death | 12 May 95 |
| restored to the throne | May 14 |
| abdicated | 1815 |
| Onorato, Duke of Valentino, carried on the government | 18 Jan 15 |
| Onorato V, succeeded his father | 1819 |
| Florestan I, m. Mlle Rouiller, succeeded his brother | 2 Oct 41 |

## MONTENEGRO

| | |
|---|---|
| Independence from Turkey was recognized by the Sultan in 1799 | |
| Peter Njegos, Prince | 1813 |
| Prince Bishop | 1830 |

## THE NETHERLANDS

| | |
|---|---|
| The United Provinces until 1795 | |
| William V of Orange-Nassau, hereditary Stadtholder, took office under the regency of his mother, Anne of England | 22 Oct 51 |
| renounced the throne | 17 Jan 95 |
| The French occupation of Jan 95 divided the Provinces; the Southern | |

33

Provinces were annexed as departments of France; the northern provinces became the Batavian Republic which was governed by councils until 1805.

| | |
|---|---|
| Roger John Schimmelpennink, Grand Pensionary (Viceroy for Napoleon) appointed | 29 Apr 05 |
| Louis Bonaparte, m. Hortense Beauharnais, created King of Holland | 5 June 06 |
| abdicated | 1 July 10 |
| Holland annexed to France | 9 July 10 |
| William I, m. (i) Wilhelmina of Prussia (ii) Countess Oultremont, created King of the United Netherlands (northern and southern provinces) and Grand Duke of Luxembourg | 16 Mar 15 |
| William became ruler of Holland and Luxembourg only in 1830 (*see* Belgium) | |
| William II of Holland and Luxembourg, m. Anna Pavlovna of Russia, succeeded his father | 7 Oct 40 |

## NORWAY

Ruled by Denmark until the Treaty of Kiel, 4 Nov 14, and then by the Kings of Sweden until 1905.

## THE PAPACY

| | |
|---|---|
| Pius VI, consecrated | 22 Feb 75–29 Aug 99 |
| Pius VII, consecrated | 21 Mar 00–20 Aug 23 |
| Leo XII, consecrated | 5 Oct 23–10 Feb 29 |
| Pius VIII, consecrated | 5 Apr 29–1 Dec 30 |
| Gregory XVI, consecrated | 6 Feb 31–1 June 46 |
| Pius IX, consecrated | 21 June 46–7 Feb 78 |

## PORTUGAL

| | |
|---|---|
| Maria I and her husband Peter III succeeded as joint rulers | 24 Feb 77 |
| Peter III died | 25 May 86 |
| French occupation | 30 Nov 07 |
| Maria I restored | Dec 13 |

John VI, having ruled in his mother's name (because of her mental illness) since 1792 and been Prince Regent since 1799, m. Carlotta of Spain, became King on his mother's death     20 Mar 16

Peter IV, m. (i) Leopoldine of Austria (ii) Amelie of Leuchtenberg, succeeded his father     27 Mar 26

    renounced the throne     2 May 26

Maria II, Da Gloria, succeeded her father in name, but her uncle Miguel, brother of Peter IV who became Regent in July 26, proclaimed himself King 25 June 28 and did not renounce the throne to his niece until 26 May 34, from which date she ruled until 1853.

## RUSSIA

Catherine II became Tsarina on the deposition of her husband Peter III     9 July 62

Paul I, m. Sophia Dorothea of Württemberg, succeeded his mother     17 Nov 96

Alexander I, m. Elizabeth of Baden, succeeded his father     3 Mar 01

Nicholas I, m. Charlotte of Prussia, succeeded his father after his elder brother Constantine had renounced the succession     7 Dec 25

## SPAIN

Charles IV, m. Maria Louisa, succeeded his father     14 Dec 88

    abdicated     20 Mar 08

Ferdinand VII, m. Maria Christina, succeeded his father     20 Mar 08

    abdicated     2 May 08

Joseph Bonaparte, brother of Napoleon, created King     6 June 08

Ferdinand VII restored     11 Dec 13

Isabella II, m. Francisco de Asís de Bourbon, succeeded her father under the regency of her mother     29 Sep 33

# SWEDEN

| | |
|---|---|
| Gustav III, m. Sofia Magdalena of Denmark, succeeded his father as King | 12 Feb 71 (assassinated) |
| Gustav IV Adolf succeeded his father under a regency | 29 Mar 92 |
| abdicated | 6 June 09 |
| Charles XIII succeeded his brother | 6 June 09 |
| Charles became King of Norway also by the Treaty of Kiel in 1814 | |
| Charles XIV John (Jean-Baptiste Bernadotte), m. Eugenia Clary de Marseille, created King of Sweden and Norway | 5 Feb 18 |
| Oscar I, m. Josephine of Leuchtenberg, succeeded his father | 8 Mar 44 |

# SWITZERLAND

Until the creation of the federal state in 1848 the country was a loose association of cantons with no single head of state. The United Helvetian Republic created by Napoleon (2 Apr 98–18 Feb 03) was headed by a directory of five.

# TURKEY

| | |
|---|---|
| Selim III succeeded his uncle as Sultan | 28 Apr 89 |
| deposed | 29 May 07 |
| Mustapha IV succeeded his cousin | 29 May 07 |
| deposed | 28 July 08 |
| Mahmud II succeeded his brother | 28 July 08 |
| Abd-el-Medjid succeeded his father | 1 July 39 |

# MINISTERS

## AUSTRIA

| Date of taking office | Prime Minister |
|---|---|
| 1753 | Wenzel Anton, Count von Kaunitz |
| 92 | Philip, Count Cobenzl |
| Mar 93 | Baron von Thugut |
| 1800 | Ferdinand, Count von Trautt- mannsdorff |
| 01 | Ludwig, Count Cobenzl |
| 25 Dec 05 | Johann, Count Stadion- Warthausen |
| 8 Oct 09 | Klemens Metternich (Prince from 1813) |

## BADEN

| Date of taking office | Prime Minister | Foreign Minister | Finance Minister |
|---|---|---|---|
| 16 | | Freiherr von Berstett | |
| 28 | | | Christian Friedrich von Boeckh |
| 30 | Georg Ludwig von Winter | | |
| 27 July 31 | | Freiherr von Turkheim | |
| Oct 35 | | Freiherr von Blittersdorf | |
| 38 | Karl Friedrich Nebenius | | |

37

(continued

## BADEN (*continued*)

| Date of taking office | Prime Minister | Foreign Minister | Finance Minister |
|---|---|---|---|
| 39 | Freiherr von Blittersdorf | | |
| Nov 43 | Christian Friedrich von Boeckh | Alexander von Dusch | Franz Anton Regenauer |
| 28 Mar 45 | Karl Friedrich Nebenius | | |
| 9 Dec 46 | Johan Baptist Bekk | | |

## BAVARIA

| Date of taking office | Prime Minister | Foreign Minister | Finance Minister |
|---|---|---|---|
| Feb 99 | Maximilian, Count von Montgelas | | |
| Feb 17 | Heinrich, Count von Reigersberg | Count von Rechberg and Rothenlöwen | Freiherr von und zu Lerchenfeld |
| Oct 25 | Georg, Freiherr von Zentner | | Joseph, Count von Armansperg |
| Apr 27 | | Georg, Freiherr von Zentner | |
| 31 Dec 31 | | Friedrich August Koch | Freiherr von und zu Lerchenfeld |
| 1 Nov 37 | Karl von Abel | | Karl, Count von Seinsheim |
| May 46 | | Otto, Count von Bray-Steinburg | |
| Feb 47 | Freiherr von Zu-Rhein | Georg Ludwig, Ritter von Maurer | Freiherr von Zu-Rhein |
| 30 Nov 47 | Ludwig, Prince of Öttingen-Wallerstein | Ludwig, Prince of Öttingen-Wallenstein | |

## BELGIUM

| Date of taking office | Prime Minister | Foreign Minister | Finance Minister |
|---|---|---|---|
| 24 Sep 30 | Charles Rogier | | |
| 24 Feb 31 | Paul Devaux (Minister of State) | | |
| July 31– Oct 32 | Provisional government | | |
| 20 Oct 32 | Charles Rogier | Albert, Count of Alviella | |
| Aug 34 | Barthélemy, Chev. de Theux de Meylandt | Barthélemy, Chev. de Theux de Meylandt | |
| Apr 40 | Joseph Lebeau | Joseph Lebeau | |
| June 41 | Baron de Nothomb | Albert Joseph Goblet | |
| June 45 | Sylvain van de Weyer | Adolphe Dechamps | Jules Malou |
| Mar 46 | Barthélemy, Chev. de Theux de Meylandt | | |
| 12 Aug 47 | Charles Rogier | C. de Hoffschmidt de Resteigne | L. Veydt |

## DENMARK

| Date of taking office | Prime Minister | Foreign Minister |
|---|---|---|
| From 1784 | Andreas, Count von Bernstorff | |
| 22 June 97 | Christian, Count von Bernstorff | |
| 1800 | | Christian, Count von Bernstorff (until 1818) |
| 10 | Friedrich, Count Moltke | |

39

(*continued*

## DENMARK (*continued*)

| Date of taking office | Prime Minister |
|---|---|
| 14 | Joachim, Count Moltke of Stridfeld and Walkendorf |
| 5 Oct 18 | Otto Joachim, Count Moltke of Stridfeld and Walkendorf |
| 42 | Adam Wilhelm von Moltke of Stridfeld and Walkendorf |

## FRANCE

| Date of taking office | Prime Minister | Foreign Minister | Finance Minister |
|---|---|---|---|
| Aug 88 | Jacques Necker | | Jacques Necker |
| 11 July 89 | Louis Auguste Le Tonnelier, Baron de Breteuil | | Charles Lambert |
| 14 July 89 | Jacques Necker | | Jacques Necker |
| July 89 | | Armand-Marc, Comte de Montmorin Saint-Hérem | |
| Sep 90 | Armand-Marc, Comte de Montmorin Saint-Hérem | | Charles Lambert |
| Dec 90 | | | Antoine de Valdec de Lessart (until Jan 91) |
| Feb 91 | Antoine de Valdec de Lessart | | |

40

(*continued*

## FRANCE (*continued*)

| Date of taking office | Prime Minister | Foreign Minister | Finance Minister |
|---|---|---|---|
| 20 Nov 91 | | Antoine de Valdec de Lessart (until 10 Mar 92) | |
| 15 Mar 92 | Jean Marie Roland de la Platière (until 13 June 92) | Charles François Dumouriez | |
| 23 Mar 92 | | | Étienne Clavière |
| 15 June 92 | Coalitions of various factions with no individual responsibilities | | |
| 12 Aug 92 | Georges Danton | Barthélemy-Louis Joseph Lebrun-Tondu | Étienne Clavière |
| 12 Sep 92 | Jean Marie de la Platière | | |
| 10 Apr 93 | | Georges Danton | Joseph Cambon (until 9 July 93) |
| 10 July 93 | Maximilien Robespierre (until 27 July 94) | Marie-Jean Hérault de Séchelles (until 30 Mar 94) | |
| 28 Oct 95 | The Directory: the following filled the 5 Directorships, 1795–99: Paul, Count de Barras; Jean François Rewbell; Louis-Marc de Larevellière-Lépeauz; Charles Le Tourneur; Lazare Carnot; François de Barthélemy; Nicolas François; Philippe de Douai; Jean Baptiste Treilhard; Louis Gohier; Jean François Moulin; Roger Ducos; Emmanuel Sièyes. | | |

Executives with responsibility:

| Date of taking office | Prime Minister | Foreign Minister | Finance Minister |
|---|---|---|---|
| Nov 95 | | | Dominique de Nogaret |
| July 97 | | Charles Maurice de Talleyrand | |
| 18 June 99 | | | Robert Lindet |
| July 99 | | Charles Reinhard | |

The Directory was overthrown by Napoleon on 9 Nov 99. Napoleon set up the Consulate, in which he filled the post of First Consul from 9 Nov 99 until 18 May 04 (alone from 4 Aug 02). His fellow-Consuls from 9 Nov 99 until 27 Dec 99 were Emmanuel Sieyès and Roger Ducos; from 27 Dec 99 until 4 Aug 02 Jean Jacques de Cambacérès and Charles Lebrun.

41

(*continued*

## FRANCE (continued)

| Date of taking office | Prime Minister | Foreign Minister | Finance Minister |
|---|---|---|---|
| | Executive responsibilities: | | |
| 9 Nov 99 | | Napoleon Bonaparte | |
| 10 Nov 99 | | | Marc Gaudin |
| Dec 99 | | Charles Maurice de Talleyrand | |
| 18 May 04 | First Empire (until 11 Apr 14) | | |
| 8 Aug 07 | | Jean Baptiste de Champigny, Duc de Cadore | |
| 17 Apr 11 | | Hugues Bernard Maret, Duc de Bassano | |
| Nov 13 | | Armand de Caulaincourt, Duc de Vicenza | |
| 13 May 14 | Pierre Louis, Duc de Blacas d'Aulps | Charles Maurice de Talleyrand | Joseph Dominique, Baron Louis |
| 20 Mar 15 | Benjamin Constant de Rebeque | Armand de Caulaincourt, Duc de Vicenza | Marc Gaudin |
| 18 June 15 | | Louis Bignon | |
| 8 July 15 | Charles Maurice de Talleyrand | Charles Maurice de Talleyrand | Louis, Comte Corvetto |
| 24 Sep 15 | Armand du Plessis, Duc de Richelieu | Armand du Plessis, Duc de Richelieu | |
| 28 Dec 18 | Jean, Marquis Dessolles | Jean, Marquis Dessolles | Joseph Dominique, Baron Louis |
| 16 Nov 19 | Élie, Comte de Décazes | Étienne, Baron de Pasquier | Antoine, Comte Roy |
| 18 Feb 20 | Armand du Plessis, Duc de Richelieu | | |
| 9 Dec 21 | Joseph, Duc de Villèle | | Joseph, Duc de Villèle |
| 24 Dec 21 | | Matthieu, Duc de Montmorency-Laval | |

(continued

## FRANCE (*continued*)

| Date of taking office | Prime Minister | Foreign Minister | Finance Minister |
|---|---|---|---|
| 28 Dec 22 | | François, Vicomte de Chateaubriand | |
| 6 June 24 | | Joseph, Duc de Villèle | |
| Oct 24 | | Ange, Baron de Damas | |
| 4 Jan 28 | Jean Baptiste, Vicomte de Martignac | Pierre Louis, Comte de la Ferronays | Antoine, Comte Roy |
| 24 Apr 29 | | Joseph, Comte Portalis | |
| 8 Aug 29 | Jules, Prince de Polignac | Jules, Prince de Polignac | André, Comte Chabrol |
| 19 May 30 | | | Guillaume Baron, Comte de Montbel |
| 29 July 30 | Victor-Louis-Victurnien, Duc de Mortemart (appointed by Charles X) | | |
| | Marie, Marquis de Lafayette (appointed by the provisional revolutionary government) | Louis Bignon | Joseph Dominique, Baron Louis |
| 13 Aug 30 | Victor, Duc de Broglie | Jean Baptiste, Comte Jourdan | |
| Sep 30 | | Louis Matthieu, Comte Molé | |
| 3 Nov 30 | Jacques Lafitte | Nicolas, Marquis de Maison | Jacques Lafitte |
| Dec 30 | | François, Comte Sebastiani | |

43

(*continued*

## FRANCE (*continued*)

| Date of taking office | Prime Minister | Foreign Minister | Finance Minister |
|---|---|---|---|
| 13 Mar 31 | Casimir Périer (died 16 May 32, replaced by M. Barthe) | | Joseph Dominique, Baron Louis |
| 11 Oct 32 | Nicholas, Duc de Dalmatie | Victor, Duc de Broglie | Jean Humann |
| 28 Mar 34 | Admiral de Rigny | | |
| 4 Apr 34 | | Admiral de Rigny | |
| 18 July 34 | Étienne, Comte Gérard | | |
| 29 Oct 34 | Victor, Duc de Broglie | Victor, Duc de Broglie | |
| 14 Nov 34 | Hugues Bernard Maret | M. Bresson | H. Passy |
| 18 Nov 34 | Eduard, Duc de Trévise | Victor, Duc de Broglie | Jean Humann |
| 12 Mar 35 | Victor, Duc de Broglie | | |
| 22 Feb 36 | Adolphe Thiers | Adolphe Thiers | Comte d'Argout |
| 7 Sep 36 | Louis Matthieu, Comte Molé | Louis Matthieu, Comte Molé | Charles, Comte Duchâtel |
| 15 Apr 37 | | | M. Lacave-Laplagne |
| 8 Mar 39 | | | M. Gautier |
| 31 Mar 39 | | Napoléon, Duc de Montebello | |
| 12 May 39 | Nicholas, Duc de Dalmatie | Nicholas, Duc de Dalmatie | H. Passy |
| 1 Mar 40 | Adolphe Thiers | Adolphe Thiers | Baron de la Lozère |
| 29 Oct 40 | Nicholas, Duc de Dalmatie | Guillaume Guizot | Jean Humann |
| Sep 47 | Guillaume Guizot | | |

## GREAT BRITAIN

| Date of taking office | Prime Minister | Foreign Minister | Finance Minister |
|---|---|---|---|
| 1783 | Chief Minister, with responsibility for Foreign Affairs and Finance, William Pitt | | |
| Feb 01 | Henry Addington | Lord Hawkesbury | |
| 10 Apr 04 | William Pitt (died 23 Jan 06) | William Pitt | William Pitt |
| 11 Feb 06 | William Wyndham Grenville | Charles James Fox (died Sep 06) | |
| 14 Sep 06 | | Charles Grey, Lord Howick | |
| 31 Mar 07 | William Cavendish-Bentinck, Duke of Portland (ministry resigned 30 Sep 09) | George Canning | |
| 4 Oct 09 | Spencer Perceval (assassinated 11 May 12) | Richard Wellesley, Duke of Mornington | |
| 9 June 12 | Robert Banks Jenkinson, Lord Liverpool | Henry Steward, Viscount Castlereagh (committed suicide 12 Aug 22) | N. Vansittart |
| Aug 22 | | George Canning | |
| 31 Jan 23 | | | F. J. Robinson |
| 10 Apr 27 | George Canning | | |
| 31 Aug 27 | Frederick Robinson, Lord Goderich | Henry Fitzmaurice, Lord Lansdowne | |
| 22 Jan 28 | Arthur Wellesley, Duke of Wellington | George Hamilton-Gordon, Lord Aberdeen | H. Goulburn |
| 16 Nov 30 | Charles, Lord Grey | Henry Temple, Lord Palmerston | Lord Althorp |
| 9 July 34 | William Lamb, Lord Melbourne | | |
| 10 Dec 34 | Robert Peel | Arthur Wellesley, Duke of Wellington | |

(continued

45

## GREAT BRITAIN (*continued*)

| Date of taking office | Prime Minister | Foreign Minister | Finance Minister |
|---|---|---|---|
| 18 Apr 35 | William Lamb, Lord Melbourne | Henry Temple, Lord Palmerston | T. Spring-Rice |
| May 39 | | | T. Baring |
| 1 Sep 41 | Robert Peel | George Hamilton-Gordon, Lord Aberdeen | H. Goulburn |
| 6 July 46 | Lord John Russell | Henry Temple, Lord Palmerston | C. Wood |

## GREECE

| Date of taking office | Prime Minister | Date of taking office | Prime Minister |
|---|---|---|---|
| 1832 | Spyridou Trikupis | 1841 | Alexander, Prince of Mavrokordatos |
| 33 | Alexander, Prince of Mavrokordatos | 15 Sep 43 | Andreas, Count Metaxis |
| 13 June 34 | John Kolettis | 11 Apr 44 | Alexander, Prince of Mavrokordatos |
| 1 July 35 | Josef, Count Armansperg | 18 Aug 44 | John Kolettis |
| 14 Feb 37 | Ignaz von Rudhart | 13 Sep 47 | Kitsos Tzavellas |
| 20 Dec 37 | King Otto took over the post of Chief Minister | 19 Mar 48 | Lazarus Kundoriotis |

## HANOVER

| Date of taking office | Prime Minister | Date of taking office | Prime Minister |
|---|---|---|---|
| May 05 | Ernst, Imperial Count Münster-Ledenburg | 28 June 37 | Georg, Baron von Schele zu Schelenburg (until June 44) |
| 13 Feb 31 | Ludwig von Ompteda | | |

## HESSE-CASSEL

| Date of taking office | Prime Minister | Date of taking office | Prime Minister |
|---|---|---|---|
| Jan 31 | Baron Schenk von Schweinsberg | May 32 | Hans Hassenpflug |

46

(*continued*

## HESSE-CASSEL (*continued*)

| Date of taking office | Prime Minister | Date of taking office | Prime Minister |
|---|---|---|---|
| July 37 | Herr Hanstein | 44 | Herr Koch (for a second term) |
| Dec 41 | Herr Koch | 47 | Friedrich Scheffer (until Mar 48) |
| Jan 43 | Herr Koch was replaced by another (anon) | | |

## HESSE-DARMSTADT

| Date of taking office | Prime Minister |
|---|---|
| 1821 | Karl von Grolmann |
| Feb 29 | Karl du Bos du Thil (until 1848) |

## NETHERLANDS

| Date of taking office | Prime Minister |
|---|---|
| 9 Nov 87 | Laurens van de Spiegel (until Jan 95) |
| 29 Apr 05 | Rutger Jan Schimmel-penninck (until 1806) |

## PORTUGAL

| Date of taking office | Prime Minister | Date of taking office | Prime Minister |
|---|---|---|---|
| 27 May 35 | João Carlos, Duke of Saldanha, Oliveira and Daun | | de Sá de Bandeira |
| 25 Nov 35 | José Loureiro | 26 Nov 39 | Count de Bomfin |
| 20 Apr 36 | António, Duke of Terceira | 19 Jan 42 | Count de Thomar |
| 36 | Bernardo da Sa Nogueira, Marquis | 10 Feb 42 | Duke of Terceira |
| | | 17 May 46 | Duke of Palmella |
| | | 6 Oct 46 | João Carlos, Duke of Saldanha, Oliveira and Daun |

## PRUSSIA

| Date of taking office | Prime Minister | Foreign Minister | Finance Minister |
|---|---|---|---|
| 1749 | Karl, Count Finck von Finckenstein | Karl, Count Finck von Finckenstein | |

47

(*continued*

## PRUSSIA (continued)

| Date of taking office | Prime Minister | Foreign Minister | Finance Minister |
|---|---|---|---|
| 1800 | | Philip, Count von Alvensleben (died 21 Oct 02) | |
| 21 Oct 02 | | Christian, Count von Haugwitz | |
| Apr 04 | | Karl, Count von Hardenberg | |
| Feb 06 | | Christian, Count von Haugwitz | |
| Nov 06 | | Karl von Beyme | |
| 26 Apr 07 | | Karl, Count von Hardenberg | |
| 30 Sep 07 | | Heinrich, Baron von und zu Stein | |
| Nov 08 | | August, Graf von der Goltz | Karl, Baron von Stein zum Altenstein |
| June 10 | | | Karl, Count von Hardenberg |
| Dec 13 | | | Ludwig von Bülow |
| June 14 | Karl, Count von Hardenberg | Karl, Count von Hardenberg | |
| 2 Dec 17 | | | Wilhelm von Klewitz |
| 16 Sep 18 | | Christian, Count von Bernstorff | |
| Nov 22 | Otto von Voss (until Jan 23) | | |
| 25 | | | Friedrich von Motz |
| 27 | Karl, Duke of Mecklenburg (died 21 Sep 37) | | |
| 1 July 30 | | | Karl Maassen |
| 32 | | Friedrich Ancillon | |
| 35 | | | Albrecht, Count von Albensleben |
| 37 | Heinrich, Baron von Werther | | |

48

(continued

## PRUSSIA (*continued*)

| Date of taking office | Prime Minister | Foreign Minister | Finance Minister |
|---|---|---|---|
| 2 Apr 38 | Karl, Baron von Müffling | | |
| 41 | | Count Maltzau | |
| Apr 42 | | Heinrich, Baron von Bülow | |
| May 42 | | | Ernst von Bodelschwingh-Velmede |
| 44 | Gustav von Rochow | | |
| 3 May 44 | | | Heinrich von Flottwell |
| 45 | | Karl, Baron von Kanitz und Dallwitz | |
| Aug 46 | | | Franz von Düesberg |

## RUSSIA

| Date of taking office | Leader of the Ministers' Committee | Foreign Minister | Finance Minister |
|---|---|---|---|
| 1800 | | Peter, Count von der Pahlen | |
| 02 | | | Count Alexei Vassiliev |
| 20 Sep 02 | | Count Alexander Voronzov | |
| 04 | | Prince Czartoryski | |
| 07 | | Count Nikolai Rumjanzev | Feodor Alexandrovič Golubzov |
| 10 | | | Count Dmitri Guriev |
| 12 | Count (later Prince) Nikolai Ivanovič Saltykov | | |
| 15 | | Ivan Andreievič Weidemeyer | |

49

(*continued

## RUSSIA (continued)

| Date of taking office | Leader of the Ministers' Committee | Foreign Minister | Finance Minister |
|---|---|---|---|
| 16 | Prince Peter Lopuchin | Anton, Count Capodistrias | |
| 17 | | Karl, Count Nesselrode (until 1856) | |
| 23 | | | Count Cancrin |
| 27 | Prince Victor Kotschubei | | |
| 34 | Count Nikolai Novosiliev | | |
| 37 | Count (later Prince) Hilarion Vasiltschikov | | |
| 44 | | | Count Feodor Vrontschenko |
| 47 | Count Vassily Levaschov | | |

## SARDINIA-PIEDMONT

| Date of taking office | Prime Minister | Foreign Minister | Finance Minister |
|---|---|---|---|
| 11 May 14 | Marquis di San Marzano (until 1821) | | |
| 31 | | | Prospero Bello |
| 21 Mar 35 | Clemente, Count Solaro della Margherita | Clemente, Count Solaro della Margherita | |
| 29 Aug 44 | | | Ottavio di Revel |

## SAXONY

| Date of taking office | Prime Minister | Foreign Minister | Finance Minister |
|---|---|---|---|
| 14 May 13 | Detlev, Count von Einsiedl | Detlev, Count von Einsiedl | |
| Sep 30 | Bernhard, Baron von Lindenau | Johannes von Minkwitz | |
| 31 | | | Heinrich von Zeschau |
| 35 | | Heinrich von Zeschau | |
| 43 | Julius von Könneritz | | |

## SPAIN

| Date of taking office | Prime Minister | Date of taking office | Prime Minister |
|---|---|---|---|
| 1789 | Don José Mõnino, Count de Floridablanca | 28 Feb 22 | Francisco Martınez de la Rosa |
| Mar 92 | Pedro, Count of Aranda | 5 Aug 22 | Evaristo San Miguel |
| 93 | Manuel de Godoy | Mar 23 | Revolutionary government until the autumn |
| 08 | Manuel Luis de Urquijo | Nov 23 | Victor Sáenz |
| 4 May 14 | Duke of Silatos | 2 Dec 23 | Carlos, Marquis de Casa-Irujo |
| 15 Nov 14 | Pedro Ceballos | 25 Dec 23 | Count of Ofalia |
| 30 Oct 16 | José Leon y Pizarro | Jan 24 | Francisco Zea-Bermudez |
| 14 Nov 18 | Carlos, Marquis de Casa-Irujo | July 24 | Luis María Salazar |
| 12 June 19 | Manuel Gonzalez Salmon | 25 Oct 25 | Duke of Infantado |
| | | 18 Aug 26 | Manuel Gonzalez Salmon |
| 12 Sep 19 | Duke of San Fernando | 20 Jan 32 | Count of Alcudia |
| 18 Mar 20 | Juan Jouvat | 1 Oct 32 | José Cafranga |
| Mar 21 | Eusebio Bardaxi y Azara | 1 Oct 33 | Francisco Zea-Bermudez |
| 23 Apr 21 | Francisco de Paula Escudero | 15 Jan 34 | Francisco Martinez de la Rosa |

(continued

## SPAIN (*continued*)

| Date of taking office | Prime Minister | Date of taking office | Prime Minister |
|---|---|---|---|
| June 35 | Count of Toreno | 9 Dec 38 | Isidore Alaix |
| 14 Sep 35 | Juan Mendizábal | 20 July 40 | Antonio Gonzalez |
| 15 May 36 | Francisco Isturiz y Montero | 12 Aug 40 | Valentin Ferraz |
| | | 16 Sep 40 | Duke of Vitoria |
| 18 July 36 | José Maria Calatrava | 21 May 41 | Antonio Gonzalez |
| 18 Aug 37 | Eusebio Bardaxi y Azara | 17 June 42 | Marquis de Rodil |
| | | 1 Dec 43 | Luis Gonzalez Bravo |
| 16 Dec 37 | Count of Ofalia | 3 May 44 | Duke of Valencia |
| 7 Sep 38 | Duke of Fraías | 4 Apr 46 | Francisco Isturiz y Montero |
| 6 Dec 38 | Evaristo Pérez de Castro | 28 Jan 47 | Duke of Sotomayor |

## TURKEY

| Date of taking office | Grand Vizier | Date of taking office | Grand Vizier |
|---|---|---|---|
| 28 May 89 | Kethüda Çerbes Hassan | June/July 12 | Hurşid Ahmed |
| | | 30 Mar 15 | Mehmed Emin Rauf |
| 2 Jan 90 | Gazi Hassan | 6 Jan 18 | Derviş Mehmed |
| 16 Apr 90 | Rusçuklu Cezairli Hassan Serif | Jan 20 | Seyyid Ali |
| | | Apr 21 | Benderli Ali |
| Feb 91 | Koca Yusuf | 30 Apr 21 | Haji Salih |
| 91 | Damad Melik Mehmed | 11 Nov 22 | Hamdullah Abdullah |
| 21 Oct 94 | Izzet Mehmed | 4 Mar 23 | Silâhtar Ali |
| 23 Oct 98 | Yusuf Ziyaeddin | Dec 23 | Galib Mehmed Said |
| 24 Sep 05 | Hafiz Ismael | 15 Sep 24 | Benderli Selim Mehmed |
| 13 Oct 06 | Hilmi Ibrahim | 26 Oct 28 | Izzet Mehmed |
| 3 June 07 | Çelebi Mustafa | Jan 29 | Reşid Mehmed |
| 29 July 08 | Mustafa Pasha Bayraktar | 17 Feb 33 | Mehmed Emin Rauf |
| | | 8 July 39 | Mehmed Hüsref |
| 16 Nov 08 | Memiş Pasha | 29 May 41 | Mehmed Emin Rauf |
| Dec 08 | Çarhaci Ali | 7 Oct 41 | Izzet Mehmed |
| Feb 09 | Yusuf Zia | 3 Sep 42 | Mehmed Emin Rauf |
| Feb 11 | Ahmed Pasha | 31 July 46 | Mustafa Reşid |

52

# TUSCANY

| Date of taking office | Prime Minister |
|---|---|
| 1815 | Vittorio, Count Fossombroni |
| Apr 44 | Prince Neri (III) Corsini (died 25 Oct 45) |
| Sep 47 | Prince Neri (IV) Corsini |

# WÜRTTEMBERG

| Date of taking office | Prime Minister | Foreign Minister | Finance Minister |
|---|---|---|---|
| 8 Nov 16 | | Ferdinand, Count von Zeppelin | Christian von Otto |
| 10 Nov 17 | | | Karl, Baron von Malchus |
| 18 Nov 17 | Hans Otto von der Lühe | | |
| 5 Sep 18 | | | Ferdinand von Weckherlin |
| 17 May 19 | | Heinrich, Count von Wintzing-gerode | |
| 29 July 21 | Christian von Otto | | |
| 2 Oct 23 | | Josef, Count von Beroldingen | |
| 29 Oct 27 | | | Karl, Baron von Varnbüler |
| 15 Nov 31 | Paul, Baron von Maucler | | |
| 23 Sep 32 | | | Johann Herdegen |
| 31 Aug 44 | | | Christian Gottlob von Gärttner |

# 3 PARLIAMENTS AND SYSTEMS OF GOVERNMENT

## AUSTRIA

Austria in 1789 included the provinces of Bohemia, Moravia, Galicia, Slovakia, Transylvania, Bukovina, Croatia-Slavonia, Carniola, Gorizia, Istria, Dalmatia, Lombardy and Venetia, and the Kingdom of Hungary. The Sovereign of Austria ruled as King (or Queen) of Austria and Hungary until 1804, when the King of Austria, who was also Holy Roman Emperor, took the title of Emperor of Austria; he remained King of Hungary. In all his dominions his power was partly limited by the existence of representative bodies, or estates, which consisted of deputies chosen to represent social groups (nobility, clergy, burghers, knights and peasants) and communities. These had varying executive powers in the management of public works and the organization of levies and supplies, but their main function was to vote taxes and be responsible for their collection. They were therefore able to obstruct the implementation of royal policies of which they did not approve. Their own effectiveness was limited in its turn because deputies were sent to the estates with limited powers, and were obliged to refer back to those whom they represented.

This system of direct royal rule, tempered by the financial control of the estates, continued in name until 1849. In effect only the Hungarian Diet attempted any real control of Hapsburg absolute government; Hungary had a central diet as well as local diets, all dominated by the nobility. The diets of the other Austrian provinces had developed into executive bodies by the end of the eighteenth century and were mainly used as machinery for local administration.

## BELGIUM

The state came into existence in 1831 with a constitution which provided for a bicameral parliament. The lower house was directly elected for a 4-year term, half retiring every 2 years. The senate sat for an 8-year term and had half the number of members of the lower house; it was elected by the same electorate. The King had the power to initiate legislation, but his acts had to be signed by his ministers. He might dissolve both houses, in which event an election had to be held within 40 days.


# DENMARK

A parliament of the various social estates had existed since the fifteenth century, but it had not been called since 1660. The King ruled through a council of ministers, although even this was not called regularly until 1814, when regular sessions began. In 1834 a constitution was introduced which allowed provincial diets to meet regularly; these were representative, not elected, bodies and their role was consultative. The Central Diet of estates was called again in 1835, also as a consultative body. This was the position until 1849.


# FRANCE

Absolute government collapsed in 1788, and the Crown called the Estates-General (parliament) to meet, for the first time since 1614. The estates consisted of 3 bodies, the nobility, the clergy and the commons. It was decided in Dec 88 that they would meet on 1 May 89 and as 3 separate bodies, with the Third Estate (the commons) having as many deputies as the other 2 combined. On 17 June 89 the third estate, joined by reformers from the nobles and clergy, declared itself to be a National Assembly; on 20 June 89 it swore never to dissolve until France had a constitution. These declarations were declared null by the Crown on 23 June, and the National Assembly was ordered to re-arrange itself into the original 3 estates, which it refused to do. On 9 July 89 the Assembly proclaimed itself the National Constituent Assembly, which devised the constitution of 22 Dec 89: franchise was to be on the basis of taxation; political rights were to be given to groups of citizens according to whether those groups were active in primary assemblies or electoral assemblies, eligible for the Legislative Assembly. Suffrage was to be granted to adult males over 25 with tax and residence qualifications, who were not domestic servants; these 'active' citizens were to elect local councils for a re-organized administrative system of cantons; they also chose delegates to elect de-

55

partmental councillors and departmental deputies in the Legislative Assembly. Delegates were eligible on property qualifications. The Assembly was given 745 deputies (for France; there were colonial deputies later), and these were allotted to the departments according to area, population and revenue.

The first Legislative Assembly was elected in Sep 91. In Aug 92 it abolished the monarchy and convoked a further constituent assembly called the Convention. This body introduced manhood suffrage, and an oath of loyalty to the Republic from electors and delegates. A further constitution (which provided for direct election to an annual assembly from single-member constituencies) was devised in 1793 but not put into operation.

Government during 1793 was by executive committees of the National Convention, but this system was disrupted and finally brought to an end by factional hostilities which ended with the execution of Robespierre in July 94.

A further constitution was then devised by the Convention in 1795. This provided for a bicameral parliament with 2 councils, the Council of Ancients with 250 members and the Council of Five Hundred. Those qualified as electors were also qualified as members, with certain age and residence qualifications. Deputies were to sit for 3 years, one-third retiring every year; they could not sit for more than 6 consecutive years. There were 711 deputies and the Convention decreed that two-thirds must be Convention members. Indirect election was re-introduced, delegates being chosen on a property qualification on the basis of 1 for every 200 registered electors in each canton. Under the Directory of 1797–8 election results were annulled because the delegates returned opposed the Directory's policies.

In 1799 Napoleon introduced a constitution which provided for manhood suffrage and indirect election by list (electors of the *arrondissement* chose one-tenth of their number whom they considered suitable to represent the commune; from that tenth a further tenth was chosen to represent the department and from that tenth a national list of about 5000 was submitted to the Senate, who selected the deputies to the Legislature from the list). The Senate was nominated by Napoleon. Members of the lists could only be replaced by a two-thirds vote of their electors. The Legislature had a Tribunate of 80 members (abolished 1807) and a legislative body of 300. There was no colonial representation.

The electoral system was changed in 1802 and electoral colleges were introduced, filled by electors who held office for life and were chosen on tax qualifications, 1 for every 500 inhabitants (*arrondissement* colleges) and one for every 1000 (departmental colleges). Seats in the Legislature were given to the departments according to their population.

(*Note*: It is thought that throughout the Revolutionary and Napoleonic period the number of those entitled to elect deputies greatly exceeded the number of actual voters; the proportion who did not exercise their right was sometimes as high as nine-tenths.)

On the overthrow of Napoleon the restored Bourbon king granted a charter which was never applied. Napoleon returned in 1815. He amended the constitution of 1802 by altering the practice of the electoral colleges and establishing a Chamber of Deputies of 629 members who were to sit for 5 years. After Napoleon's final defeat this chamber was retained, and some of the provisions of the Bourbon charter of 1814 were applied to it. This charter had stressed the function of the Legislature rather than the electoral system, which it did not define. The King was to make all appointments and to initiate all legislation. Parliament might petition him to initiate, and no law could be passed or tax levied without its consent. Parliament was obliged to meet at least once a year. A new Chamber was elected in Aug 15; electoral colleges were retained and their practices altered. An electoral law was passed in 1817 which abolished the colleges. Electors of a department were to meet in one place and vote for deputies in 3 successive ballots. Electors were chosen on age and tax qualifications, as were deputies; annual direct tax paid by an elector was at least 300 francs, by a deputy at least 1000.

In 1820 the electoral district was changed from department to *arrondissement*, each returning one member to a total of 258. The remaining 172 members were elected at the chief towns of the departments by those voters who paid most taxes, ensuring a double vote for about 12,000 richer voters.

In 1824 the term of office for deputies was altered to 7 years, the Chamber being renewable as a whole.

The Parliamentary Commission of 1830 revised the Constitutional Charter. Both the Chamber of Deputies and the Crown-appointed Chamber of Peers (which was introduced by the 1814 charter) gained the right to initiate laws. The term for deputies was altered again to 5 years. The age of electors was lowered from 30 to 25.

In 1831 the tax qualification for electors was lowered to 200 francs (100 for some professional classes). This doubled the size of the electorate to about a 150th of the population.

## GERMANY

The Holy Roman Empire had a Reichstag which sat permanently as a negotiating and consulting body. Deputies attended from individual states owing allegiance to the Emperor. The Reichstag did not legislate or impose taxes.

The Empire came to an end in 1806. The Confederation of the Rhine formed by Napoleon in that year consisted of 16 states headed by a Protector whom Napoleon appointed. Its constitution provided for a diet of 2 colleges; one for member-kings and the other for the remaining states. This diet was to have no power to interfere in the affairs of member states.

The German Confederation was formed in 1815 with a Federal Diet which met in Frankfurt. Delegates were sent and instructed by the 38 member states (39 after 1817). There was one chamber, with powers to make war or peace, organize a federal army, enact laws to apply the constitution and decide disputes between states. It had no executive; its decisions were enacted by the governments of member-states if they were willing to do so. If they refused, the Diet could ask another member-state to intervene with force.

The Diet sat as a full assembly or as a small council or *curia*. In the latter the 11 large states had 1 vote each and the rest 6 votes between them. In the full assembly there were 70 votes cast, of which Austria, Prussia, Saxony, Hanover, Bavaria and Württemberg had 4 each. A two-thirds majority was necessary for a decision. The small councils dealt with ordinary business, the full assembly discussed constitutional matters and questions of war and peace.

Austria held the Presidency by permanent right, and Prussia the Vice-Presidency.

Between 1832 and 1834 there was conflict between the Diet and the state diets, the Diet insisting that princes had supreme power in their states and that their parliaments must not hinder them in their duty to the Confederation, that the Diet alone had the right to interpret federal law and that the state diets must not infringe it; that the Diet would support princes against their parliaments, who might be called to account by the Federal Court. The Vienna Conference of 1834 affirmed the superiority of the Diet over the state parliaments.

# GERMAN STATES

## PRUSSIA

The separate provinces had diets or estates which had been established in the Middle Ages, but most had fallen into disuse. There was no central representative body. The King ruled through an executive General Directory and his *Kabinett* of secretaries. Ministers of the General Directory were responsible to the King; the powers of the Directory were divided according to subject (e.g. mines) and geographical areas. In 1808 a Council of State was introduced as the sole organ of government under the King. This consisted of ministers of the Crown, the King, princes of the royal house and privy councillors nominated for their expert knowledge. The Council had a president and met regularly. Full sessions were necessary for legislation; a smaller body called the Council of Ministers met to transact routine business. There were 5 ministries.

In 1811, and from 1812 to 1815, a central representative body met to administer newly imposed taxation. In 1847 a central diet was called; it consisted of members of the provincial diets and met as 2 houses. The upper house consisted of nobility, the lower of knights, burghers and peasants. The Diet was dismissed by the King in the same year.

## BAVARIA

In the separate provinces of Bavaria there were estates, and there was also a central Bavarian *Landtag*. By the end of the eighteenth century the former were still functioning and the latter met only as a standing committee to administer taxes and the budget. In 1808 both were abolished and a parliament was established. There was a single chamber of deputies, composed partly of nominees representing 15 administrative *Kreise* (circles) and partly of members indirectly elected in these *Kreise* by highly taxed landowners, businessmen and merchants. The ruler did not share his power with this body as he had done with the old estates; he remained superior to it. The executive body was the Council of Ministers which was composed of the heads of ministries (5), the heads of departments within ministries, the Sovereign and the Crown Prince. This body had existed before 1808 as a consultative body which drafted policy; after 1808 it also legislated and passed the budget. Individual ministers were responsible to the King for the conduct of their ministries.

In 1818 a constitution was granted which provided for a bicameral parliament. Ministers were still responsible to the King and not to the parliament, but his executive power was shared with them and they had to countersign all his acts. The upper house of parliament held hereditary, nominated and *ex-officio* members. The lower house was composed of members elected on a tax-based franchise from electoral districts whose representation varied with population. Budget and taxation were now controlled by parliament. Members of both houses had a limited right to interpellate ministers and to question and debate policies, but parliament had no legislative initiative and no power to reject the bills proposed by the King and his Council of Ministers.

## SAXONY

The executive power was in the hands of the King who acted through a Council of Ministers. The estates consisted of representatives of the social

59

classes and special interests; it had no legislative power. In 1831 a constitution was granted which changed the estates into a two-chamber parliament by the addition of an elected lower house. The deputies were directly elected on a tax-based franchise, one for every 30,000 population. The term of office was 6 years, one-third retiring every 2 years.

The King still controlled all legislation. His acts had to be countersigned by his ministers, but he appointed and dismissed ministers himself. Both houses of parliament were required to accept or reject a bill in the form in which the King presented it.

### HANOVER

A constitution was drafted in 1814 but never put into operation. Government was by the Sovereign who executed his decisions through ministers responsible to him. The representative estates formed an advisory body with limited powers regarding taxation and the budget. In 1833 a constitution was granted which created a bicameral parliament, still dominated by the King through nominations to office. It had some legislative power and some power to control the budget. This constitution was abrogated in 1837.

### WÜRTTEMBERG

The estates representative of social groups had suffered an erosion of their powers during the eighteenth century. In 1770 their rights were restored; they met regularly and functioned as an advisory body with some control over finance. Government was by the King and his ministers who were appointed by and responsible to him.

A constitution was granted in 1819 which provided for a bicameral parliament. The King still had the sole right to initiate legislation for financial purposes; he enjoyed considerable emergency powers even if parliament were not sitting and his ordinances need not be submitted to the house for approval. All statutory laws, appropriations and taxes required parliament's consent. Both chambers met annually; the lower house only was elected, election being on a tax-based franchise and indirect. There were 92 deputies.

The members of either house might question ministers on their decisions, but the ministers were not obliged to give account of their policies.

### BADEN

Government was by the Sovereign acting through his appointed ministers. A constitution of 1810 was drafted but never enforced. In 1818 a further constitution was drafted and applied. This provided for a bicameral parliament with an elected lower house. The deputies (73) were indirectly elected on a tax-based franchise from electoral districts, their numbers being according to the district's population. Both chambers were required to meet at least every other year and were given competence to deal with taxes, loans, expenditures and laws regarding the freedom and property of citizens. All other matters could be dealt with by royal ordinance not requiring parliament's consent. Parliament's real power was in voting funds; the Crown still controlled all administration and the execution of laws.

## HESSE-CASSEL AND HESSE-DARMSTADT

In both states there was absolute government, and the power of the estates had gone. The estates of Hesse-Darmstadt were dismissed in 1803 and never summoned again. The Elector of Hesse-Cassel and the Grand Duke of Hesse-Darmstadt ruled through Councils of Ministers responsible to their sovereign, appointed and dismissed by him.

A constitution was granted in Hesse-Darmstadt in 1820. This provided for a bicameral parliament with an elected lower house. The deputies (50) were indirectly elected on a tax-based franchise for a 6-year term. The parliament had no initiative and acted as an advisory body; real legislative and executive power remained with the Sovereign. A similar constitution was granted in Hesse-Cassel in 1831.

## BRUNSWICK

The Sovereign exercised absolute power through his own appointed ministers until 1832, when a constitution was granted. This provided for a parliament which resembled the old estates in that its deputies represented special groups. Members were elected on a tax-based franchise for a 6-year term. The house was obliged to meet at least every 2 years. Parliament had limited legislative powers, and ministers were still responsible to the sovereign.

## MECKLENBURG-SCHWERIN AND MECKLENBURG-STRELITZ

There was no written constitution. A parliament evolved through the sixteenth, seventeenth and eighteenth centuries. There was a common *Landtag* for both duchies, which the Grand Duke of Mecklenburg-Schwerin was obliged to summon at least once a year. There was one chamber for each duchy, but sittings were always in joint session. Representation was the same as in the ancient estates; deputies attended on behalf of the knights or of the towns.

Either duke might submit measures to parliament, having advised the other of his intention. He did so in writing, as his ministers did not appear in the house. The chamber, after debate, sent its acceptance, rejection or amendment.

61

The Crown then either accepted or modified the chamber's vote, and this process continued until agreement was reached or seen to be impossible.

Parliament's consent was needed for laws affecting the various estates of the realm and their members, and Crown revenue. In laws affecting Crown domains the Crown was absolute. In other laws the parliament was consulted but its consent was not necessary.

# GREAT BRITAIN

Parliament consisted of the Sovereign, the House of Lords and the House of Commons. Executive power was nominally in the hands of the Sovereign but actually exercised by the Cabinet of ministers who were responsible to the 2 houses. The upper house consisted of peers and bishops who held their seats either by appointment, hereditary right or election (the last being the case with Scottish and Irish peers). The lower house consisted of directly elected members chosen to represent counties and boroughs. Counties had 2 members each. Parliamentary boroughs (203) also had 2 members each, elected on widely differing franchise based on property and civic rights.

Parliament had initiative in all legislation, and its consent was necessary for all measures. Bills were introduced first in the lower, and then in the upper, house, the latter having the right to reject them; if passed, they became law with the Sovereign's assent. Parliament was also the highest court of justice.

The Reform Act of 1832 rationalized the franchise, which remained on a property basis, and re-distributed constituencies according to population. In the counties the franchise belonged to freeholders of property worth 40 shillings a year, and certain leasehold tenants. In the boroughs, householders with a £10 property qualification could vote, as well as freeholders.

Irish members first sat in parliament following the Act of Union between England and Ireland in 1800.

# GREECE

Government was by the Sovereign or his regent through his ministers, appointed by him, until 1844. A constitution was granted in that year which established a parliament with 2 chambers, the upper house (Senate) being nominated by the King and the lower (Chamber of Deputies) being elected on universal manhood suffrage. The executive power was held by a cabinet who were responsible to parliament.

## ITALIAN STATES

The only exceptions to absolute government were the republics of Venice and Genoa as they existed in 1789, the states established by Napoleon between 1796 and 1815, and the government of councillors in Lucca which lasted from the fifteenth century until 1799.

Venice was governed by a doge with a republican council until the French occupation of 1797. Its territory was then divided between the Napoleonic Cisalpine Republic and the Austrian Empire. It became part of the Kingdom of Italy (with Napoleon as King) in 1806 and returned to Austrian rule in 1814.

Genoa was governed by a doge with a republican council until 1797, when it became part of the Napoleonic Ligurian Republic. It was united with the Kingdom of Sardinia in 1815.

The government of Lucca by 120 councillors and 40 elders was brought to an end by the French occupation of 1799. The republican council was reconstituted in 1801 with a council of 12 elders, and suppressed by Napoleon in 1805. Lucca became a Bourbon duchy in 1817.

The Napoleonic republics were each given 2 legislative councils and an executive directory whose members were to be elected by members of the councils. The members of the legislative councils were indirectly elected by special groups, but their decisions could always be over-ruled by the executive. In the Roman and Parthenopean Republics the upper house (Senate) had the exclusive right to initiate legislation. Joseph Bonaparte as King of Naples granted a constitution in 1808: this provided for a Council of State of 26–36 members, and a Legislative Assembly of 100 chosen to represent various classes of society. In the Assembly 80 members were to be nominated by the King and 20 indirectly elected. This constitution did not come into operation until 1815, and then only for a short time. The reinstated Bourbon King abrogated it.

## THE NETHERLANDS (HOLLAND)

In 1789 Holland was ruled by a Hereditary Stadtholder (William of Orange-Nassau) and a parliament or States-General of 24 members chosen to represent the various social estates. Government was executed through provincial states which were semi-independent.

A revolutionary republic was proclaimed in 1795 and obtained its constitution as the Batavian Republic in 1798. Government was by a directory of 5 and 2 councils, one having 60 and the other 30 members. In 1801 the directory was increased in size to 12 members and the 2 councils were replaced by a single council of 35. In 1805 Napoleon introduced the office of Grand Pensionary, the Grand Pensioner to act as his viceroy. In 1806 this office was abolished and Holland became a monarchy; the councils remained as advisory bodies. In 1810 the country was annexed to France, and became independent once more with a new monarchical constitution in 1815.

This re-established the States-General as a two-chamber parliament, of which the upper house was composed of members representing the provinces and qualified to sit either because of official status or level of taxation. The lower house was elected on a tax-based franchise. Executive power was in the hands of the King and his Council of Ministers; legislative power was shared between the King, the Council and the States-General.

# NORWAY

The country was ruled by Denmark until 1814, when it was united with Sweden by a union of the Swedish and Norwegian crowns. Norway had its own constitution, however, and was semi-autonomous. The Constitution of 1814 provided for a monarchy with limited powers. Executive power was held by the King and a ministerial council of his choice. The King was bound by oath to uphold the constitution. His decrees could only be issued if they were not at variance with it. The counter-signature of ministers was required for his acts.

Legislative power was held by the parliament. Deputies were indirectly elected on a property and residence franchise, and served for 3 years. A single legislature was elected which, after election, split itself in two; the whole body elected one-quarter of its members to form a second chamber. The lower house retained the right to initiate laws, which were then passed to the higher chamber and finally to the King. Bills rejected by the higher chamber twice could still be adopted by a two-thirds majority in a joint session. The King had a suspensive veto. The lower house controlled finance.

# PORTUGAL

A representative diet of estates had existed since the thirteenth century, but this had not been summoned since the mid-eighteenth century. Government was carried on by the Sovereign acting through chosen ministers. In 1807 Portugal was occupied by the French and the Sovereign deposed, but there was no effective substitute government. The monarchy was restored in 1813, but the monarch had fled to Brazil (which was a Portuguese possession), and in his absence a governing junta was set up in 1820; this in turn summoned a constitutional assembly to draw up a liberal constitution. The King returned from Brazil in 1821 and accepted the constitution in 1822. It provided for a single-chamber parliament which would have full legislative powers, subject only to the suspensive veto of the King. This constitution was abrogated in 1823. In 1826 a charter was granted which provided for a parliament of 2 chambers; the upper house was composed of hereditary and nominated peers, the lower house of deputies was elected on a property and education franchise. Executive power still rested with the King and his ministers, but legislative initiative lay with parliament, to whom the ministers were responsible. The King had powers of suspensive veto; measures which were passed by both houses twice became law. The King also decided points of dispute between the 2 houses.

## RUSSIA

Central government had been reorganized by Peter I and remained in similar form until the end of the nineteenth century. Administration was carried out by colleges of which there were normally 12; each college had a specific responsibility and was managed by a director under a board. There was a Senate of appointed members whose function was to supervise the work of the colleges, but it had no real power to co-ordinate or plan.

Under Catherine II (1762–96) the directors of the colleges received increased powers at the expense of the boards. A Cabinet of ministers was established, but its exact role was not defined. The Senate's powers were also increased; it was given more power of administrative control, and it was the supreme court of appeal.

Paul I (1796–1801) and Alexander I (1801–25) had no Cabinet or formal Council of Ministers, although ministries replaced the former colleges in 1801. There was a co-ordinating 'committee of ministries' with a permanent secretary. Nicholas I continued this system.

There was no parliament or central representative body.

## SPAIN

In 1789 the King governed through a central executive council, with a representative Cortes or diet of estates whose task was mainly to vote taxes. There had originally been separate Cortes for Aragon, Castile and Catalonia; by the end of the eighteenth century that of Castile had become dominant.

Napoleon forced the abdication of the King in 1808 and installed his brother Joseph Bonaparte as King. He continued to rule through a central council, but as insurrection against the French was followed by British invasion, he established no effective government. He was replaced by a reinstated Bourbon King in 1813.

In 1810 a partisan central junta summoned a Cortes for the purposes of raising money for the war against the French. This Cortes also devised a constitution which was published in 1812. It provided for a monarchy and a single-chamber parliament. The King was to exercise power through responsible ministers, and was to have the power of suspensive veto only. Legislative initiative lay with parliament, which might still pass laws which the King had vetoed provided those laws had been passed by the house 3 years in succession. The King might also initiate bills, which required the assent of parliament. The chamber had one deputy for every 70,000 population, indirectly elected for a 2-year term. The executive was responsible to parliament. The King abolished this constitution in 1814. It was restored in 1820 and abolished again in 1823. A similar liberal constitution was drawn up in 1833, but civil war prevented its application.

# SWEDEN

The King ruled through ministers; there was a diet of 4 estates – nobles, clergy, burghers and peasants – which had formerly had considerable powers of legislation, but Gustav III summoned it only in 1789 and never again. Government through ministers continued under Gustav IV after 1792. In 1809 he was forced to abdicate, and a new constitution was granted by his successor. This revived the diet of 4 estates and laid down that it should meet at least once every 5 years. The presidents of the burgher and peasant estates were to be appointed by the King. The estates had exclusive power to raise taxes and levies. They shared legislative power with the King and the assent of both was necessary for a bill to become law; the royal veto or the estates' rejection was final.

Ministers were appointed by the King and were not responsible to the estates; their counter-signature was needed for all acts of the King, and they might refuse it if a measure was thought unconstitutional.

In 1840 the ministers became heads of departments.

## SWITZERLAND

In 1789 there was a loose confederation. The diet was the only central body, and all cantons had one vote; it met regularly and the representatives were responsible only to their own governments. Of the separate cantons, 6 had primary assemblies and direct democracy. Three had representative governments chosen on a limited franchise and 4 were oligarchies.

In 1798 Napoleon established the Helvetic Republic, with one central government. There was a bicameral legislature: the Grand Council was composed of deputies indirectly elected, and the Senate had members appointed to represent each canton (4 for each). The senators and councillors together elected a Directory of 5. There were 4 administrative heads of department, and each canton had a prefect and an elected legislature.

In 1803 this system was replaced by a federal constitution. In the new Federal Diet cantons with 100,000 inhabitants or less had 1 vote and others 2. Executive authority was vested in the governments of Berne, Freiburg, Lucerne, Zürich, Basle and Solothurn by turns.

In 1815 there was a return to the original loose confederation. Each canton had a primary assembly of its own and 1 vote in the Central Diet. Executive authority in the diet was vested in Berne, Zürich and Lucerne for a period of 2 years each.

(*Note*: the Helvetic Republic of Napoleon is generally regarded as having been unsuccessful and generally inoperative. Four draft constitutions were considered before it was finally abandoned in 1803.)


## TURKEY

In 1789 the Sultan ruled through the Grand Vizier, in whose hands all executive power was concentrated. During the reign of Mahmud II (1808–39) this system was replaced by a number of ministries, each with specific responsibility. In 1838 the Supreme Council of Judicial Ordinances was created as a consultative body to advise the Sultan. There was no parliament or other representative body.

67

# 4 THE GROWTH OF LIBERALISM AND NATIONALISM: 1815–48

## CHRONOLOGY OF MAJOR EVENTS

THE ITALIAN RISORGIMENTO

| | |
|---|---|
| 23 June 17 | Rising at Macerata collapses. |
| 2 July 20 | Outbreak of rebellion in Naples, led by Morelli and Salvati. Joined by General Guglielmo Pepe. Inspired by Cadiz revolt in Spain in Jan 1820, which forced a return to 1812 constitution. Early success of revolt. |
| 6 July 20 | Constitution promised to Naples. |
| Aug 20 | Membership of the Carbonari declared high treason throughout Lombardy-Venetia. Wave of arrests. |
| Feb 21 | Austria accedes to Ferdinand's request to dispatch army to Naples. |
| 13 Mar 21 | Victor Emanuel leaves Piedmont after constitutionalist rising. Charles Albert left as Regent, proclaims the 1812 Spanish constitution. Charles Felix of Modena disowns these actions and calls on Austrian military aid. |
| 23 Mar 21 | Austrian troops, called in to crush the Naples revolt, enter Naples. Pepe's army beaten earlier at Rieti. Execution of Morelli. |
| 8 Apr 21 | Battle of Novara; triumph of Austrian forces; De la Tour, and Count Bubna, the Austrian commander, enter Turin and Alessandria without opposition. |
| Sep 23 | Leo XII elected Pope; continuation of reactionary misgovernment in the Papal States. |
| 13 June 24 | Accession of Grand Duke Leopold II in Tuscany. |
| 4 Jan 25 | Death of Ferdinand I, King of the Two Sicilies; accession of the weak Francis I. |

| | |
|---|---|
| 29 | Death of Count von Neipperg, effective ruler of Parma. Replaced by reactionary Baron Werklein. |
| 2 Feb 31 | Election of Cardinal Mauro Capellari as Pope Gregory XVI. Rising in Modena, led by Menotti against Francis IV; flight of Werklein from Parma. Rebellion in Papal States. |
| 4 Mar 31 | New Austrian invasion of Italy in response to an appeal by Gregory XVI. |
| 21 Mar 31 | Austrian troops enter Bologna. |
| 10 May 31 | Memorandum agreed by ambassadors of great powers on reform of government in the Papal States. Largely ignored. |
| Jan 32 | Further rising in Romagna quelled by Austrian troops; French troops sent by Louis-Philippe to occupy Ancona. Mazzini founds 'Young Italy'. |
| 10 Oct 38 | With the exception of Ferrara, Austrian troops evacuate Papal States. |
| 39 | Scientific congresses in Italy discuss problem of unity. |
| 43 | Gioberti advocates a united Italy under Papal sovereignty in his book *The Moral and Civil Supremacy of Italy*. |
| 25 July 44 | Bandiero brothers shot for attempting revolt in Calabria. |
| 15 June 46 | Pius IX (Pio Nono) elected Pope. Major liberal concessions, including a political amnesty; modification of press censorship; formation of Civic Guard and establishment of a Council of State. |
| | Charles Albert (in Piedmont) embarks on anti-Austrian policy. D'Azeglio advocates end of papal misrule in his publication *Ultimi casi di Romagna*. |
| 47 | Misgovernment in Naples exposed by Settembrini in *Protests of the People of the Two Sicilies*. Austrian occupation of Ferrara (17 July); protest by Pio Nono helps secure subsequent withdrawal. |
| | Imprisonment of Manin and Tommaseo after pleas for unity at Venice Scientific Congress. |
| 21 Oct 47 | Charles Albert of Piedmont dismisses reactionary ministers. |
| 12 Jan 48 | Revolt in Sicily. A provisional independent government proclaimed. |
| 10 Feb 48 | Constitution proclaimed in Naples by Ferdinand II. |
| 4 Mar 48 | Charles Albert proclaims constitution in Piedmont. |
| 14 Mar 48 | Pius IX grants constitution in Rome. |
| 17 Mar 48 | Daniele Manin leads revolution in Venice. |

| | |
|---|---|
| 18 Mar 48 | Uprising in Milan; Radetsky evacuates city. |
| 20 Mar 48 | Revolt in Parma. |
| 22 Mar 48 | Republic proclaimed in Venice. |
| 24 Mar 48 | Sardinia declares war on Austria. |
| 8 Apr 48 | Piedmontese troops defeat Austrians at Gioto. |
| 13 Apr 48 | Sicily declares independence from Naples. |
| 25 Apr 48 | Papacy joins war against Austria. |
| 29 Apr 48 | Pius IX withdraws support from nationalist movement. |
| 30 Apr 48 | Further Austrian reverse at Patrengo. |
| 15 May 48 | Collapse of Naples revolt. |
| 29 May 48 | Battle of Curtatone; Austrians defeat Tuscany. |
| 22 July 48 | Battle of Custozza. Major victory for Radetsky. Sardinian troops driven from Milan and remainder of Lombardy. |
| 9 Aug 48 | Armistice of Vigevano between Sardinia and Austria. |
| 11 Aug 48 | Sardinian troops expelled from Venice. |
| 15 Nov 48 | Assassination of Count Rossi, premier of Papal States. |
| 24 Nov 48 | Pius IX escapes to Gaeta. |
| 7 Feb 49 | Flight of Grand Duke of Tuscany to Gaeta. |
| 9 Feb 49 | Mazzini proclaims republic in Rome. |
| 12 Mar 49 | Sardinia ends truce with Austria. |
| 23 Mar 49 | Battle of Novara; major Austrian victory. Abdication of Charles Albert; accession of Victor Emanuel II. |
| 25 Apr 49 | French troops land in Papal States. |
| 15 May 49 | Troops from Naples occupy Palermo. |
| 4 July 49 | French troops enter Rome. Pius IX restored. |

GERMAN NATIONALISM

| | |
|---|---|
| Nov 16 | Diet of German Confederation opens at Frankfurt-am-Main. |
| Sep 19 | 'Carlsbad' decrees promulgated; aimed at suppressing revolutionary activity. |
| Oct 19 | Prussia signs trade treaty with Schwarzburg-Sonderhausen. Beginning of the *Zollverein*. |
| 2 Dec 23 | Provincial diets established in Prussia. |
| 22 Sep 30 | Succession of revolts in Saxony, Hesse and Brunswick. Rulers dethroned; constitutions granted. |
| 5 Jan 31 | Constitution granted in Hesse-Cassel. |
| 8 Mar 31 | Constitution granted in Hanover. |
| 4 Sep 31 | Saxony granted a constitution. |
| 27 May 32 | Hambach Festival advocates revolt against Austrian rule. |

| | |
|---|---|
| 28 June 32 | Metternich's 'Six Articles'. |
| 23 Mar 33 | Prussia establishes *Zollverein*, with Austria excluded. |
| 12 May 35 | Baden joins *Zollverein*. |
| 10 July 37 | Hanover constitution suppressed by Ernest Augustus. |
| 7 June 40 | Accession of Frederick William IV of Prussia. |
| 3 Feb 47 | Frederick William IV summons United Diet. |
| 17 Mar 48 | Uprising in Berlin; Frederick William IV grants constitution. |
| 31 Mar 48 | The *Vorparlament* meets at Frankfurt. |
| 2 May 48 | Prussia invades Denmark over Schleswig-Holstein question. |
| 18 May 48 | German National Assembly meets at Frankfurt. |
| 22 May 48 | Berlin meeting of Prussian National Assembly. |
| 26 Aug 48 | Treaty of Malmo between Denmark and Prussia. |
| 5 Dec 48 | Dissolution of Prussian National Assembly. |
| 23 Jan 49 | Prussia advocates union of Germany without Austria. |
| 27 Mar 49 | German National Assembly offers title 'Emperor of the Germans' to an unwilling Frederick William IV. |
| 3 May 49 | Revolt in Dresden suppressed by Prussia. |
| 6 June 49 | National Assembly moves to Stuttgart. |
| 18 June 49 | Troops dissolve Stuttgart assembly. |
| 23 July 49 | Baden rebels surrender to Prussia. |

## DECLINE OF THE OTTOMAN EMPIRE

| | |
|---|---|
| 5 Nov 17 | Serbia granted partial autonomy by the Turks. |
| 6 Mar 21 | Rebellion in Moldavia-Wallachia against Turks. Rebels appeal for aid to Alexander I. |
| 22 Apr 21 | Greek massacre of Turks at Morea; beginning of Turkish repression. |
| 19 June 21 | Turks defeat Greek rebels at Dragashan. |
| 5 Oct 21 | Greek rebels capture Tripolitza in Morea. |
| 13 Jan 22 | Proclamation of Greek independence. |
| 22 Apr 22 | Turks capture Chios; Greeks massacred. |
| 15 July 22 | Turks invade Greece. |
| 19 Apr 24 | Death of Byron at Missolonghi. |
| 4 Apr 26 | St Petersburg Protocol; Britain and Russia agree on autonomy for Greece. |
| 5 Apr 26 | Russian ultimatum to Turkey concerning Serbia and the Danube provinces. |
| 27 Oct 26 | Akkermann Convention; Russian gains Serbia and Danube. |

| | |
|---|---|
| 5 June 27 | Turks enter Athens. |
| 6 July 27 | Treaty of London. Russia, France and Britain agree to recognize autonomy of Greece. |
| 16 Aug 27 | Turkey rejects Allied demands. |
| 20 Oct 27 | Battle of Navarino; destruction of Turkish and Egyptian fleets. |
| 8 Dec 27 | Allied ambassadors leave Constantinople. |
| 26 Apr 28 | Russian declaration of war on Turkey. |
| 19 July 28 | London Protocol signed. |
| 6 Aug 28 | Turks under Mahomet Ali agree to leave Greece. |
| 11 Oct 28 | Russians occupy Varna. |
| 16 Nov 28 | Independence of Greece recognized. |
| 14 Sep 29 | Russo-Turkish war ended by Treaty of Adrianople. |
| 3 Feb 30 | London Conference; Greek independence under guarantee of Britain, France and Russia. |
| 10 Apr 32 | Turkey declares war on Mahomet Ali. |
| 27 Apr 32 | Acre falls to Mahomet Ali. |
| 21 Dec 32 | Turks heavily defeated at Battle of Konieh. |
| 3 May 33 | Turkey grants independence to Egypt. |
| 8 June 33 | Treaty of Unkiar-Skelessi; Russo-Turkish alliance. |
| 10–20 Sep 33 | Congress of Müchengratz. |
| 15 Oct 33 | Prussia, Austria and Russia agree to support integrity of the Ottoman Empire. |
| 21 Apr 39 | Turkish army invades Syria. |
| 24 June 39 | Turkish army defeated at Nezib. |
| 1 July 39 | Death of Sultan Mahmud; accession of Abd-el-Medjid surrender of Turkish fleet at Alexandria. |
| 3 Nov 39 | Reform decree promulgated throughout Ottoman Empire. |
| 15 June 40 | Quadruple Alliance (Russia, Prussia, Austria and Britain) in support of Turkey against Mahomet Ali. |
| 11 Sep 40 | Beirut bombarded by British navy. |
| 3 Nov 40 | Acre captured by British, Syria evacuated by Mahomet Ali. |
| 5 Nov 40 | Convention of Alexandria; Mahomet Ali accedes to terms of Treaty of London. |
| 13 July 41 | Ottoman integrity guaranteed. Straits closed to warships of all nations. |
| 28 July 48 | Russian invasion of Danube principalities to suppress revolts. |
| 1 May 49 | Convention of Balta Liman. Joint 7-year Russo-Turkish occupation of Danubian principalities. |

INDEPENDENCE OF BELGIUM

| | |
|---|---|
| 31 May 15 | Belgium, Holland and Luxembourg are united to constitute the Netherlands. |
| 25 Aug 30 | Revolt in Belgium against union with Holland. |
| 18 Nov 30 | National Congress in Belgium declares independence. |
| 22–4 Nov 30 | Belgium votes for a monarchy, but vetoes the House of Orange. |
| 20 Dec 30 | Britain, France, Austria, Prussia and Russia agree at the London Conference on separation of Belgium from Holland. |
| 22–7 Jan 31 | Protocols by the powers for the separation of Belgium. Accepted by Dutch, rejected by Belgians. |
| 3 Feb 31 | Duc de Nemours elected King by the Belgians. Nomination rejected by Louis-Philippe to placate Britain. |
| 7 Feb 31 | Belgian constitution proclaimed. |
| 26 June 31 | The '18 Articles' of the London Conference rejected by Holland. |
| 2 Aug 31 | Dutch invasion of Belgium. |
| 20 Aug 31 | French army enters Belgium; Dutch forced to retreat. |
| 21 Oct 31 | The '21 Articles' of the London Conference again rejected by Holland. |
| 15 Nov 31 | A treaty, incorporating 24 articles, is accepted by the powers. |
| 23 Dec 32 | Antwerp falls to France; Dutch forced to recognize independence of Belgium. |
| 21 May 33 | Indefinite armistice concluded between Dutch and Belgians. |
| 19 Apr 39 | Treaty of London. Final agreement of territorial boundaries of Holland and Belgium. Luxembourg created a Grand Duchy. |

THE POLISH INSURRECTION OF 1830

| | |
|---|---|
| 9 June 15 | Congress of Vienna ends; eastern Poland ceded to Russia, western Poland to Prussia. Cracow becomes an independent city republic. |
| 27 Nov 15 | Poland granted a constitution by Russia. |
| 29 Nov 30 | Polish revolt against Russia, partly caused by Tsar's intention of using Polish troops in France and Belgium. |

| | |
|---|---|
| 25 Jan 31 | Polish Diet declares independence. |
| 26 May 31 | Russian defeat of Polish forces at Ostrolenke. |
| 8 Sep 31 | Russians capture Warsaw; collapse of Polish revolt. |
| 26 Feb 32 | Polish constitution abolished. |

THE REVOLUTION OF 1830 IN FRANCE

| | |
|---|---|
| 13 Feb 20 | Duc de Berri murdered. |
| 5 May 21 | Napoleon I dies. |
| 16 Sep 24 | Louis XVIII succeeded by Charles X. |
| 30 Apr 27 | National Guard disbanded. |
| 5 Nov 27 | 76 new peers created. |
| 19–20 Nov 27 | Election riots in Paris; barricades, some deaths. |
| 4 Jan 28 | Villèle ministry replaced by Martignac. |
| 10 Dec 28 | Beranger imprisoned for political songs. |
| 8 Aug 29 | Polignac administration formed. |
| 16 May 30 | Chamber of Deputies dissolved. |
| 26 July 30 | Ordinances against the press and reconstruction of the Chamber of Deputies. |
| 27 July 30 | Revolution begins with erection of barricades. Fighting between people, helped by the National Guard, and the army. |
| 2 Aug 30 | Charles X retires to Rambouillet and abdicates on 31 July; flight of his ministry. |
| 7 Aug 30 | Duke of Orleans accepts the throne as Louis-Philippe I. |
| 14 Aug 30 | Constitutional Charter of July published. |
| 17 Aug 30 | Charles X retires to England. |
| 21 Dec 30 | Polignac and other ministers sentenced to perpetual imprisonment. |
| 27 Dec 31 | Abolition of the hereditary peerage decreed by both chambers after the creation of 36 new peers. |
| 5–6 Jun 32 | The ABC (*abaissés*) insurrection in Paris suppressed. |
| 18 Mar 33 | Bergeron and Benoît tried for an attempt on the life of Louis-Philippe, and acquitted. |

RISINGS IN RUSSIA

| | |
|---|---|
| 16 | Rise of League of Salvation – first secret organization of the Decembrists. |
| 19 | Rising of military settlers in Chuguev. |
| 19–20 | Rising in Imeretia. |
| 20 | Disturbance in Semenov Guards Regiment in St Petersburg. |

| | |
|---|---|
| 21 | Rise of secret societies of Decembrists – the northern and southern societies. |
| 23 | Formation of Society of United Slavs – the Decembrists. |
| Dec 25 | Rising of Decembrists in the Senate Square (now the Square of the Decembrists) in St Petersburg. |
| Dec 25–Jan 26 | Rising of Chernigov Regiment in the Ukraine (led by the Decembrists). |
| 27 | Activities of student revolutionary circle of the Kritsky brothers in Moscow. |
| 30 | Rising in Sevastopol. |
| 30–1 | 'Cholera Riots'. |
| | Polish rising (see p. 73). |
| 31 | Rising by military settlers in Novgorod province. |
| 32–5 | Peasant movement of the Ukraine at its height, led by U. Ya. Karmalyuk. |
| 41 | Peasant rising in Guria. |
| 41–5 | Disturbances among state peasants in a number of provinces in connection with the Kiselev reform. |
| 42–5 | Peasant disturbances in the Baltic. |

THE REVOLUTIONS OF 1848–9

### 1848

| | |
|---|---|
| 12 Jan | Revolt in Sicily; provisional independent government formed. |
| 10 Feb | Constitution proclaimed by Ferdinand II in Naples. |
| 22 Feb | Revolution in Paris. |
| 24 Feb | Abdication of Louis-Philippe; a Republican provisional government proclaimed under Alphonse de Lamartine. |
| 27 Feb | National Workshops erected in France. Inauguration of Louis Blanc's plan for public relief. |
| 4 Mar | Charles Albert proclaims constitution in Piedmont and Sardinia. |
| 12 Mar | Student demonstrations herald revolution in Vienna. |
| 13 Mar | Resignation of Metternich. |
| 14 Mar | Pius IX grants constitution in Rome. |
| 15 Mar | Hungarian Diet accepts reforms of Mar 1847. |
| 17 Mar | Revolution in Venice under Daniele Manin; revolution in Berlin; constitution granted by Frederick William IV. |
| 18 Mar | Revolution in Milan against Austrian rule; Radetzky forced to evacuate the city. |
| 20 Mar | Revolt in Parma. |

| | |
|---|---|
| 22 Mar | Republic proclaimed in Venice. |
| 24 Mar | Sardinia declares war on Austria. |
| 31 Mar | German *Vorparlament* meets at Frankfurt. |
| 8 Apr | Austrians defeated at Gioto by Piedmontese troops. |
| 13 Apr | Sicily declares independence from Naples. |
| 25 Apr | Papacy joins war against Austria; constitution, including responsible government, granted to Austria. |
| 29 Apr | Pius IX withdraws support from nationalist movement. |
| 30 Apr | Further Austrian reverse at Patrengo. |
| 2 May | Prussia invades Denmark over Schleswig-Holstein question. |
| 4 May | French National Assembly meets; elections based on universal male suffrage return majority for moderate Republicans. |
| 7 May | Polish rebels surrender in Warsaw. |
| 15 May | Fresh rising in Paris after news of the suppression of the Polish revolt; second rising in Vienna; collapse of the revolt in Naples. |
| 17 May | Ferdinand flees Vienna to Innsbruck. |
| 18 May | German National Assembly meets at Frankfurt and suspends German Confederation. |
| 22 May | Prussian National Assembly meets in Berlin. |
| 29 May | Battle of Curtatone; Austrians defeat Tuscany. |
| 2 June | Pan-Slav Congress meets at Prague. |
| 17 June | Czech rising suppressed by Austrians. |
| 23 June | The June 'Days' in France; Louis Cavaignac suppresses workmen in effort to close workshops; thousands killed. |
| 22 July | Battle of Custozza results in major victory for Austrians under Radetzky. |
| 9 Aug | Armistice of Vigevano between Sardinia and Austria. |
| 11 Aug | Sardinian troops expelled from Venice. |
| 12 Aug | Ferdinand I returns to Vienna. |
| 26 Aug | Treaty of Malmo between Denmark and Prussia. |
| 7 Sep | Serfdom abolished in Austria. |
| 24 Sep | Louis Kossuth proclaimed president of the committee for the national defence of Hungary. |
| 6 Oct | Third Revolution in Vienna. |
| 31 Oct | Government troops fully in control in Vienna. |
| 4 Nov | Republican constitution in France promulgated. |
| 15 Nov | Assassination of Count Rossi, premier of Papal States. |
| 24 Nov | Escape of Pius IX to Gaeta. |

| | |
|---|---|
| 2 Dec | Abdication of Ferdinand I; accession of Franz Joseph. |
| 5 Dec | Dissolution of Prussian National Assembly. |

### 1849

| | |
|---|---|
| 23 Jan | Prussia advocates union of Germany without Austria. |
| 7 Feb | Flight of Grand Duke of Tuscany to Gaeta. |
| 9 Feb | Mazzini declares republic in Rome. |
| 4 Mar | Proclamation of an Austrian constitution. |
| 7 Mar | Austrian Assembly dissolved. |
| 12 Mar | Sardinia ends truce with Austria. |
| 23 Mar | Decisive Battle of Novara ends in Austrian victory; abdication of Charles Albert. |
| 27 Mar | German National Assembly offers title 'Emperor of the Germans' to an unwilling Frederick William IV. |
| 14 Apr | Hungarian Diet proclaims independence, with Kossuth as leader. |
| 25 Apr | French troops land in Papal States. |
| 3 May | Revolt in Dresden suppressed by Prussia. |
| 15 May | Troops from Naples occupy Palermo. |
| 6 June | German National Assembly moves to Stuttgart. |
| 18 June | Troops dissolve Stuttgart assembly. |
| 4 July | French troops enter Rome; Pius IX restored. |
| 23 July | Baden rebels surrender to Prussia. |
| 6 Aug | Peace of Milan ends Austria-Sardinia conflict. |
| 13 Aug | Battle of Vilagas; Hungarians defeated by Austrians aided by Russians. |
| 28 Aug | Venice finally surrenders to Austrians. |

# 5 DEFENCE AND WARFARE

## THE WARS OF THE FRENCH REVOLUTION AND NAPOLEON

1791  2 Aug   In the Declaration of Pilnitz, Frederick William II of Prussia and the Emperor Leopold II of Austria declared themselves ready to join other European powers in restoring the authority of the French monarchy.

14 Dec   The French formed three new armies for the defence of their northern and eastern frontiers.

1792  7 Feb   Alliance between Austria and Prussia, later joined by Sardinia.

20 Apr   French Assembly declared war on Austria. The French Army of the North advanced into the Austrian Netherlands, but was thrown back by the Duke of Saxe-Teschen.

24 Jul   Prussia declared war on France. Allied army under the Duke of Brunswick assembled at Koblenz for invasion of France.

19 Aug   Brunswick's army crossed the French frontier, capturing Longwy on 23 Aug and Verdun on 2 Sep.

20 Sep   Brunswick's infantry halted by accurate fire from 54 French guns in the 'Cannonade of Valmy'. The Allies withdrew into Germany, evacuating Verdun and Longwy. The French under Custine took the offensive, capturing Mainz and Frankfurt. However, Brunswick drove Custine back to the Rhine, retaking Frankfurt on 2 Dec.

In the north, the Austrians failed to capture Lille and were defeated by Dumouriez at Jemappes on 6 Nov. Dumouriez entered Brussels on 14 Nov, and the Austrians evacuated the country.

19 Nov   The French declared themselves ready to help all peoples against their kings, and proclaimed the Scheldt an open river.

In the south, French forces seized Nice and Savoy from the King of Sardinia.

**1793**  21 Jan   Louis XVI executed. When England expelled the French ambassador, France declared war on England and Holland on 1 Feb, and on Spain on 7 Mar. Belgium was declared to be incorporated into France.

1 Mar   Allied offensive opened, as Austrian army of 40,000 men under the Prince of Saxe-Coburg advanced into Belgium.

18 Mar   Dumouriez attacked Coburg at Neerwinden but was routed.

21 Mar   After a further defeat at Louvain, Dumouriez opened negotiations with the enemy and deserted to the Austrians on 5 Apr. Coburg captured Condé on 10 Jul and Valenciennes on 29 Jul.

On the Rhine, Brunswick retook Mainz on 23 Jul.

23 Aug   With the situation now desperate for France, the Committee of Public Safety ordered the conscription of the entire male population, the *Levée en masse*.

28 Aug   Hood seized Toulon, but was forced to evacuate it on 18 Dec.

6 Sep   Houchard attacked the Duke of York, who had invested Dunkirk, driving him back with the loss of his siege artillery.

13 Sep   Houchard defeated the Prince of Orange at Menin, but was guillotined for his failure to follow up the victory.

16 Oct   Jourdan defeated the Austrians at Wattignies, forcing them to raise the siege of Maubeuge.

On the Rhine, Hoche was victorious over the Austrians and Prussians at Fröschwiller on 22 Dec and Geisberg on 26 Dec.

**1794**  18 May   The Army of the North, temporarily commanded by Souham, defeated the Austrians, British and Hanoverians under Coburg at the Battle of Tourcoing.

22 May   A French attack on the Allied entrenched camp at Tournai was repulsed.

17 Jun   The French defeated an Austrian attempt to relieve Ypres at the Battle of Hooglede.

26 Jun   Battle of Fleurus; Coburg, advancing to the relief of Charleroi, which had already fallen, was defeated by Jourdan, in command of the newly formed Army of the Sambre and Meuse.

10 Jul   The French entered Brussels, and Antwerp on 27 Jul. The Austrians withdrew across the Rhine, while the British retreated into Holland and on into Germany. The French under Pichegru invaded Holland.

1795 Jan The French entered Amsterdam. Holland was renamed the Batavian Republic on 16 May.

5 Apr Treaty of Basle; peace treaty between France and Prussia, establishing neutrality of Prussia and northern states of Germany. Spain signed a peace treaty on 22 Jul, and by the end of 1795 France had also made peace with Saxony, Hesse, Naples and Parma.

27 Jun Landing of French émigrés and British troops at Quiberon. Hoche defeated these forces on 16–20 Jul, and the British were evacuated.

5 Sep Jourdan crossed the Rhine and advanced on Frankfurt, but was defeated by the Austrians under Count von Clerfayt. Clerfayt then attacked Pichegru commanding the Army of the Rhine and Moselle, defeated him on 29 Oct and invaded the Palatinate.

31 Dec Pichegru concluded an armistice with the Austrians.

## WAR BETWEEN FRANCE AND AUSTRIA, 1796–7

### Campaign in Germany

1796 20 May The Austrians denounced the armistice of 31 Dec 1795.

10 Jun Jourdan, commanding the Army of the Sambre and Meuse, crossed the Rhine to draw the Austrians northwards. He was defeated by Archduke Charles on 16 Jun at Wetzler, and retreated across the Rhine.

24 Jun Moreau, commanding the Army of the Rhine and Moselle, crossed the Rhine at Strasbourg. After an indecisive battle at Malsch on 9 Jul, Archduke Charles retreated across the Danube.

28 Jun Jourdan again crossed the Rhine. The Archduke marched north and decisively defeated Jourdan at Amberg on 24 Aug. But on the same day Moreau defeated Latour at Friedberg.

3 Sep The Archduke defeated Jourdan at Würzburg, and again on the River Lahn at Biberach on 2 Oct, but was beaten at Emendingen on 19 Oct. He re-crossed the Rhine on 26 Oct.

1797 Hoche, who had succeeded Jourdan, crossed the Rhine and defeated General Werneck in the Battle of the Lahn on 18 Apr. On 21 Apr Moreau fought his way across the Rhine near Kehl. The Austrians fell back to Rastatt.

### Campaign in Italy

1796 2 Mar Bonaparte appointed to replace Schérer as commander of the Army of Italy. He took command on 27 Mar of an army consisting of 37,000 effectives.

10 Apr    The Austrians under Beaulieu captured Voltri.

12 Apr    Seizing the initiative, Bonaparte drove a wedge between the Austrian and Piedmontese armies at the Battle of Montenotte. The French then captured Dego on 13 Apr and held it against Austrian attacks.

Bonaparte then attacked the Piedmontese army under Baron Colli, driving it from Ceva on 18 Apr and defeating it at Mondovi on 22 Apr.

28 Apr    The Piedmontese signed the Armistice of Cherasco.

7 May    Bonaparte crossed the Po at Piacenza. Beaulieu retreated eastwards.

10 May    Bonaparte took the vital bridge over the River Adda at Lodi.

15 May    Bonaparte entered Milan. King Victor Amadeus signed a treaty surrendering Savoy and Nice to the French.

30 May    Bonaparte broke Beaulieu's line on the Mincio at Borghetto, and as the Austrians retreated over the Adige, he besieged Mantua, which was defended by 12,000 men and 316 guns.

Jul    The Austrians began their first attempt to relieve Mantua. By dividing their forces into three, however, they enabled Bonaparte to attack them in turn.

3 Aug    Bonaparte defeated Quasdanovich at Lonato.

5 Aug    The Austrians under Würmser were defeated at Castiglione and retreated into the Tyrol. The siege of Mantua was renewed on 24 Aug.

French forces now marched northwards and defeated Davidovich at Roveredo on 4 Sep. Learning that Würmser had resumed the offensive, Bonaparte pursued the main Austrian army and defeated it at Bassano on 8 Sep. Würmser withdrew into Mantua on 12 Sep.

A new Austrian offensive was now mounted by Baron d'Alvintzi. After an unsuccessful attack at Caldiero on 12 Nov, Bonaparte defeated the Austrians in the Battle of Arcola on 15–17 Nov. D'Alvintzi was forced to retreat.

1797    14 Jan    A fourth Austrian attempt to relieve Mantua ended when d'Alvintzi was defeated at Rivoli.

2 Feb    Würmser surrendered Mantua to the French.

Mar    The Archduke Charles replaced d'Alvintzi. Bonaparte launched an offensive. The Archduke was defeated by Masséna at

81

Malborgetto on 23 Mar, and Bonaparte advanced on Vienna. Whilst maintaining his advance, fears about his lines of communication led him to offer an armistice.

7 Apr   Armistice of Leoben concluded.

16 May   The French occupied Vienna.

17 Oct   Treaty of Campo Formio; Austria recognized French possession of Belgium and the Rhine frontier, and acknowledged the independence of the Cisalpine Republic; in return, Austria was compensated with Venetian territory.

## EGYPTIAN CAMPAIGN, 1798–1801

**1798**   12 Apr   Army of the Orient created with Bonaparte as commander.

19 May   Bonaparte sailed from Toulon with 36,000 troops, secured the surrender of Malta on 12 Jun and landed in Egypt on 1 Jul.

2 Jul   The French captured Alexandria and advanced on Cairo.

21 Jul   Bonaparte routed the Egyptian army at the Battle of the Pyramids, and occupied Cairo on the following day.

1 Aug   Nelson destroyed the French fleet at the Battle of Aboukir Bay, isolating the French army in Egypt.

**1799**   31 Jan   Bonaparte invaded Syria with 13,000 men. Jaffa was captured on 7 Mar and Acre invested on 17 Mar.

17 Apr   An attempt by the Turks to relieve Acre was defeated at the battle of Mount Tabor. Nevertheless, Acre continued to resist, supported by an English squadron under Sir Sydney Smith. When plague broke out in his army, Bonaparte was forced to raise the siege on 20 May and retreat to Egypt.

25 Jul   Bonaparte defeated a Turkish force which had been landed from Rhodes at Aboukir.

22 Aug   Leaving Kléber in command, Bonaparte sailed for France, landing at Fréjus on 9 Oct.

**1800**   21 Jan   Kléber agreed to evacuate Egypt by the Convention of El Arish, but Britain refused to ratify the agreement.

20 Mar   Kléber defeated the Turks at Heliopolis.

14 Jun   Assassination of Kléber.

**1801**   8 Mar   British troops under Abercromby landed at Aboukir Bay.

13 Mar   A British attack on Alexandria failed, but a French counter-attack was beaten off on 21 Mar, though Abercromby was fatally wounded. His successor, Hutchinson, advanced on Cairo, which the French agreed to evacuate on 28 Jun.

31 Aug   French forces remaining in Alexandria surrendered.

WAR OF THE SECOND COALITION, 1798–1801

*Operations in Italy, 1798–1800*

1798      29 Nov  A Neapolitan army under General Mack captured Rome.

15 Dec  The Neapolitan forces were driven out by the French under Championnet, who then took Naples on 24 Jan 1799 and proclaimed the Parthenopean Republic.

1799      12 Mar  Austria declared war on France. Schérer, commanding the Army of Italy, moved against the Austrians under Kray, hoping for an early victory.

26 Mar  Schérer was repulsed at Verona and defeated at Magnano on 5 Apr. Suvarov, who now succeeded Kray, pursued the French, defeating them at Cassano on 27 Apr and entering Milan on 28 Apr.

17–19 Jun  Macdonald, who had marched north with the French forces in southern Italy, was defeated at Trebbia. He retreated to join Moreau, who had replaced Schérer, at Genoa. Moreau was himself replaced by Joubert on 5 Aug.

15 Aug  Joubert attacked Suvarov at Novi, but was defeated and killed. Suvarov was then ordered to take 20,000 Russian troops into Switzerland.

4 Nov  Suvarov's successor, Melas, defeated Championnet at the battle of Genoa, and the French retreated across the Alps.

1800      7 Jan  Bonaparte, now First Consul of France, ordered the formation of an Army of Reserve around Dijon.

6 Apr  Masséna, commanding the Army of Italy, was defeated and besieged in Genoa by the Austrians under Ott, supported by the British navy. Genoa finally surrendered on 4 Jun.

14–24 May  Bonaparte crossed the Great St Bernard Pass with the Army of Reserve, seized Milan and Pavia and threatened Melas' lines of communication. Melas moved east and ordered a concentration at Alessandria.

9 Jun  Ott, marching north from Genoa, encountered French forces under Lannes at Montebello. He was driven towards Alessandria.

14 Jun  Melas advanced from Alessandria and attacked the French at Marengo. After early reverses, Bonaparte was joined by Desaix's 9000-strong corps and counter-attacked. The Austrians were defeated and Melas was forced to ask for an armistice on 15 Jun.

*Russo-British Expedition to Holland, 1799*
1799      27 Aug   British troops under Abercromby landed at the Helder.
The Dutch navy in the Texel surrendered on 30 Aug.
On the arrival of 9000 Russians, the combined force, commanded by the Duke of York, planned to advance on Amsterdam.
19 Sep   Battle of Bergen; lack of coordination resulted in a defeat for the Allies by Franco-Batavian forces under Brune.
Further attacks on enemy positions on 2 Oct and 6 Oct made little progress.
18 Oct   By the Convention of Alkmaar the Allies agreed to evacuate Holland, but retained the Dutch fleet.

*Operations in Germany and Switzerland, 1799–1800*
1799      1 Mar   Jourdan's Army of the Danube crossed the Rhine at Kehl and advanced against Austrian forces under the Archduke Charles.
Jourdan was defeated at Ostrach on 21 Mar and Stockach on 25 Mar. He retreated to the Rhine and resigned his command.
Meanwhile, Masséna, commanding the Army of Helvetia, had crossed the Rhine near Mayenfeld and captured 7000 Austrians around Chur. Masséna then took over Jourdan's army as well as his own.
4 Jun   Masséna repulsed an Austrian attack at Zurich, but when he attempted to advance he was defeated on 14 Aug.
Austria then ordered Archduke Charles to move north to observe Allied progress in Holland.
25 Sep   Masséna defeated the weakened Allied army under Korsakov at Zurich.
:800      The French under Moreau defeated Kray at Stockach on 3 May, Möskirch on 5 May, Ulm on 16 May and Hochstadt on 19 Jun. An armistice was effective from 15 Jul to 13 Nov.
3 Dec   Moreau defeated the Archduke John, who had replaced Kray, at Hohenlinden. Moreau then advanced on Vienna, while Macdonald invaded the Tyrol and Brune moved towards the Julian Alps.
25 Dec   The Austrians sued for peace.
1801      9 Feb   Peace of Lunéville between France and Austria, confirming the terms of the Treaty of Campo Formio.

## *Defeat of Austria and Russia, 1805*

1803      18 May   Britain declared war on France.

1804      6 Nov   The Emperor Francis of Austria made a secret treaty with Tsar Alexander of Russia to resist French aggression in Italy.

1805      11 Apr   Treaty of alliance between Britain and Russia.

9 Aug   Austria secretly joined the alliance on promise of a subsidy from Britain. Sweden also joined the coalition.

2 Sep   Austria set in motion her armed forces to attack France. An Austrian army of 72,000 under the Archduke Ferdinand and General Mack von Leiberich marched towards Ulm to deter the Elector of Bavaria, who had signed a treaty with Napoleon on 24 Aug. In northern Italy the Archduke Charles with 95,000 men prepared to attack Masséna, while the Archduke John with 23,000 men held the Tyrol. Three Russian armies, totalling 95,000 men, were marching to reinforce the Austrians, who planned a united advance on Strasbourg when the Russians arrived.

In the meantime, Napoleon had abandoned his planned invasion of Britain and broken up his camp at Boulogne on 23 Aug. The Grand Army of 200,000 men was ordered to march eastwards.

25 Sep   The French army crossed the Rhine. While Murat thrust through the Black Forest to fix the attention of Mack, the main body wheeled south towards the Danube. Corps led by Marmont and Bernadotte violated the territory of Prussia by passing through Ansbach, and the French army crossed the Danube east of Ulm, cutting Mack's lines of communication.

20 Oct   After skirmishes in which he unsuccessfully attempted to break out, Mack was forced to surrender with 30,000 men at Ulm.

26 Oct   Napoleon advanced eastwards towards Vienna.

29 Oct   Masséna attacked the Archduke Charles at Caldiero, but was driven off, and the Archduke continued his withdrawal. On the same day Kutusov retreated with his Russo-Austrian forces from his positions on the River Inn.

8 Nov   Austrian forces under Merveldt were beaten by Davout at Maria Zell, but on 9 Nov Kutusov crossed safely to the north bank of the Danube at Krems.

11 Nov   While Murat marched on Vienna, Kutusov attacked Mortier's corps at Dürrenstein, inflicting heavy casualties.

13 Nov   Murat and Lannes personally bluffed the Austrian

85

guards into surrendering the principal bridge across the Danube at Vienna. The city was then occupied. Russo-Austrian forces concentrated at Olmütz.

17 Nov   Leaving 20,000 men in Vienna, Napoleon marched his army northwards towards Brünn. He feigned uncertainty and weakness to tempt the Allies into battle. The Allies took the bait. They planned to move from Olmütz round Napoleon's right flank and cut his lines of communication.

Napoleon drew up his army facing east near Austerlitz, deliberately leaving his right wing weak.

2 Dec   Battle of Austerlitz; the Allied army attacked the French right wing, driving it back. By 9 a.m. a third of the Allied army was engaged in the attack on that wing. At that moment Napoleon sent Soult's corps in the French centre to take the Pratzen Heights, splitting the Allied front. Soult then swung right, rolling up the Allied left wing, while Bernadotte drove on through the gap that was created. On the French left Lannes led the advance, and the Allied forces were finally routed by Murat's cavalry.

4 Dec   After this crushing defeat, Austria surrendered unconditionally, while Alexander withdrew his forces towards Russia.

26 Dec   Peace of Pressburg; Austria was forced to cede Venetia to the Kingdom of Italy, and surrendered territory to Bavaria, Baden and Württemberg.

### Defeat of Prussia, 1806

1805   15 Dec   Prussia, which had been on the point of entering the war before the French victory at Austerlitz, was forced to sign the Treaty of Schönbrunn with France. All Prussia's other diplomatic alliances were declared void. Cleves and Neuchâtel were ceded to France and Ansbach to Bavaria. In return Prussia received Hanover.

1806   12 Jul   Napoleon abolished the Holy Roman Empire and on 25 Jul he formed the Confederation of the Rhine.

7 Aug   After learning that Napoleon had offered to restore Hanover to George III, Prussia secretly decided for war.

6 Sep   Prussia invaded Saxony and forced it into an alliance.

26 Sep   Prussia sent an ultimatum to Napoleon containing clearly unacceptable terms.

8 Oct   French forces, which had been assembled in north-eastern Bavaria, advanced through the Thuringian Forest in three columns on a 30-mile front.

10 Oct   Lannes defeated Prince Louis Ferdinand at Saalfeld.

Prince Louis was killed and Prussian morale suffered a severe blow.

Napoleon sent Davout and Bernadotte northwards to Naumberg to cut the line of communications of the Prussian forces concentrated round Jena. He himself moved on Jena. Learning of the French movements, the Duke of Brunswick marched northwards, leaving Prince Friedrich Hohenlohe in the area between Weimar and Jena to protect his rear.

14 Oct   Napoleon inflicted a crushing defeat on Hohenlohe at Jena. On the same day Davout was attacked by Brunswick at Auerstadt. After withstanding a series of assaults, Davout emerged victorious, even though Bernadotte only arrived with his corps at the end of the day.

After a single day's fighting the Prussian army had virtually ceased to exist. Napoleon now pursued its remnants. Berlin was occupied on 24 Oct, and on 6 Nov the last sizeable Prussian force in the field under Blücher surrendered near Lübeck.

Napoleon advanced into Poland and occupied Warsaw on 18 Dec. A Russian army under Bennigsen evaded him after fighting a desperate rearguard action at Pultusk on 26 Dec and Napoleon went into winter quarters.

*Campaign against Russia, 1807*

1807        18 Jan   Bennigsen attacked Ney's corps south of Königsberg, forcing him to withdraw. Napoleon now concentrated his forces and Bennigsen retreated.

8 Feb   Napoleon attacked Bennigsen in a heavy snowstorm at Eylau.

Bennigsen withdrew during the night, but both the French and the Russians had suffered heavy casualties. Both sides retired to their winter quarters.

15 Mar   French forces besieged Danzig, which surrendered on 27 May.

26 Apr   Treaty of Bartenstein; Russia, Prussia and later Britain and Sweden undertook to continue the struggle against France.

5 Jun   Bennigsen returned to the offensive and forced Ney back. When Napoleon again concentrated his forces, Bennigsen retired to a series of entrenched redoubts at Heilsberg. A French attack on the redoubts was repulsed on 10 Jun, but Bennigsen again retreated.

Napoleon ordered Lannes to seize the town of Friedland. He

encountered the whole Russian army, and Napoleon moved forces to his support.

14 Jun   Battle of Friedland; Napoleon inflicted a decisive defeat on the Russians. Massed French artillery commanded by Sénarmont exacted a heavy toll on the Russian army, which suffered 20,000 casualties, compared to 8000 French.

15 Jun   Lestocq evacuated Königsberg and retreated to Tilsit.

19 Jun   Napoleon occupied Tilsit. The Russians asked for an armistice, which came into effect on 23 Jun.

25 Jun   Napoleon met Alexander on a raft on the Niemen to discuss peace terms.

7–9 Jul   Treaties of Tilsit; Prussia surrendered the territory taken in the partitions of Poland to the Grand Duchy of Warsaw, ruled by the King of Saxony. All its possessions west of the Elbe were to be included in the new Kingdom of Westphalia. The Prussian army was reduced to 42,000 men and an indemnity of 140 million francs imposed. Russia ceded the Ionian Islands and Dalmatian coast to France in return for a free hand with regard to European Turkey, and received the province of Bialystock in Poland. Russia recognized the Grand Duchy of Warsaw, and agreed to an alliance with France against Britain if no general peace was forthcoming.

PENINSULAR WAR, 1807–14

1807      Nov   French forces under Junot invaded Portugal to close one of the remaining gaps in Napoleon's Continental System. Lisbon was occupied on 30 Nov.

1808      Mar   A French army under Murat marched into Spain and occupied Madrid on 24 Mar.

6 May   Napoleon signed a decree creating Joseph Bonaparte King of Spain. There was a general uprising of the Spanish people.

20 Jul   Dupont, surrounded by 35,000 Spanish levies, was forced to capitulate with 20,000 men at Baylen.

1 Aug   A British army under Sir Arthur Wellesley landed near Lisbon. The French were defeated at Roliça on 17 Aug and Vimeiro on 21 Aug.

30 Aug   The Convention of Cintra was signed, allowing Junot to evacuate the French army.

25 Sep   Sir John Moore took command of the British army and advanced into Spain.

5 Nov   Napoleon joined his army in Spain and entered Madrid

on 4 Dec. Moore retreated north-westwards, pursued by the French.

1809    16 Jan   Battle of Corunna; Soult's attack was repulsed and the British army evacuated, though Sir John Moore was killed. Napoleon now left Spain, arriving in Paris on 23 Jan.

22 Apr   Wellesley landed at Lisbon and took command of British and Portuguese forces. He drove Soult out of Oporto on 12 May.

12 Jun   Wellesley invaded Spain in conjunction with a Spanish army.

28 Jul   Wellesley defeated Victor and Joseph at Talavera. The French fell back on Madrid, but Wellesley had to retire to Portugal when his Spanish contingent was withdrawn.

19 Nov   The Spanish under Areizago were defeated by Soult and Joseph at Ocana.

1810    10 Jul   The French took Ciudad Rodrigo and invaded Portugal.

27 Sep   Masséna attacked Wellington at Busaco Ridge but was defeated.

On 10 Oct Wellington retired behind the fortified lines of the Torres Vedras. Masséna found them to be impregnable, and shortage of supplies forced him to retreat in Nov.

1811    5 May   Masséna was defeated at Fuentes de Onoro as he attempted to relieve Almeida, which fell to Wellington on 10 May.

16 May   As he moved to relieve Badajoz, Soult was defeated at Albuera by Beresford.

1812    Jan   Wellington took the offensive, capturing Ciudad Rodrigo on 19 Jan and Badajoz on 19 Apr.

22 Jul   Wellington defeated Marmont at Salamanca.

12 Aug   Wellington entered Madrid, but when he failed to take Burgos in Nov, he fell back to Ciudad Rodrigo.

1813    Wellington again advanced, and defeated Joseph at Vitoria on 21 Jun. He defeated Soult at Sorauren 26 Jul–1 Aug and drove him across the Pyrenees. The French suffered further defeats in the Battle of Nivelle on 10 Nov and the Battle of the Nive on 9–13 Dec.

1814    27 Feb   Wellington defeated Soult at Orthez, and again at Toulouse on 10 Apr. Hostilities were suspended when the news of Napoleon's abdication was received.

WAR WITH AUSTRIA, 1809

1809    8 Feb   Seeking to take advantage of Napoleon's involvement in Spain, Austr. secretly decided to go to war again with France.

9 Apr   An Austrian army under the Archduke Charles invaded Bavaria, while the Archduke John invaded Italy.

16 Apr   Prince Eugène de Beauharnais attacked the Archduke John at Sacile, but he was defeated and retired behind the Piave. A popular uprising against the Bavarians took place in the Tyrol, led by Andreas Hofer (he was eventually defeated on the Iselberg on 1 Nov 1809 and later shot).

17 Apr   Napoleon reached Donauwörth and took command in Germany. The slowness of the Austrian advance enabled him to order the concentration of the French forces, which his chief of staff, Berthier, had failed to do.

20 Apr   Napoleon attacked the Austrians at Abensberg. The Austrian right wing was driven towards Ratisbon, where the French garrison was overwhelmed, and the left wing towards Landshut.

21 Apr   Napoleon defeated the Austrian left wing under Baron Hiller, who retreated across the Isar.

22 Apr   The Archduke Charles on the Austrian right attacked Davout at Eckmühl, but the French were able to hold on until Napoleon brought up reinforcements to defeat the Austrians.

23 Apr   Napoleon captured Ratisbon but allowed a large part of the Austrian army to escape.

29 Apr   Eugène defeated the Archduke John at Caldiero.

13 May   Napoleon occupied Vienna.

21–22 May   Battle of Aspern-Essling; Napoleon prepared to attack the Austrians, moving troops to the north bank of the Danube by way of the island of Lobau. However, the Austrians floated heavy objects down the river and broke the French bridge from the south bank to the island, curtailing the flow of reinforcements. In the ensuing battle the French were defeated and forced to withdraw from the bridgehead on the north bank to the island of Lobau.

14 Jun   Eugène defeated the Archduke John at Raab and marched to join Napoleon.

3–4 Jul   During the night Napoleon began moving troops to the island of Lobau.

5 Jul   Napoleon's army crossed from Lobau to the north bank of the Danube and attacked the Austrians around Wagram. The battle continued the following day and ended in a decisive Austrian defeat.

12 Jul   Austria signed the armistice of Znaim.

14 Oct   Treaty of Schönbrunn; Austria ceded 32,000 sq. miles of

territory, and agreed to join the Continental System against Britain. The Austrian army was reduced to 150,000 men, and an indemnity of 85 million francs imposed.

## INVASION OF RUSSIA, 1812

1812    May   Napoleon assembled an army of 450,000 men in Poland for the invasion of Russia.

23 Jun   At 10 p.m. Napoleon's army began to cross the River Niemen at Kovno. He was opposed by Barclay de Tolly with 127,000 men north of the Niemen, Bagration with 48,000 men between the Niemen and the Pripet Marshes, and Tormassov with 43,000 men defending the south-west frontier.

28 Jun   Napoleon entered Vilna, but the pace of the French advance was already slackening due to the effects of heavy rain on the Russian roads, the slowness of the supply convoys and lack of information about Russian moves.

8 Jul   Davout occupied Minsk and defeated Bagration at Mohilev on 23 Jul.

3 Aug   The armies of Bagration and Barclay combined at Smolensk under the latter's command.

17 Aug   Napoleon attempted to destroy Barclay at Smolensk, but he failed to press his advantage, and Barclay retired the following day. After heavy fighting at Volutino on 19 Aug, Barclay escaped with his army, due largely to French mistakes and particularly Junot's refusal to attack the Russian flank.

24 Aug   Napoleon continued his advance on Moscow.

7 Sep   Kutusov, who had replaced Barclay on 29 Aug, made a stand at Borodino. In the ensuing battle he was defeated but inflicted heavy casualties on the French. He retreated to Moscow on 8 Sep, but then evacuated the capital, moving his army 60 miles south-east to Kolumna.

14 Sep   A French army of 95,000 men entered Moscow, large parts of which were destroyed by fire. Napoleon then made overtures for peace to Alexander but these were rebuffed.

19 Oct   As his lines of communication were increasingly threatened, Napoleon began to withdraw his army towards Smolensk. His first intention was to retreat by way of Kaluga, a rich food area, and to attack Kutusov. He was opposed by the Russians at the bridge over the Lusha at Maloyaroslavets. After an indecisive battle on 24 Oct, Napoleon turned to withdraw through Mojaisk, following the wasted route of his advance.

91

3 Nov   First snowfalls experienced by the French army; discipline and morale began to deteriorate rapidly.

9 Nov   The French army reached Smolensk. After news was received of the surrender of d'Hilliers' reinforcements to the southwest of the city, the retreat continued.

16–17 Nov   Napoleon defeated Kutusov's attempt to bar his way at Krasnoi, and on 26–8 Nov successfully crossed the Beresina near Borisov.

5 Dec   Giving Murat command of the army in Russia, Napoleon left for France, arriving in Paris on 18 Dec.

13 Dec   The French army crossed the Niemen and the Russian pursuit stopped. It struggled on to Königsberg on 19 Dec, having lost some 570,000 men in the 6-month campaign.

## LEIPZIG CAMPAIGN, 1813

| | |
|---|---|
| 1812 | 30 Dec   A Prussian contingent under Yorck signed the Convention of Tauroggen, declaring itself neutral. |
| 1813 | 9 Feb   Frederick William III issued an edict calling all Prussians to arms. |

27 Feb   By the Treaty of Kalisch, Russia and Prussia formed an alliance against France.

17 Mar   Prussia declared war on France. French forces under Eugène withdrew to the Elbe.

30 Apr   Napoleon joined Eugène with 120,000 men, and advanced on Leipzig.

2 May   Battle of Lützen; Ney's failure to carry out adequate reconnaissance led to his corps' being taken by surprise when Wittgenstein attacked. But Napoleon concentrated his forces against the Allied centre, breaking their line and forcing them to retreat.

9 May   Napoleon captured Dresden, and the Allies continued their withdrawal to Bautzen.

20–1 May   Battle of Bautzen; Napoleon launched a series of frontal assaults on the Allied positions on the east bank of the Spree. Ney, commanding the northern part of the French army, was supposed to envelop the right wing of the Allied army and cut off their retreat. Ney mismanaged the operation, and the Allies escaped.

2 Jun   Hostilities were suspended, and at a conference at Plestwitz on 4 Jun Napoleon agreed to a 7-week armistice, which was extended to 17 Aug.

19 Jun   By the Convention of Reichenbach, Russia, Prussia and Austria agreed on peace terms to be put to the French. These were rejected and Austria declared war on 12 Aug.

14 Aug   Blücher, who had replaced Wittgenstein, broke the armistice and began to advance. Napoleon with 300,000 men was now opposed by Allied armies under Schwarzenberg, Blücher and Bernadotte, totalling 450,000 men.

Napoleon advanced towards Dresden, held by French forces under Saint-Cyr. The Allies adopted a policy of avoiding battle if Napoleon was present but attacking his lieutenants. Bernadotte defeated Oudinot at Grössbeeren on 23 Aug, and Blücher defeated Macdonald at Katzbach on 26 Aug.

26–7 Aug   Battle of Dresden; Schwarzenberg attacked Saint-Cyr, but Napoleon arrived and drove the Allies back. However, he failed to coordinate an effective pursuit. Vandamme's corps, left unsupported, was crushed at Kulm on 29–30 Aug.

6 Sep   Ney's attempt to take Berlin ended in his defeat by Bernadotte at Dennewitz.

24 Sep   Napoleon withdrew across the Elbe and chose Leipzig as the centre of his operations.

8 Oct   By the Treaty of Ried Bavaria joined the Allies.

16–19 Oct   Battle of the Nations; the Allies closed in on the French at Leipzig and threatened to overwhelm them by weight of numbers after two days' fighting. Napoleon's planned withdrawal, which began at 2 a.m. on 19 Oct, ended in disaster when the bridge over the Elster was destroyed prematurely, leaving thousands of Frenchmen stranded.

30–1 Oct   Napoleon routed the Bavarians and Austrians who were attempting to block his retreat at Hanau.

1–5 Nov   The French army crossed the Rhine at Mainz.

## INVASION OF FRANCE, 1814

1813     22 Dec   After abortive peace negotiations, Allied forces crossed the Rhine and besieged Hunigen.

29 Dec   Blücher began to cross the Rhine at Caub, Lahnstein and Mannheim. Three Allied armies were now advancing on Paris: Schwarzenberg with 150,000 men was marching towards Langres; Blücher with 75,000 men was advancing up the Moselle Valley into Lorraine; and Winzingerode was operating in the Low Countries. To oppose them Napoleon had 118,000 men, many of them inexperienced recruits, spread out between Antwerp and Lyons.

1814     26 Jan   Napoleon arrived at Châlons-sur-Marne and assumed direct control of the French forces.

29 Jan   Napoleon attacked and defeated Blücher at Brienne. He was victorious again the following day at La Rothière, but when Blücher counter-attacked on 1 Feb, he withdrew to Troyes.

9 Feb   Having concentrated the main body of his army at Nogent-sur-Seine, Napoleon now marched north to strike at Blücher.

10 Feb   Napoleon defeated Olsuviev's corps of Blücher's army at Champaubert. He inflicted further defeats on Sacken and Yorck's corps at Montmirail on 11 Feb and Château Thierry on 12 Feb.

14 Feb   Napoleon defeated Blücher himself at Vauchamps. The Prussians retreated north of the Marne. Napoleon marched speedily south to face Schwarzenberg.

18 Feb   Napoleon defeated Schwarzenberg at Montereau.

1 Mar   Treaty of Chaumont; the Allies agreed not to make a separate peace until France was reduced to her 1791 frontiers.

27 Feb   Blücher crossed the Marne at La Ferté, marching towards Paris. His advance was checked by Marmont and Mortier on 28 Feb and 1 Mar.

Napoleon marched north, leaving Macdonald to watch Schwarzenberg. Macdonald was defeated at Bar-sur-Aube on 27 Feb and had to withdraw north of the Seine on 6 Mar.

Blücher retreated before Napoleon, crossing the Aisne at Soissons when the French garrison there surrendered. Napoleon crossed further upstream and defeated an attack by Blücher at Craonne on 7 Mar.

9–10 Mar   Battle of Laon: Napoleon attacked Blücher's army, but a successful night attack by Blücher on the French right wing under Marmont forced Napoleon to withdraw to Soissons.

13 Mar   Napoleon defeated an isolated Prussian corps at Rheims and recaptured the city. Blücher withdrew to Laon.

20–1 Mar   Battle of Arcis-sur-Aube; Napoleon managed to avoid a heavy defeat when he unexpectedly encountered the whole of Schwarzenberg's army, and withdrew to St Dizier.

25 Mar   The Allies, disregarding Napoleon, marched on Paris, and defeated Marmont and Mortier at La Fère-Champenoise.

27 Mar   In his last victory of the campaign, Napoleon defeated Winzingerode at St Dizier.

31 Mar   Marmont surrendered Paris to the Allies.

11 Apr   Abdication of Napoleon. He withdrew to Elba on 4 May.

30 May    First Treaty of Paris; France was reduced to her 1792 frontiers.

WATERLOO CAMPAIGN, 1815

1815      1 Mar   Napoleon landed at Cannes and entered Paris on 20 Mar.
25 Mar   Austria, Britain, Prussia and Russia concluded a new alliance against Napoleon.
11 Jun   Napoleon left Paris, heading north. His intention was to defeat the Allied armies in Belgium – Wellington's Anglo-Dutch army of 95,000 men and Blücher's 124,000 Prussians – before the arrival of the Austrians and Russians.
15 Jun   The French army captured Charleroi.
16 Jun   Napoleon attacked Blücher's Prussians at Ligny, while Ney engaged the Anglo-Dutch army at Quatre Bras. Ney was unable to achieve a speedy victory, which would have enabled him to help Napoleon to crush the Prussians. Ney recalled d'Erlon's corps, which he had sent to help Napoleon, but it failed to reach him in time. Both Allied armies were able to conduct orderly retreats.
17 Jun   Napoleon sent Grouchy to pursue Blücher and prevent his joining Wellington. But Blücher had retreated towards Wavre and not Liége as believed. When Grouchy eventually caught up with Blücher's rearguard on 18 Jun at Wavre, it was too late to influence the outcome of the campaign.
18 Jun   Battle of Waterloo; French attacks failed to drive Wellington's Anglo-Dutch army from its defensive position, and the arrival of Blücher in the late afternoon ensured the total defeat of the French.
22 June   Abdication of Napoleon.
20 Nov   Second Treaty of Paris; France was now reduced to her 1790 frontiers.

NAVAL OPERATIONS AND MINOR EXPEDITIONS, 1793–1815

1793      28 Aug   British fleet under Hood seized Toulon. French pressure from the landward side, directed by Bonaparte, forced Hood to evacuate on 18 Dec.
Nov   British force of 7000 men under Grey sent to the West Indies. By 1796 military action, including the suppression of slave revolts, and disease had resulted in 40,000 dead and a similar number incapacitated. The campaign was brought to an end in Oct 1798.

1794      1 Jun   Howe defeated the French fleet off Ushant, but a vital food convoy of 130 merchant ships from the United States was allowed to reach Brest.

10 Aug   British forces captured Corsica.

1797      14 Feb   Jervis defeated a Spanish fleet under Admiral José de Córdova at Cape St Vincent.

11 Oct   Duncan defeated a Dutch fleet under de Winter at Camperdown.

1798      1 Aug   Nelson destroyed the French fleet in Aboukir Bay.

22 Aug   Humbert landed with 1200 French troops at Killala Bay to support the Irish rebels. He was forced to surrender to Cornwallis on 8 Sep. A French squadron with reinforcements was destroyed by Warren on 12 Oct.

19 Nov   The British occupied Minorca.

1800      5 Sep   French forces on Malta surrendered to the British after a lengthy siege of Valetta.

15 Dec   Tsar Paul revived the Armed Neutrality of the North with Sweden, Denmark and Prussia to resist British interference with their shipping.

1801      2 Apr   Parker and Nelson destroyed the Danish fleet at Copenhagen. Tsar Paul had been assassinated on 24 Mar, and his successor, Alexander, made peace with Britain on 17 Jun.

12 Jul   A British fleet under Saumarez defeated a Franco-Spanish fleet at Algeçiras.

1805      21 Oct   Battle of Trafalgar; Nelson's defeat of a Franco-Spanish fleet under Villeneuve finally ended the threat of a French invasion of Britain.

1806      8 Jan   A British expedition of 6000 men under Baird captured the Cape of Good Hope from the Dutch.

6 Feb   A British fleet under Duckworth destroyed the French West Indian Squadron at Santo Domingo.

Jun   5000 British troops under Stuart landed in Calabria in Italy to assist the opposition to Joseph Bonaparte. The British defeated a French army at Maida on 4 Jul, but then withdrew to Sicily.

Jun   Popham landed a small force under Beresford which occupied Buenos Aires. Local militia forced Beresford to surrender on 12 Aug. A further expedition led by Whitelocke took Montevideo in Jul 1807, but a popular uprising forced it to withdraw.

1807      2–7 Sep   British land and naval forces under Cathcart and Gambier bombarded the Danish capital in the second Battle of Copenhagen. The Danish fleet surrendered.

1809 30 Jun A British and Spanish expedition captured Martinique and Santo Domingo.

   Jul Walcheren Expedition; a British fleet of 35 ships of the line escorted 40,000 men under Chatham to the Scheldt estuary to take Antwerp. The advance was delayed by the resistance of Flushing, which held out until 16 Aug, and there were heavy losses when fever broke out. Half the force returned to England in Sep; the rest remained to garrison Walcheren, but were evacuated in Dec.

1810 Dec The British captured Mauritius and Réunion from the French.

1811 Aug The British captured Batavia from the Dutch.


# PRINCIPAL EUROPEAN ARMED CONFLICTS, 1815–48

### SPANISH CIVIL WAR, 1820–3

A revolution which began with a mutiny at Cadiz on 1 Jan 1820 forced King Ferdinand VII to accept the liberal constitution of 1812. Ferdinand appealed to the Holy Alliance, and after the Congress of Verona in 1822 a French army led by the Duke of Angoulême entered Spain on 17 Apr 1823. The rebel government fled to Cadiz, and its forces were defeated at the Battle of the Trocadero on 31 Aug 1823. Ferdinand was restored to power and took harsh reprisals against his opponents.

### REVOLTS IN ITALY, 1820–1

General Pepe led an army revolt against Ferdinand IV of Naples in Jul 1820, but he was defeated by an Austrian army at Rieti on 7 Mar 1821. A revolt in Sardinia in Mar 1821 was suppressed by loyalist forces at the Battle of Novara on 8 Apr.

### GREEK REVOLT, 1821–32

The Greek revolt against the Ottoman Empire began in Mar 1821, and independence was proclaimed at Epidauros on 13 Jan 1822. Attempting to suppress the revolt, the Turks besieged Missolonghi in Jul 1822 but had to withdraw in Jan 1823. In 1825 Mahomet Ali of Egypt sent forces to aid the Turks. His son, Ibrahim, subdued the Morea. A Turkish army captured the Acropolis in Jun 1825, and Missolonghi fell in Apr 1826 after a second siege lasting nearly a year. The Great Powers now intervened in support of the Greeks. On 6 Jul 1827 Britain, France and Russia signed the Treaty of

London, calling for an Egyptian withdrawal and an armistice. Their navies destroyed a joint Turkish and Egyptian fleet in Navarino Bay on 20 Oct 1827. After defeat in war with Russia, Turkey was forced to accept Greek independence, which was established by the Treaty of London on 7 May 1832.

### CIVIL WAR IN PORTUGAL, 1826–34

King John of Portugal died on 10 Mar 1826. His son, Dom Pedro, succeeded him but remained in Brazil as Emperor of that country. His infant daughter, Maria, became Queen, with his younger brother, Miguel, acting as Regent. Civil war broke out when Miguel attempted to seize power, but a British force under Sir William Clinton landed in Portugal in Jan 1827 to support the constitutional government. When it withdrew, Miguel seized the throne in Jul 1828. Maria's supporters occupied the Azores and defeated Miguel's fleet in Praia Bay on 12 Aug 1828. Pedro now abdicated the throne of Brazil and landed in Portugal in Jul 1832, occupying Oporto. He was besieged there by Miguel. Admiral Sir Charles Napier, commanding Pedro's squadron of ships, defeated an opposing flotilla off Cape St Vincent on 5 Jul 1833, and captured Lisbon on 24 Jul. Miguel was finally defeated at the Battle of Santarem on 16 May 1834, and surrendered at Evora-Monte on 24 May.

### RUSSO-TURKISH WAR, 1828–9

Russia declared war on Turkey on 26 Apr 1828, and launched offensives in the Balkans and on the Caucasus front. Russian forces defeated the Turkish at Kulevcha on 11 Jun 1829, and took Adrianople on 20 Aug. The Turks were obliged to make peace at the Treaty of Adrianople on 14 Sep 1829, surrendering the mouth of the Danube and the eastern coast of the Black Sea.

### BELGIAN REVOLT, 1830–9

Rioting began in Brussels on 25 Aug 1830, and Belgium declared its independence from the Netherlands on 4 Oct. This was recognized by a conference of the Great Powers in a preliminary agreement on 20 Jan 1831, and by the Treaty of London on 15 Nov. A Dutch force of 50,000 men invaded Belgium on 2 Aug 1831, but a French army under Marshal Gérard intervened to restore the situation. Franco-British forces compelled the Dutch troops in the citadel of Antwerp to surrender, and the Dutch accepted the *status quo* on 21 May 1833. The independence and neutrality of Belgium were guaranteed by the Treaty of London on 19 Apr 1839.

### POLISH INSURRECTION, 1830–1

Insurrection broke out in Warsaw on 29 Nov 1830. A Russian Army under

General Diebitsch was defeated by Prince Radziwell at the Battle of Grochow on 20 Feb 1831. However, the Poles were defeated at the Battle of Ostrolenka on 26 May. Warsaw fell on 8 Sep 1831, and the insurrection was ruthlessly suppressed.

## CIVIL WARS IN SPAIN, 1833–43

Ferdinand VII of Spain died on 29 Sep 1833. He had named his infant daughter, Isabella, as his successor, with his widow, Maria Christina, as Regent, but this was contested by his brother, Carlos. An army of 10,000 men, known as the Spanish Legion, sailed from England under Sir George de Lacy Evans, and France sent its Foreign Legion to Spain to support Isabella's Government. A long period of guerrilla warfare ensued. The Carlists were defeated at Terapegui on 26 Apr 1836 and Huesca on 24 Mar 1837. They finally capitulated by the Convention of Gergara on 31 Aug 1839, and Carlos went into exile in France.

In 1840 General Espartero seized power from Isabella and Maria Christina. After suppressing two uprisings, he himself was ousted in 1843 by General Narvaez, who restored Isabella to the throne.

## HUNGARIAN INSURRECTION, 1848–9

The revolt in Hungary began on 15 Mar 1848. Austrian forces invaded Hungary to reassert control in Sep 1848, but were driven out by the Hungarians, who advanced on Vienna. A popular revolt in Vienna was suppressed by General Windischgrätz, who then repulsed the Hungarians and occupied Budapest on 5 Jan 1849. An Hungarian Republic was established on 13 Apr with Lajos Kossuth as president, and the Austrians were again driven out of Hungary. However, on 17 Jun 1849 Russian troops invaded Hungary in support of the Austrians. The Hungarians were defeated in the battles of Segesvar on 31 Jul and Temesvar on 9 Aug, and surrendered to the Russians at Vilagos on 13 Aug 1849.

## AUSTRO-SARDINIAN WAR, 1848–9

The war was precipitated by a revolt in Milan, 18–23 Mar 1848. Charles Albert of Sardinia declared war on Austria on 22 Mar 1848, but was defeated by General Radetsky in battles around Custozza 23–5 Jul. An armistice was arranged at Vigevano on 9 Aug 1848. Fighting was renewed in Mar 1849, and the Austrians were victorious at Novara on 23 Mar. Charles Albert abdicated, and his son, Victor Emanuel, made peace by the Treaty of Milan on 6 Aug 1849. The Roman Republic, proclaimed on 9 Feb 1849, was suppressed by a

French expeditionary force in Jun 1849, and the Republic of Venice, established on 26 Mar 1848, surrendered in Aug 1849.

### PRUSSO-DANISH WAR, 1848–52

The Duchies of Schleswig-Holstein declared their independence of Denmark on 24 Mar 1848. A Prussian army under General Wrangel intervened in support of the rebels in Apr 1848. Sweden sent troops to aid Denmark, and Britain threatened naval action against Prussia. A truce was signed at Malmo on 26 Aug 1848. Fighting broke out again in Apr 1849, but a fresh truce was arranged, after international pressure, on 10 Jul. The Treaty of Berlin was signed in Jul 1850, and a final settlement, including a Great Power guarantee of Danish integrity, was made by the Treaty of London on 8 May 1852.

PRINCIPAL BATTLES, 1789–1848

LAND BATTLES

| Battle | Date | Combatants | Numbers engaged | Casualties | Commanders |
|---|---|---|---|---|---|
| Albuera | 16 May 1811 | British, Portuguese, Spanish | 35,000 | 6000 | Beresford |
| | | French | 24,000 | 8000 | Soult |
| Alexandria | 13 Mar 1801 | French | 6000 | 500 | Friant |
| | | British | 10,000 | 1300 | Abercromby |
| Alexandria | 21 Mar 1801 | British | 10,000 | 1400 | Abercromby |
| | | French | 11,000 | 2000 | Ménou |
| Alkmaar | 2 Oct 1799 | British, Russians | 30,000 | 2000 | Duke of York |
| | | French, Dutch | 30,000 | 2000 | Brune |
| Amberg | 24 Aug 1796 | Austrians | 46,000 | 500 | Charles |
| | | French | 34,000 | 1200 | Jourdan |
| Arcis-sur-Aube | 20–1 Mar 1814 | Allies | 80,000 | 4000 | Schwarzenberg |
| | | French | 28,000 | 3000 | Napoleon |
| Arcola | 15–17 Nov 1796 | French | 20,000 | 4500 | Bonaparte |
| | | Austrians | 17,000 | 7000 | D'Alvintzi |
| Aspern-Essling | 21–2 May 1809 | Austrians | 95,800 | 23,400 | Charles |
| | | French | 70,000 | 21,000 | Napoleon |
| Auerstadt | 14 Oct 1806 | French | 27,000 | 7000 | Davout |
| | | Prussians | 50,000 | 10,000 | Brunswick |
| Austerlitz | 2 Dec 1805 | French | 73,200 | 9000 | Napoleon |
| | | Austrians, Russians | 85,400 | 27,000 | Kutusov |

(continued

101

## PRINCIPAL BATTLES, 1789–1848 (continued)

LAND BATTLES (continued)

| Battle | Date | Combatants | Numbers engaged | Casualties | Commanders |
|---|---|---|---|---|---|
| Barrosa | 5 Mar 1811 | British, Portuguese, Spanish | 4500 | 1200 | Graham |
| | | French | 9000 | 2000 | Victor |
| Bautzen | 20–1 May 1813 | French and allies | 167,000 | 21,000 | Napoleon |
| | | Allies | 97,000 | 11,000 | Witgenstein |
| Beretsina | 27–8 Nov 1812 | French | 40,000 | 25,000 | Napoleon |
| | | Russians | 64,000 | 20,000 | Kutusov |
| Bergen-op-Zoom | 19 Sep 1799 | French, Dutch | 18,000 | 3000 | Vandamme |
| | | British, Russians | 20,000 | 4000 | Duke of York |
| Bidassoa | 7–9 Oct 1813 | British, Portuguese, Spanish | 32,000 | 1600 | Wellington |
| | | French | 14,000 | 1100 | Soult |
| Borodino | 7 Sep 1812 | French | 133,000 | 30,000 | Napoleon |
| | | Russians | 120,000 | 44,000 | Kutusov |
| Brienne | 29 Jan 1814 | French | 36,000 | 3000 | Napoleon |
| | | Prussians, Russians | 30,000 | 3000 | Blücher |
| Busaco Ridge | 27 Sep 1810 | British, Portuguese | 51,300 | 1250 | Wellington |
| | | French | 66,000 | 4600 | Masséna |
| Caldiero | 29–31 Oct 1805 | Austria | 49,000 | 5700 | Charles |
| | | French | 46,000 | 6300 | Masséna |
| Castella | 13 Apr 1813 | British, Portuguese, Spanish | 17,000 | 600 | Murray |
| | | French | 15,000 | 800 | Suchet |

| Battle | Date | Combatants | Numbers | Losses | Commander |
|---|---|---|---|---|---|
| Castiglione | 5 Aug 1796 | French | 30,000 | 1500 | Bonaparte |
| | | Austrians | 25,000 | 3000 | Würmser |
| Corunna | 16 Jan 1809 | British | 14,000 | 800 | Moore |
| | | French | 16,000 | 2000 | Soult |
| Dresden | 26–27 Aug 1813 | French and allies | 120,000 | 10,000 | Napoleon |
| | | Austrians, Russians | 170,000 | 38,000 | Schwarzenberg |
| Eckmuhl | 22 Apr 1809 | French, Bavarians | 60,000 | 6000 | Napoleon |
| | | Austrians | 35,000 | 12,000 | Charles |
| Eylau | 8 Feb 1807 | French | 75,000 | 25,000 | Napoleon |
| | | Russians | 76,000 | 15,000 | Benningsen |
| Fleurus | 26 Jun 1794 | French | 81,000 | 5000 | Jourdan |
| | | Austrians, Dutch | 46,000 | 5000 | Coburg |
| Friedland | 14 Jun 1807 | French | 80,000 | 8000 | Napoleon |
| | | Russians | 60,000 | 20,000 | Benningsen |
| Fuentes de Onoro | 5 May 1811 | British, Portuguese | 37,600 | 1450 | Wellington |
| | | French | 48,300 | 2260 | Masséna |
| Hanau | 30–1 Oct 1813 | French | 60,000 | 6000 | Napoleon |
| | | Austrians, Bavarians | 40,000 | 5000 | Wrede |
| Heilsberg | 10 Jun 1807 | French | 49,000 | 12,500 | Napoleon |
| | | Russians, Prussians | 53,000 | 9000 | Benningsen |
| Hohenlinden | 3 Dec 1800 | French | 55,000 | 2500 | Moreau |
| | | Austrians, Bavarians | 57,000 | 5500 | John |
| Hondschoote | 8 Sep 1793 | French | 24,000 | 3000 | Houchard |
| | | British, Dutch, Austrians, Hanoverians | 16,000 | 1600 | Freytag |

(continued

103

PRINCIPAL BATTLES, 1789–1848 (*continued*)

LAND BATTLES (*continued*)

| Battle | Date | Combatants | Numbers engaged | Casualties | Commanders |
|--------|------|-----------|----------------|-----------|-----------|
| Jemappes | 6 Nov 1792 | French | 45,000 | 2000 | Dumouriez |
| | | Austrians | 13,200 | 1000 | Albert |
| Jena | 14 Oct 1806 | French | 96,000 | 5000 | Napoleon |
| | | Prussians, Saxons | 53,000 | 25,000 | Hohenlohe |
| Katzbach | 26 Aug 1813 | Prussians, Russians | 80,000 | 4000 | Blücher |
| | | French | 60,000 | 12,000 | Macdonald |
| Kulm | 29–30 Aug 1813 | Russians, Prussians, Austrians | 103,000 | 11,000 | De Tolly |
| | | French | 37,000 | 9000 | Vandamme |
| Laon | 9–10 Mar 1814 | Allies | 85,000 | 4000 | Blücher |
| | | French | 47,000 | 6000 | Napoleon |
| La Rothière | 1 Feb 1814 | Allies | 110,000 | 6000 | Blücher |
| | | French | 40,000 | 6000 | Napoleon |
| Leipzig | 16–19 Oct 1813 | Russians, Austrians, Prussians, Swedes | 365,000 | 54,000 | Schwarzenberg |
| | | French and allies | 195,000 | 73,000 | Napoleon |
| Ligny | 16 Jun 1815 | French | 80,000 | 11,500 | Napoleon |
| | | Prussians | 84,000 | 25,000 | Blücher |
| Lodi | 10 May 1796 | French | 17,500 | 900 | Bonaparte |
| | | Austrians | 9500 | 400 | Beaulieu |

| Battle | Date | Combatants | Strength | Casualties | Commander |
|---|---|---|---|---|---|
| Lonato | 3 Aug 1796 | French | 20,000 | 2000 | Bonaparte |
| | | Austrians | 15,000 | 3000 | Quasdanovich |
| Lützen | 2 May 1813 | French | 110,000 | 20,000 | Napoleon |
| | | Prussians, Russians | 73,000 | 18,000 | Wittgenstein |
| Magnano | 5 Apr 1799 | Austrians | 46,000 | 4000 | Kray |
| | | French | 41,000 | 3500 | Schérer |
| Maida | 4 Jul 1806 | British | 5100 | 330 | Stuart |
| | | French | 6500 | 2200 | Reynier |
| Mainz | 29 Oct 1795 | Austrians | 36,000 | 1600 | Clerfayt |
| | | French | 33,000 | 3000 | Pichegru |
| Maloyaroslavets | 24 Oct 1812 | French | 24,000 | 6000 | Napoleon |
| | | Russians | 24,000 | 8000 | Kutusov |
| Marengo | 14 Jun 1800 | French | 28,000 | 7000 | Napoleon |
| | | Austrians | 31,000 | 14,000 | Melas |
| Mincio | 25–6 Dec 1800 | French | 66,000 | 4000 | Brune |
| | | Austrians | 50,000 | 4100 | Bellegarde |
| Mondovi | 22 Apr 1796 | French | 17,500 | 600 | Bonaparte |
| | | Sardinians | 13,000 | 1600 | Colli |
| Montenotte | 12 Apr 1796 | French | 10,000 | 880 | Bonaparte |
| | | Austrians | 4500 | 2500 | Argenteau |
| Mount Tabor | 17 Apr 1799 | French | 4500 | 62 | Kléber, Bonaparte |
| | | Turks | 35,000 | unknown | Pasha of Damascus |
| Neerwinden | 18 Mar 1793 | Austrians | 43,000 | 2600 | Coburg |
| | | French | 41,000 | 3000 | Dumouriez |

(*continued*

105

## PRINCIPAL BATTLES, 1789–1848 (continued)

LAND BATTLES (continued)

| Battle | Date | Combatants | Numbers engaged | Casualties | Commanders |
|---|---|---|---|---|---|
| Neresheim | 11 Aug 1796 | French<br>Austrians | 50,000<br>48,000 | 1200<br>1100 | Moreau<br>Charles |
| Nive | 9–13 Dec 1813 | British, Portuguese, Spanish<br>French | 60,000<br>60,000 | 5000<br>8000 | Wellington<br>Soult |
| Nivelle | 10 Nov 1813 | British, Portuguese, Spanish<br>French | 80,000<br>63,000 | 2700<br>4300 | Wellington<br>Soult |
| Novi | 15 Aug 1799 | Russians, Austrians<br>French | 50,000<br>35,000 | 7000<br>7000 | Suvarov<br>Joubert |
| Orthez | 27 Feb 1814 | British, Portuguese, Spanish<br>French | 44,000<br>36,000 | 2000<br>4000 | Wellington<br>Soult |
| Pultusk | 26 Dec 1806 | French<br>Russians | 26,000<br>44,000 | 3300<br>3500 | Lannes<br>Bennigsen |
| Pyramids | 21 Jul 1798 | French<br>Mamelukes, Fellahin | 25,000<br>21,000 | 300<br>5000 | Bonaparte<br>Murad Bey |
| Pyrenees | 25 Jul–<br>1 Aug 1814 | British, Portuguese, Spanish<br>French | 40,000<br>53,000 | 7000<br>13,500 | Wellington<br>Soult |
| Quatre Bras | 16 Jan 1815 | British and allies<br>French | 36,000<br>25,000 | 4300<br>4700 | Wellington<br>Ney |
| Ratisbon | 23 Apr 1809 | French<br>Austrians | 72,000<br>47,000 | 2000<br>2000 | Napoleon<br>Charles |

| Battle | Date | Nationality | Commander | | |
|---|---|---|---|---|---|
| Rivoli | 14–15 Jan 1797 | French | Bonaparte | 22,000 | 2200 |
| | | Austrians | D'Alvintzi | 28,000 | 4000 |
| Roliça | 17 Aug 1808 | British | Wellesley | 14,000 | 480 |
| | | French | Laborde | 4000 | 600 |
| Salamanca | 22 Jul 1812 | British, Portuguese, Spanish | Wellington | 48,500 | 4800 |
| | | French | Marmont | 50,000 | 14,000 |
| Smolensk | 17–18 Aug 1812 | French | Napoleon | 45,000 | 10,000 |
| | | Russians | De Tolly | 30,000 | 6000 |
| Stockach | 25–6 Mar 1799 | Austrians | Charles | 46,000 | 2900 |
| | | French | Jourdan | 38,000 | 2000 |
| Stockach | 3 May 1800 | French | Moreau | 84,000 | 3000 |
| | | Austrians | Kray | 72,000 | 3000 |
| Talavera | 28 Jul 1809 | British, Spanish | Wellesley | 55,000 | 5600 |
| | | French | Joseph | 46,000 | 7300 |
| Toulouse | 10 Apr 1814 | British, Portuguese, Spanish | Wellington | 50,000 | 4600 |
| | | French | Soult | 42,000 | 3200 |
| Tourcoing | 18 May 1794 | French | Souham | 70,000 | 3000 |
| | | Allies | Coburg | 74,000 | 4000 |
| Tournai | 22 May 1794 | Allies | Coburg | 50,000 | 3000 |
| | | French | Pichegru | 45,000 | 5500 |
| Trebbia | 17–19 Jun 1799 | Austrians, Prussians | Suvarov | 37,000 | 5000 |
| | | French | Macdonald | 33,000 | 9500 |
| Valmy | 20 Sep 1792 | French | Dumouriez, Kellermann | 59,000 | 300 |
| | | Prussians | Brunswick | 35,000 | 200 |
| Vimeiro | 21 Aug 1808 | British | Wellesley | 17,000 | 720 |
| | | French | Junot | 13,000 | 2000 |

*(continued)*

PRINCIPAL BATTLES, 1789–1848 (continued)

LAND BATTLES (continued)

| Battle | Date | Combatants | Numbers engaged | Casualties | Commanders |
|---|---|---|---|---|---|
| Vitoria | 21 Jun 1813 | British, Portuguese, Spanish | 79,000 | 4900 | Wellington |
| | | French | 66,000 | 5200 | Joseph |
| Wagram | 5–6 Jul 1809 | French | 170,000 | 32,000 | Napoleon |
| | | Austrians | 146,000 | 40,000 | Charles |
| Waterloo | 18 Jun 1815 | British and allies | 67,000 | 22,000 | Wellingon |
| | | Prussians | 53,000 | | Blücher |
| | | French | 72,000 | 32,000 | Napoleon |
| Wattignies | 16 Oct 1793 | French | 45,000 | 5000 | Jourdan |
| | | Allies | 30,000 | 2500 | Coburg |
| Wavre | 18 Jun 1815 | French | 33,000 | 2500 | Grouchy |
| | | Prussians | 17,000 | 2500 | Thielmann |
| Würzburg | 3 Sep 1796 | Austrians | 44,000 | 1200 | Charles |
| | | French | 30,000 | 2000 | Jourdan |
| Zurich | 4 Jun 1799 | Austrians | 55,000 | 2200 | Charles |
| | | French | 45,000 | 1300 | Masséna |
| Zurich | 25–6 Sep 1799 | French | 33,500 | 4000 | Masséna |
| | | Russians | 23,000 | 6000 | Korsakov |

SEA BATTLES

| Battle | Date | Combatants | Ships engaged | Ships lost | Casualties | Commanders |
|---|---|---|---|---|---|---|
| Camperdown | 11 Oct 1797 | British | 16 | 0 | 1000 | Duncan |
| | | Dutch | 16 | 9 | 1100 | De Winter |
| Cape St Vincent | 14 Feb 1797 | British | 15 | 0 | 300 | Jervis |
| | | Spanish | 27 | 4 | 800 | De Cordova |
| Copenhagen | 2 Apr 1801 | British | 18 | 6 | 1000 | Parker |
| | | Danes | 17 | 17 | 1700 | Fischer |
| Navarino | 20 Oct 1827 | British, French, Russians | 27 | 0 | 696 | Codrington, De Rigny, Heiden |
| | | Turks, Egyptians | 89 | 60 | 8000 | Tahir Pasha |
| Nile | 1 Aug 1798 | British | 14 | 0 | 1000 | Nelson |
| | | French | 13 | 11 | 10,000 | Brueys |
| Trafalgar | 21 Oct 1805 | British | 27 | 0 | 1700 | Nelson |
| | | French | 33 | 20 | 6900 | Villeneuve |
| Ushant | 1 Jun 1794 | British | 25 | 0 | 1000 | Howe |
| | | French | 26 | 7 | 3000 | Villaret-Joyeuse |

# 6 TREATIES AND DIPLOMACY

## PRINCIPAL EUROPEAN TREATIES, 1789–1848

### 1790

| | |
|---|---|
| 9 Jan | Treaty of Berlin between Britain, Prussia and the Netherlands |
| Feb | Treaty of alliance between Prussia and Turkey |
| Mar | Treaty of alliance between Prussia and Poland |
| 27 Jul | Convention of Reichenbach between Prussia and Austria |
| 15 Aug | Treaty of Varala between Russia and Sweden |
| Sep | Truce of Guirgevo between Austria and Turkey |

### 1791

| | |
|---|---|
| 4 Aug | Treaty of Sistova between Austria and Turkey |
| 11 Aug | Preliminaries of peace between Russia and Turkey |
| Oct | Treaty of friendship between Sweden and Russia |

### 1792

| | |
|---|---|
| 9 Jan | Treaty of Jassy between Russia and Turkey |
| 7 Feb | Treaty of Berlin between Prussia and Austria for mutual guarantee of territory and support against France |

### 1793

| | |
|---|---|
| 23 Jan | Treaty between Prussia and Russia for the partition of Poland |
| 12 Feb | Convention concluded in London by Britain and Spain |
| 25 Mar | Treaties between Britain and Russia on commerce and for concerted action against France |
| 25 Apr | Treaty of alliance between Britain and Sardinia |
| 25 May | Convention concluded at Aranjuez by Britain and Spain |
| 12 Jul | Convention concluded at Naples by Britain and Sicily |
| 14 Jul | Convention concluded at Mainz by Britain and Prussia |
| 30 Aug | Convention concluded in London by Britain and Austria |

| | |
|---|---|
| 23 Sep | Treaty for partition of Poland between Prussia and Russia |
| 26 Sep | Treaty of London between Britain and Portugal |

## 1794

| | |
|---|---|
| 11 Jan | Agreement concluded at Madrid between Britain and Spain |
| 19 Apr | Subsidy treaty concluded at The Hague by Britain, Prussia and the Netherlands |
| 8 Nov | Subsidy treaty between Britain and the Duke of Brunswick |
| 19 Nov | Treaty of amity, commerce and navigation between Britain and the United States |

## 1795

| | |
|---|---|
| Jan | Secret treaty of assistance between Austria and Russia |
| 18 Feb | Defensive alliance concluded at St Petersburg by Britain and Russia |
| 5 Apr | Treaty of Basle between France and Prussia |
| 4 May | Loan convention concluded in Vienna by Britain and Austria |
| 16 May | Treaty between Holland and France |
| 20 May | Defensive alliance concluded in Vienna by Britain and Austria |
| 22 Jul | Treaty between Spain and France |
| 24 Oct | Treaty for partition of Poland between Austria, Prussia and Russia |

## 1796

| | |
|---|---|
| 28 Apr | Armistice of Cherasco between France and Sardinia |
| 5 Jun | Armistice between France and Naples |
| 23 Jun | Armistice of Foligno between France and the Papacy |
| 5 Aug | Secret treaty between France and Prussia concerning the French frontier and the Rhine |
| 19 Aug | Treaty of San Ildefonso between France and Spain renewing the Family Compact |
| 10 Oct | Peace treaty between France and Naples |

## 1797

| | |
|---|---|
| 26 Jan | Treaty concerning Poland between Austria, Prussia and Russia |
| 19 Feb | Treaty of Tolentino between France and the Papacy |

| | |
|---|---|
| 21 Feb | Treaty of commerce concluded at St Petersburg by Britain and Russia |
| 12 May | Treaty of Milan abolishing the Venetian Great Council |
| 16 May | Loan convention concluded in London by Britain and Austria |
| 10 Aug | Peace treaty between France and Portugal |
| 17 Aug | Preliminaries of Leoben between Austria and France |
| 17 Oct | Peace of Campo Formio between Austria and France |

## 1798

| | |
|---|---|
| 21 Feb | Treaty between France and the Cisalpine Republic |
| 1 Dec | Treaty of alliance concluded at Naples by Britain and the Two Sicilies |
| 29 Dec | Provisional treaty concluded at St Petersburg by Britain and Russia |

## 1799

| | |
|---|---|
| 5 Jan | Treaty of alliance concluded at Constantinople by Britain and Turkey |
| 22 Jun | Convention concluded at St Petersburg by Britain and Russia |

## 1800

| | |
|---|---|
| 21 Jan | Convention of El Arish for evacuation of Egypt by French forces |
| 16 Mar | Subsidy treaty concluded in Munich by Britain and Bavaria |
| 20 Jun | Convention concluded in Vienna by Britain and Austria |
| 15 Jul | Armistice of Parsdorf between France and Austria |
| 29 Aug | Convention concluded at Copenhagen by Britain and Denmark |
| 15 Dec | Treaty establishing the Armed Neutrality of the North between Russia, Sweden and Denmark (accession: Prussia, 18 Dec) |
| 25 Dec | Armistice of Steyr between France and Austria |

## 1801

| | |
|---|---|
| 15 Jan | Armistice of Treviso between France and Austria |
| 9 Feb | Peace of Lunéville between France and Austria |
| 21 Mar | Treaty of Aranjuez between France and Spain |
| 28 Mar | Treaty of Florence between France and Naples |
| 18 May | Peace between Britain and Sweden |

| | |
|---|---|
| 28 May | Peace between Britain and Denmark |
| 6 Jun | Treaty of Badajoz between Portugal and Spain/France |
| 17 Jun | Convention concluded at St Petersburg between Britain and Russia (accessions: Denmark, 2 Oct 1801; Sweden, 30 Mar 1802) |
| 1 Oct | Preliminary articles of peace between France and Britain |

### 1802

| | |
|---|---|
| 27 Mar | Treaty of Amiens for peace between Britain, France, Spain and the Batavian Republic |
| 11 Oct | Treaty of alliance between Russia and France |

### 1803

| | |
|---|---|
| 19 Oct | Subsidy treaty between Spain and France |

### 1804

| | |
|---|---|
| 6 Nov | Secret treaty between Austria and Russia to resist French aggression in Italy |
| Dec | Alliance between Britain and Sweden |

### 1805

| | |
|---|---|
| | Treaty of alliance between Sweden and Russia |
| 11 Apr | Treaty of concert concluded at St Petersburg between Britain and Russia (accession: Austria, 9 Aug) |
| Jul | Treaty between France and Naples |
| 24 Aug | Treaty between France and Bavaria |
| 3 Oct | Treaty of Beckascog between Britain and Sweden |
| 15 Dec | Treaty of Schönbrunn between Prussia and France |
| 26 Dec | Peace of Pressburg between Austria and France |

### 1806

| | |
|---|---|
| 15 Feb | Treaty of Paris between Prussia and France |
| Jul | Secret defensive alliance between Prussia and Russia |
| 11 Dec | Peace of Posen between France and Saxony |

## 1807

| | |
|---|---|
| 28 Jan | Articles of treaty of peace and amity concluded at Memel between Britain and Prussia |
| 18 Apr | Armistice between France and Sweden |
| 26 Apr | Treaty of Bartenstein between Russia and Prussia (accessions: Sweden and Britain) |
| 17 Jun | Convention concluded in London by Britain and Prussia |
| 23 Jun | Subsidy convention concluded at Stralsund by Britain and Sweden |
| 27 Jun | Subsidy convention concluded in London by Britain and Prussia |
| 9 Jul | Treaty of Tilsit between France and Russia |
| 22 Oct | Convention of friendship concluded in London by Britain and Portugal |
| 27 Oct | Treaty of Fontainebleau between France and Spain for partition of Portugal |
| 30 Oct | Treaty of alliance between France and Denmark |

## 1808

| | |
|---|---|
| 8 Feb | Subsidy convention concluded at Stockholm by Britain and Sweden |
| 30 Mar | Treaty of alliance and subsidy concluded at Palermo by Britain and Naples |
| 30 Aug | Convention of Cintra between Britain and France for evacuation of Portugal by French army |
| 12 Oct | Treaty of Erfurt between Russia and France |

## 1809

| | |
|---|---|
| 5 Jan | Treaty of peace and commerce between Britain and Turkey |
| 14 Jan | Treaty of peace, friendship and alliance concluded in London by Britain and Spain |
| 1 Mar | Convention concluded in Stockholm by Britain and Sweden |
| 24 Apr | Treaty of alliance concluded in London by Britain and Austria |
| 13 May | Treaty of alliance and subsidy concluded in Palermo by Britain and Naples |
| 12 Jul | Armistice of Znaim between Austria and France |
| 17 Sep | Treaty of Fredericksburg between Russia and Sweden |
| 14 Oct | Peace of Schönbrunn between France and Austria |

## 1810

| | |
|---|---|
| 6 Jan | Treaty of Paris between Sweden and France |
| 19 Feb | Treaty of commerce, navigation and friendship concluded in Rio de Janeiro by Britain and Portugal |

## 1812

| | |
|---|---|
| 24 Feb | Treaty between France and Prussia concerning Russian campaign |
| 9 Apr | Treaty of Abo between Sweden and Russia |
| 28 May | Treaty of Bucharest between Russia and Turkey |
| 18 Jul | Treaty of Orebro for peace and friendship between Britain and Russia |
| 18 Jul | Treaty of Orebro for peace and friendship between Britain and Sweden |
| 12 Sep | Treaty of alliance and subsidy concluded in Palermo by Britain and Naples |
| 30 Dec | Convention of Tauroggen between Prussia and Russia |

## 1813

| | |
|---|---|
| 27 Feb | Treaty of Kalisch between Russia and Prussia |
| 3 Mar | Treaty of concert and subsidy concluded in Stockholm by Britain and Sweden |
| 4 Jun | Armistice of Plestwitz between Napoleon and the Allies. |
| 14 Jun | Convention of Reichenbach between Britain and Prussia |
| 15 Jun | Convention of Reichenbach between Britain and Russia |
| 27 Jun | Convention of Reichenbach between Austria, Prussia and Russia. |
| 9 Sep | Treaty of Teplitz confirming alliance between Austria, Prussia and Russia |
| 3 Oct | Preliminary treaty of alliance between Austria and Britain |
| 8 Oct | Treaty of Ried between Bavaria and the Allies |
| 12 Oct | Treaty of Gulistan between Russia and Persia |

## 1814

| | |
|---|---|
| 11 Jan | Alliance between Austria and Naples |
| 14 Jan | Treaty of peace concluded at Kiel by Britain and Denmark |

| | |
|---|---|
| 15 Feb | Convention of Troyes between Britain, Austria, Prussia and Russia concerning territorial arrangements of peace with France |
| 1 Mar | Treaty of Chaumont between Austria, Britain, Prussia and Russia |
| 6 Apr | Treaty of Fontainebleau between Napoleon and the Allies |
| 11 Apr | Treaty between Austria, Prussia, Russia and Napoleon (accession: Britain, 27 Apr) |
| 23 Apr | Convention for suspension of hostilities with France |
| 28 May | Military convention between Britain, Austria, Prussia, Russia and France |
| 30 May | Definitive treaty of peace and amity with France |
| 14 Jun | Protocol of conference between Austria, Britain, Prussia and Russia concerning union of Holland and Belgium |
| 5 Jul | Treaty of friendship and alliance concluded in Madrid by Britain and Spain |
| 24 Dec | Treaty of Ghent between Britain and the United States |

## 1815

| | |
|---|---|
| 3 Jan | Defensive alliance between Austria, Britain and France (accessions: Bavaria, 26 Jan; the Netherlands, 31 Jan) |
| 22 Jan | Treaty between Britain and Portugal restricting the slave trade |
| 8 Feb | Declaration by Austria, Britain, France, Portugal, Prussia, Russia, Spain and Sweden concerning universal abolition of the slave trade |
| 20 Mar | Declaration of the Eight Powers (as above) on the affairs of the Swiss Confederation (accession: Swiss Confederation, 27 May) |
| 25 Mar | Treaty of alliance between Austria, Britain, Prussia and Russia against Napoleon (accessions: France, 27 Mar; Hanover, 7 Apr; Portugal, 8 Apr; Sardinia, 9 Apr; Bavaria, 15 Apr; Princes and Free Towns of Germany, 27 Apr; Netherlands, 28 Apr; Baden, 13 May; Switzerland, 20 May; Hesse-Darmstadt, 23 May; Saxony, 27 May; Württemberg, 30 May; Denmark, 1 Sep). Supplemented by convention of 30 Apr |
| 30 Apr | Additional convention of alliance and subsidy between Austria, Britain, Prussia and Russia |
| 2 May | Subsidy treaty between Britain and Sardinia |
| 13 May | Naval convention between Britain and Naples |
| 20 May | Territorial treaty between King of Sardinia and Austria, Britain, France, Prussia and Russia (accession: Switzerland, 20 May) |

| | |
|---|---|
| 31 May | Treaty between the Netherlands and Austria, Britain, Prussia and Russia concerning the Kingdom of the Netherlands |
| 9 Jun | Act of the Congress of Vienna signed by Austria, Britain, France, Portugal, Prussia, Russia and Sweden (accessions: Netherlands, 20 Oct; Naples, 1 Feb 16; Sardinia, 15 Oct 16; Spain, 7 Jun 17; Parma, 25 Jan 18; Hesse-Darmstadt, 1 Mar 18; Saxony, 10 Mar 18; Württemberg, 14 Apr 18; Denmark, 20 Apr 18; Tuscany, 22 Apr 18; Hesse-Cassel, 11 Jan 19; Bavaria, 7 May 20) |
| 3 Jul | Commercial convention between Britain and the United States |
| 26 Sep | Treaty between Austria, Prussia and Russia establishing the Holy Alliance (accessions: France, Spain, Naples and Sardinia) |
| 3 Nov | Protocol of conference between Austria, Britain, Prussia and Russia to regulate disposition of territories ceded by France |
| 5 Nov | Treaty between Austria, Britain, Prussia and Russia concerning Ionian Islands (accessions: France, 27 Sep 16; Turkey, 24 Apr 19) |
| 20 Nov | Treaty of alliance and friendship between Austria, Britain, Prussia and Russia |
| 20 Nov | Definitive treaty of Paris signed by Austria, Britain, France, Prussia and Russia (accessions: Hesse-Cassel, 15 Oct 16; Spain, 8 Jun 17; Bavaria, 20 Dec 17; Parma, 30 Jan 18; Hesse-Darmstadt, 1 Mar 18; Saxony, 21 Mar 18; Sardinia, 9 Apr 18; Denmark, 21 Apr 18; Tuscany, 24 Apr 18; Württemberg, 14 Aug 18; Netherlands, 8 Feb 22) |
| 20 Nov | Convention concerning French indemnity to the Allied Powers between Austria, Britain, Prussia, Russia and France |
| 20 Nov | Convention concerning Allied army of occupation in France between Austria, Britain, Prussia, Russia and France |
| 20 Nov | Act guaranteeing Swiss neutrality signed by Austria, Britain, France, Prussia and Russia |
| 20 Nov | Convention concerning claims of subjects of Allied Powers upon France between Austria, Britain, Prussia, Russia and France |
| 21 Nov | Treaty between Austria, Britain, Prussia and Russia regarding the fortification of the Netherlands, Germany and Savoy |

## 1816

| | |
|---|---|
| 26 Sep | Convention of commerce and navigation concluded in London by Britain and Naples |

16 Nov    Treaty concluded at Frankfurt by Britain and the Netherlands concerning Luxembourg

## 1817

28 Jul    Convention concluded in London by Britain and Portugal for the prevention of the slave trade

23 Sep    Treaty concluded in Madrid by Britain and Spain for the abolition of the slave trade

## 1818

25 Apr    Convention between Austria, Britain, Prussia, Russia and France for the final liquidation of private claims upon the French government (additional articles, 4 Jul)

4 May     Treaty concluded at The Hague by Britain and the Netherlands for preventing subjects engaging in the slave trade (additional articles, 31 Dec 22 and 25 Jan 23)

9 May     Convention concluded at Aix-la-Chapelle by Austria, Britain, Prussia, Russia and France regarding the evacuation of French territory by Allied troops

12 Nov    Agreement concluded at Aix-la-Chapelle by Austria, Britain, Prussia, Russia and France for the readmission of France to conferences of the Great Powers

15 Nov    Agreement concluded at Aix-la-Chapelle by Austria, Britain, France, Prussia and Russia for the preservation of the established order and peace

## 1819

2 Feb     Definitive arrangement with France relative to the liquidation of French indemnity, signed in Paris by Austria, Britain, France, Prussia and Russia

10 Jul    Treaty concluded at Frankfurt by Austria, Britain, Prussia, Russia and Baden

20 Jul    General treaty of territorial commission assembled at Frankfurt, signed by Austria, Britain, Prussia and Russia (accessions: Baden, 4 Aug 20; Parma, 15 Aug 20; Tuscany, 10 Nov 20; Saxony, 18 Dec 20; Sardinia, 30 Dec 20)

## 1820

15 May — Final act of ministerial conferences in Vienna on the organization of the Germanic Confederation

## 1822

12 Jul — Convention concluded at St Petersburg by Britain, Russia (as mediator) and the United States concerning the slave trade

22 Nov — Declaration of the Congress of Verona concerning the abolition of the slave trade, signed by Austria, Britain, France, Prussia and Russia

## 1823

12 Mar — Convention concluded in Madrid by Britain and Spain for settlement of British claims against Spain

17 Nov — Convention concluded at Vienna by Austria and Britain for definitive settlement of the Austrian loan

## 1824

17 Mar — Commercial treaty concluded in London by Britain and the Netherlands

2 Apr — Commercial treaty concluded in London by Britain and Prussia

16 Jun — Commercial treaty concluded in London by Britain and Denmark

16 Jul — Declaration by Britain and Sweden concerning navigation and trade

6 Nov — Treaty concluded at Stockholm by Britain and Sweden for preventing the slave trade

## 1825

9 Apr — Convention concluded at St Petersburg by Britain and Russia concerning the north-west coast of America and the Pacific Ocean

## 1826

| | |
|---|---|
| 26 Jan | Convention of commerce and navigation concluded in London by Britain and France |
| 18 Mar | Convention of commerce and navigation concluded in London by Britain and Sweden |
| 4 Apr | Protocol of conference at St Petersburg between Britain and Russia on mediation between the Greeks and Turks |
| 7 Oct | Treaty of Akkerman between Russia and Turkey |
| 13 Nov | Convention concluded in London between Britain and the United States |

## 1827

| | |
|---|---|
| 19 Jan | Convention concluded at Brighthelmstone by Britain and Portugal for maintaining corps of British troops sent to Portugal (additional article, 13 Mar) |
| 6 Jul | Treaty of London between Britain, France and Russia for pacification of Greece |
| 6 Aug | Conventions concluded in London by Britain and the United States concerning commerce and the north-west coast of America |
| 29 Sep | Convention concluded in London by Britain and the United States concerning boundaries |

## 1828

| | |
|---|---|
| 22 Feb | Treaty of Turkmanchai between Russia and Persia |
| 6 Aug | Convention concluded in Alexandria by Britain and the ruler of Egypt concerning the Morea |
| 28 Oct | Convention of claims between Britain and Spain |

## 1829

| | |
|---|---|
| 14 Sep | Treaty of Adrianople between Russia and Turkey |
| 21 Dec | Convention of commerce and navigation concluded in London by Austria and Britain |

## 1830

| | |
|---|---|
| 3 Feb | Protocol of conference in London between Britain, France and Russia concerning Greek independence |

## 1831

| | |
|---|---|
| 20 Jan | Protocol of conference between Austria, Britain, France, Prussia and Russia on the separation of Belgium and Holland |
| 15 Nov | Treaty of London between Austria, Britain, France, Prussia and Russia on the separation of Belgium and Holland |
| 14 Dec | Convention concluded in London by Austria, Britain, France, Prussia and Russia concerning the Belgian fortresses |

## 1832

| | |
|---|---|
| 7 May | Convention between Bavaria, Britain, France and Russia concerning the sovereignty of Greece |
| 21 Jul | Treaty concluded at Constantinople by Britain, France, Russia and Turkey concerning the continental limits of Greece |
| 22 Oct | Treaty concluded in London by Britain and France for the enforcement of the treaty of 15 Nov 31 |
| 10 Nov | Convention concluded in Brussels by Belgium and France for the entry of a French army into Belgium |

## 1833

| | |
|---|---|
| 22 Mar | Supplementary convention between Britain and France concerning the slave trade |
| 8 Jul | Defensive alliance concluded at Constantinople by Russia and Turkey |

## 1834

| | |
|---|---|
| 29 Jan | Agreement concluded at St Petersburg by Russia and Turkey concerning Moldavia and Wallachia |
| 22 Apr | Treaty of Quadruple Alliance concluded in London between Britain, France, Portugal and Spain for the pacification of the peninsula |
| 5 Sep | Agreement between Britain and Russia to respect the integrity and independence of Persia |

## 1839

19 Apr     Treaties concluded in London between Austria, Belgium, Britain, France, the Netherlands, Prussia and Russia concerning the separation of Belgium and the Netherlands

## 1840

15 Jul     Convention concluded in London by Austria, Britain, Prussia, Russia and Turkey for the pacification of the Levant

## 1841

13 Jul     Convention concluded in London by Austria, Britain, France, Prussia, Russia and Turkey concerning the straits of the Dardanelles and the Bosphorus

20 Dec     Treaty between Austria, Britain, France, Prussia and Russia concerning the suppression of the African slave trade

## 1842

9 Aug     Convention between Britain and the United States concerning boundaries, the slave trade and the giving-up of criminals

## 1846

15 Jun     Treaty between Britain and the United States concerning the settlement of the Oregon boundary

6 Nov     Treaty concluded at Cracow by Austria, Prussia and Russia uniting the Free City of Cracow to the Austrian monarchy

## 1847

21 May     Protocol of conference in London between Britain, France, Portugal and Spain for the pacification of Portugal

# 7 THE CHURCH

## AUSTRIA

The Napoleonic Wars had little influence on the position of the Roman
Catholic Church in Austria. The Jesuits, reconstituted as an order in 1814 by
Pope Pius VII, were not allowed to return.

| | |
|---|---|
| 1815 | 26 Sep Holy Alliance to establish mutual relations on the 'sublimest truths of the religion of God our Saviour'. To Metternich it was 'just verbiage'. |
| 1817 | Francis II visited Rome and promised to sign a concordat, but negotiations failed. |
| 1820 | Jesuits, exiled from Russia, allowed into Galicia and Hungary. |
| 1829 | Jesuits allowed into Styria. |
| 1836 | Jesuits formally admitted to Venice and (1838) the Tyrol. |
| 1848 | Redemptionists driven from Vienna, Jesuits from Graz. |

## BELGIUM

Belgium was more than 90 per cent Roman Catholic.

| | |
|---|---|
| 1813 | Belgian notables objected to the Fundamental Law because it proposed religious equality. The Roman Catholic hierarchy was strong and backed by the Pope.<br>King William I, determined to enlighten his Catholic provinces, sent Protestant inspectors to Catholic schools. Candidates for Catholic orders were forced to attend College of Philosophy at Louvain. Jesuits banished. The King supported the schismatic Jansenist Bishop of Deventer. But Leo XII counselled Catholics to 'maintain an attitude of passivity'. |
| 1829 | Hatred of the Dutch united the liberals and Catholics, normally enemies. |

1830    25 Aug   Belgian revolt.

1831    7 Feb   Belgian constitution proclaimed freedom of worship, recognition of religious orders, appointment of bishops by the Pope, and the rights of the Church. But the régime stood for the separation of State and Church, and civil marriage before religious. The State paid Roman Catholic, Protestant and Jewish ministers, as under the concordat of 1801. Clergy were exempt from military service and were to supervise religious teaching in schools.

Church founded primary schools, secondary colleges and the University of Malines (1834), which moved to Louvain in 1835.

1841    After ten years of negotiation Gregory XVI agreed to establish diplomatic relations. The first papal nuncio, Mgr Fornari, was so clumsy in attempts to control Belgian bishops and Catholics that he was recalled.

1842    Religious instruction obligatory in primary schools.

1843    New nuncio, Mgr Pecci (afterwards Leo XIII), conciliatory.

1845    Pecci was rebuked for lack of energy in defence of papal rights by Cardinal Antonelli, Papal Secretary of State, and recalled after dispute between the Society of Jesus and professors of Louvain.

1847    Catholic alliance with liberals ended; liberals now anti-clerical.


# BULGARIA

In 1393 the Turks overcame the Bulgars and exiled their Orthodox Patriarch to Macedonia. 1393–1767 the Greco-Bulgarian Patriarch of Okhrida controlled the Bulgarian Church. Greeks from the Phanar quarter of Constantinople bought all posts of importance in the patriarchal organization. They suppressed the last traces of Bulgarian nationality in the Church, abolishing independent patriarchates (1767). Bulgars who adopted the Moslem creed were called Pomaks.

In the early nineteenth century the revival of Bulgaria was fostered by 2 committees of rich Bulgarian merchants in Bucharest and Odessa. The Bucharest committee favoured violence, the Odessa committee change by reform in Church and education.

## DENMARK

1537  Lutheran Church Order. All old bishops deposed. Evangelical superintendents consecrated by Luther's collaborator, Johann Bugenhagen, an ordained priest.

1569  All foreigners who wished to remain in Denmark had to subscribe to 25 articles containing teachings of Lutheranism. For 250 years only Lutheran faith allowed.

## FRANCE

1789  At the French Revolution Catholicism was the official religion of France. Clergy numbered 130,000, of whom 70,000 were regulars, 60,000 seculars. The Church was the biggest landowner. It received tithes, paid no direct tax, but voted a fiscal contribution every 5 years. The Church supported nearly 2200 hospitals, 600 colleges and 25,000 primary schools. Bishops of the 135 dioceses were recruited from the older aristocracy. Parish priests in towns were reasonably well off but in the country had only a bare living.

The Assembly abolished annates and tithes, and authorized the transfer of all Church property to the State. The State became responsible for reasonable expenses of worship, sustenance of ministers, Catholic, Protestant or Jewish, and relief of poor. The taking of monastic vows was suspended.

The principle of freedom of religion was stated in the Declaration of the Rights of Man. Protestants could hold all public appointments from Sep 89, Jews from Sep 91.

1790  By the Civil Constitution of the Clergy dioceses were reduced to 83, coinciding with departments, and parishes redistributed. Bishops and parish priests were elected by the people. Bishops were to be invested by 10 metropolitans, not by the Pope.

1792  The clergy were ordered to swear loyalty to the constitution, which split the Church. Exile declared for non-juring priests. Many were massacred (e.g. 225 in Paris, 90 at Nantes, 130 at Lyons) and 30,000 fled abroad. In La Vendée non-juring priests and their supporters revolted in alliance with Royalists. Constitutional clergy suffered when anti-Christian movement grew. All churches were secularized, many destroyed in the cult of Reason.

1801  Napoleon, requiring the support of the Church, concluded a concordat with the Papacy. France acknowledged that the 'Catholic, Apostolic and Roman religion' was that of the 'majority of French citizens'. Public worship was guaranteed. New bishops were to be nominated by the First Consul, the Pope conferring spiritual powers. Bishops were to appoint parish priests from lists approved by the government. Before consecration they were to take an oath to obey 'the government established by the constitution'. The Pope was not to protest about loss of church property. All churches and chapels not alienated were to be at the disposal of the bishops. The government was to pay the clergy, Catholic, Protestant or Jewish, a 'reasonable salary', and foundations with land or money were allowed. But 77 Organic Articles severely restricted the rights of the Holy See in France. The concordat, with slight modifications, lasted for 100 years.

1815    At Marseilles, Toulouse, Nîmes and Uzes Catholic mobs massacred Protestants and supporters of Napoleon. Article VI of the Bourbon Charter declared Catholicism the state religion, not just that of the majority of Frenchmen. In a close alliance between Church and State the observance of Sunday was imposed, divorce suppressed, teaching passed to clerical control and the profanation of the Host or theft of sacred vessels made a capital crime (1825). But 2,741,000 copies of the *philosophes* were printed between 1817 and 1824, including 12 editions of Voltaire, 13 of Rousseau.

1828    Growing attack on the Church as the ally of reaction. Gallican Catholics saw the Jesuits as the spearhead of ultramontanism and with support of liberals obtained an ordinance banning scholastic establishments belonging to 'an unauthorized religious congregation', i.e. Society of Jesus. (The ban of 1761 had never been repealed.) The Jesuits then disguised themselves as secular priests. In 1829 they numbered 108 priests, 212 coadjutors. Another ordinance limited to 20,000 the number of pupils to be admitted to church schools and junior seminaries.

1830    Freemasons accused of collaborating in revolution which ejected Charles X. During anti-clerical outburst priests were attacked and churches sacked. Notre Dame narrowly escaped destruction.
Catholic liberal movement, led by Abbé Lamennais, a Dominican priest, Lacordaire, and the Count de Montalembert, with their journal *L'Avenir*, sought to separate altar and throne and abolish the concordat.

1845    The government, faced with demands to expel the Jesuits, persuaded Pope Gregory XVI to sacrifice them. In effect the Jesuits closed their houses but remained dispersed in small groups.

1848    New constitution, increasing electors from 240,000 to 9 million, gave great power to the peasants over whom the Church had preponderant influence. Workers' rising. The Archbishop of Paris, Mgr Affre, fatally wounded while seeking a truce on the Paris barricades. The Church joined forces with reaction. 'Democracy is the heresy of our time' – Mgr Gousset, Archbishop of Rheims.

# GERMANY

### BADEN

| | |
|---|---|
| 1810 | *Code Napoléon* adopted voluntarily. |
| 1818 | Concordat with Papacy. |
| 1821 | Lutherans merged with Reformed Church to become United Evangelical Church. The Roman Catholic Bishop of Freiburg, appointed by the Pope, and the Superintendent of the Protestant Church sat in the upper chamber. |

### BAVARIA

Bavaria was strongly Catholic but not ultramontane. Napoleon confiscated and secularized church lands. Monteglas, under the influence of Napoleon, introduced religious toleration, curbed ecclesiastical jurisdiction, dissolved monasteries and promoted churchmen by merit.

| | |
|---|---|
| 1803 | Bavaria gained episcopal territories of Freising, Augsburg (principal residence, Dillingen), Bamberg (approximately 2400 sq. miles), Würzburg (40 towns and villages), secularized by Talleyrand. |
| 1805 | Lost Würzburg, gained Trent. |
| 1810 | Gained territories of Archbishop of Salzburg; university abolished. |
| 1815 | Gained Würzburg and Mainz. Mainz, approximately 1000 sq. miles, had not been secularized in 1803. Its Archbishop, as an Elector of the Empire, was also Sovereign of Eichfeld, Eisfeld and the city and territory of Erfort. Secularized land not returned to the Church. |
| 1816 | Lost Salzburg territories to Austria (approximately 6000 sq. miles). |
| 1817 | Constitution guaranteed religious liberty. All eligible for civil offices and military appointments. Members of the upper house included the 2 archbishops (Munich and Bamberg), a Roman |

Catholic bishop and a Protestant clergyman nominated by the King.

Concordat with Papacy.

Lutheran opposition to an immediate merger with the numerically negligible Reformed Church was too strong to allow the formation of a United Evangelical Church.

| | |
|---|---|
| 1830 | Tercentenary of Augsburg Confession. |
| 1832 | Papal brief told bishops that mixed marriages would not be tolerated. |
| 1837 | Jesuits active to prevent fraternization between faiths. |
| | Ultramontane movement grew. |
| 1846–7 | Roman Catholic party sought to expel the dancer Lola Montez, mistress of King Ludwig I and patron of the liberals. |

## HANOVER

Most inhabitants Lutheran. *Code Napoléon* adopted voluntarily.

1817    Lutheran opposition to immediate merger with the numerically negligible Reformed Church was too strong to allow the formation of a United Evangelical Church.

Lutheran Church composed of 5 consistories: Hanover, Stade, Otterndorf, Osnabrück, Aurich. All members of Protestant consistories nominated by Crown. Pastors of towns paid from municipal funds; country pastors from land formerly ecclesiastical. Inhabitants of parish bound to cultivate glebe but glebe usually leased instead of being cultivated by forced labour. All tithes the property of Crown or large landowners. Calvinist church council of Aurich; sub-committee at Neustadt and Nordhorn. Roman Catholic Bishops of Hildesheim and Osnabrück.

## HESSE-CASSEL

Protestant majority. Reigning family Calvinist.

1813    Acquired territories of Bishopric of Fulda.

## HESSE-DARMSTADT

Lutheran majority.

1820    Chief Protestant superintendent and Roman Catholic bishop sat in upper chamber.

PRUSSIA

Under Napoleonic influence Prussia secularized Church property in Catholic Silesia.

1817    Prussia imposed a merger on the Lutheran and Reformed Churches, thus producing the United Evangelical Church of Prussia. Some smaller states followed this example. Lutherans in Silesia, objecting to being merged in the United Evangelical Church of Prussia, were crushed by police and troops.
        Prussian government exercised exclusive right of appointment, promotion and dismissal, but church congregations paid for more than 90 per cent of clergy. Separate ministry, the *Kultusministerium*, made responsible for ecclesiastical and educational affairs.
1819    Prussia rewarded clergy who helped to ensure political loyalty to established order. Bishop R. F. Eylert, court preacher, denounced all political opposition as blasphemy. His sermon was the signal for persecution. Friedrich Ernst Daniel Schleiermacher (1768–1834), theologian and patriotic preacher of national struggle against Napoleon, removed from chair at Berlin University. Protestant Neo-Pietists of the Awakening believed in a union of throne and altar against liberalism, and allied themselves with conservatives.
        Frederick William III imposed his new service book.
1827    *Evangelische Kirchen-Zeitung (EKZ)* founded, with Ernst Wilhelm Hengstenberg (1802–69) as editor, to support interests of aristocracy: 'Our politics consist of unconditional obedience to the God-given order.'
1830    *EKZ*'s attack on rationalists at Halle University, Saxony, led to major political battle between liberal and conservative clergy. Frederick William III supported Protestant Neo-Pietists and Hengstenberg opposed social reform and the ideas of the July 1830 revolution in France.
1832    Old Lutherans, who had been allowed to use pre-merger Lutheran liturgy in Silesia in attempt to win support for merger, sought leave to form separate church. They were now accused of inciting the population against the Prussian government; meetings were broken up by troops, and the property of congregations confiscated.
1834    International reaction at persecution of Old Lutherans resulted in 1000 being allowed to leave for United States (1839) to form

Buffalo Synod, (now 1.5 million strong). Further emigration from Saxony in 1845 developed into Missouri Synod (1.3 million strong).

1835    Professor of Theology at Tübingen, Ferdinand Christian Baur (1792–1860), a disciple of Hegel, founded the 'Tübingen School'. Its teaching was so unorthodox, especially regarding the New Testament, that great antagonism resulted. Lecturer in philosophy at Tübingen, David Friedrich Strauss (1808–74), published his *Life of Jesus*. Regarded Christianity as an ordinary pseudo-mythological religion and Christ as a Jewish Socrates. Bitter controversy followed. English translation by George Eliot, 1846.

1837    Growth of ultramontane movement among Catholics in Rhenish Prussia, now freed from dead hand of Prince-Bishops. Conflict over brief on mixed marriages, 25 Mar 30, resulted in Prussia imprisoning the Catholic Archbishop of Cologne, Mgr zu Droste-Vischering, 20 Nov 37 (the *Event of Cologne*), and the Archbishop of Gniesen-Posen (Polish Prussia), Mgr von Dunin.

1841    Frederick William IV released the archbishops. Special department in the *Kultusministerium* for Catholic affairs. Prussia allowed Catholics freedom of worship, autonomy in ecclesiastical appointments, freedom of communication with Rome, right to open schools and right of association.

Bishop Alexander, Prussian native, Jewish Christian, Anglican by confession, consecrated Anglo-Prussian Bishop of Jerusalem. But Frederick William IV's experiment came to nothing.

1845    Ban on Friends of Light movement which had used mass meetings to agitate for a Church based on a free constitution, with abolition of hereditary privilege.

1846    Activities of Hengstenberg's intolerant faction resulted in a drop in numbers of theological students at universities.

SAXE-WEIMAR

Large Protestant majority.

1817    Wortburg Festival. Students celebrating the tercentenary of Luther's Theses burnt emblems of reaction, to the great alarm of Metternich and other reactionaries.

1827    Lutherans merged with Reformed Church to become the United Evangelical Church.

SAXONY

Royal family Roman Catholic but most inhabitants Protestant.

1817    Lutheran opposition to immediate merger with numerically
        negligible Reformed Church was too strong to allow the for-
        mation of a United Evangelical Church.

1830    Attack by Hengstenberg's *Evangelische-Kirchen-Zeitung* on ra-
        tionalists at Halle University led to a major political battle
        between liberal and conservative clergy.
        Upper chamber included one deputy of the (Lutheran)
        Archbishop of Meissen, the Lutheran *Oberhofprediger* of
        Dresden, the Dean of the Roman Catholic chapter of St Peter at
        Bautzen as 'Apostolic Vicar at Dresden', and the Superintendent
        at Leipzig.

1832    Gustavus Adolphus Union for strengthening Protestant witness
        founded in Saxony. 2000 churches built by 1914, £2 million raised
        for struggling congregations.

1845    Emigration of Old Lutherans to Missouri, United States, after
        persecution; now 1.3 million strong.

WÜRTTEMBERG

Large Protestant majority.

1815    Secularized lands increased wealth of kingdom and were not
        returned to the Church.

1827    Lutherans merged with Reformed Church to form United
        Evangelical Church. Superintendents at Ulm, Ludwigsburg,
        Reutlingen, Hall, Heilbronn, Tübingen.
        Supreme direction vested in King.
        In the Chamber of Deputies 6 superintendents of Protestant
        Church, 1 Roman Catholic bishop and 2 other representatives of
        Roman Catholics. Roman Catholics under bishop at Rotenberg,
        with council appointed by government. Jews under board nomi-
        nated by Minister of Ecclesiastical Affairs.

# GREECE

Christian subjects of the Porte were free to exercise their religion and choose their education. Orthodox bishops, regarded as important functionaries, could settle civil cases among co-religionists. Orthodox priests kept the Greeks a distinct people while under Turkish rule.

1821 Beginning of Greek revolt. Orthodox clergy headed by Archbishop Germanos of Patras proclaimed war of extermination against infidel; 25,000 killed in 6 weeks. Orthodox Patriarch Gregory of Constantinople, held responsible for good behaviour of his flock, hanged by Sultan as reprisal and body flung into Bosphorus. Turks massacred 40,000 Greeks in Chios. Sultan proclaimed Holy War but the powers intervened and Greece became free.

1828 Greek government would not treat with Patriarch of Constantinople who had refused to sanction revolt. 300 smaller monasteries closed and revenues secularized.

1833 National synod decided that Orthodox Church of Greece, which recognized no spiritual head but Jesus Christ, was dependent on no external authority. In administration acknowledged King of Greece as supreme head. Permanent synod of bishops, who were selected by King, to be highest ecclesiastical authority.


# HUNGARY

Many leading Roman Catholics died in the Turkish victory of Mohacs, 1526, and Calvinism spread rapidly. In 1572 the Diet recognized the Roman Catholic, Lutheran, Calvinist and Unitarian creeds as established religious with freedom of worship and equal political rights. Orthodox had freedom of worship without political equality. In early seventeenth century many magnates were won back to Roman Catholicism, resulting in the persecution of Protestants. In 1731 Roman Catholicism became the state religion. Protestant services were allowed only in special places and conversion was forbidden. Protestants had to keep Roman Catholic festivals and were subject to visitation by Roman Catholic bishops.

1781 Patent of Toleration. Non-Catholic Christians were granted freedom of worship and equality. Jews, estimated at 1 per cent of population, were granted freedom of worship without full civic rights.

# ITALY

## LOMBARDY-VENETIA

1815    Austria did not restore to the Church its courts or ecclesiastical
        law, but the bishops were directly under the Pope.
        In Lombardy: Archbishop of Milan, Bishops of Bergamo, Brescia,
        Como, Cremona, Lodi, Mantua and Pavia.
        Higher clergy favoured Austrian rule.

1846    *Pensieri sull' Italia* by Un Anonimo Lombardo (Count Luigi
        Torelli) attacked papal government of Gregory XVI and urged
        that the papal territories should be reduced to Rome and Elba.
        Forbidden in Papal States.

## THE PAPACY

Events of the Revolutionary and Napoleonic periods had so much influence
on the later history of the Papacy that they have been included.

### Pius VI (249) 1775–99

1790    Pope Pius VI strongly opposed Gallicanism and condemned the
        French Assembly's Civil Constitution of the Clergy.

1796    Democratic revolution in Rome encouraged by the French who
        set up puppet republic.

1797    By Treaty of Tolentino the Pope gave up the legations of Ferrara,
        Bologna and Romagna to Cisalpine Republic, and Avignon to
        France.

1798    Pius VI deported by French to Siena and later to Valence, where he
        died.

### Pius VII (250) 1800–23

1800    Pope Pius VII elected by Sacred College, meeting at Venice.
        Napoleon, seeking support of Catholics, restored Papal States.

1801    Concordat, extracted by Napoleon, reconciled Papacy and
        France.

1804    Pius VII summoned to crown Napoleon in Notre Dame, Paris.

1806    Pius ignored Napoleon's orders to close Papal States to British
        trade.

1807    Napoleon occupied Papal States.

1809    Papal States annexed. Pius taken as prisoner to Savona, near

Genoa, and (1812) to Fontainebleau. This encouraged many Catholics to oppose Napoleon and later support the Bourbons.

1814 Napoleon freed Pius before his first abdication. Pius re-established the Jesuit order, suppressed in 1773 by Pope Clement XIV.

1815 Congress of Vienna confirmed the 1797 transfer of Avignon to France but, because of efforts by Cardinal Ercole Consalvi (1757–1824), Secretary of State until 1823, the Pope regained other territories – the legations of Bologna, Urbino, Ravenna and Ferrara; the 5 territories of Perugia, Orvieto, the Patrimony, the Roman Campagna and Sabinia; the Duchies of Spoleto, Castro, Benevento and the Marches of Ancona; Citta del Castello, Rome. Consalvi halted reaction by provisional government under Mgr (later Cardinal) Agostino Rivarola which had restored Inquisition, ordered Jews back to ghettos, and even abolished vaccination and street lighting as French innovations. Sanfedisti, claiming to defend Holy See, took terrible revenge on collaborators.

1816 Constitution, inspired by French principles, imposed unity and uniformity. Civil and penal code, a disguised *Code Napoléon*, introduced. But efforts to laicize administration failed and Italianization of Sacred College continued (e.g. at conclave of 1829 43 of 49 Cardinals present were Italians).

### Leo XII (251) 1823–9

1823 Consalvi dismissed.

Encyclicals denounced liberalism, condemned 'indifferentism' and de-Christianization of society, freemasonry, secret societies.

1825 To demonstrate Papacy's strength jubilee held, first since 1775, when Pius moved from Quirinal to Vatican.

### Pius VIII (252) 1829–30

1830 Pius without hesitation recognized regime of Louis-Philippe after revolution in France.

### Gregory XVI (253) 1831–46

In a world of turmoil Gregory XVI was hostile to change and chiefly concerned with clarifying doctrine.

1830 Insurrections became frequent, Austrian troops twice called in to restore order in papal territories.

French occupied Ancona.

1831      Pope declared that on changes of regime Roman pontiffs would recognize those who were *de facto* in power.

Papal brief *Superiori anno* condemned Polish rebellion and ordered obedience to Russian repression.

Although Gregory XVI was an austere monk, papal ceremonies became more magnificent, protocol stricter, and monumental building was encouraged in Rome.

*Pius IX (254) 1846–78*

PAPAL STATES

1814      The return of Pope Pius VII to Rome and the defeat of Napoleon were regarded as the finger of God, and were confidently quoted when Pius IX faced his enemies after 1848 and 1860.

1815      Papal territories, except Avignon, were returned to the Pope, thanks to the skill at Vienna of Cardinal Ercole Consalvi (1757–1824), Secretary of State. The Papal States were composed of 21 geographical territories, most of which were also governmental units. The number of governmental units, legations and delegations, was often changed 1815–60. Bologna, Ferrara, Ravenna and Forli, the legations, were each under a legate, always a cardinal. The rest of the units, called delegations, were administered by a delegate, usually a bishop. Legates and delegates were responsible to the Secretary of State.

Mgr (later Cardinal) Agostino Rivarola in the absence of Consalvi restored feudal justice and the Holy Roman Inquisition, which was advised not to use torture.

The Index forbade all political books; 724 charges of heresy were pending.

1816      Consalvi continued the principle of centralization adopted by Napoleon, who had abolished many important local rights.

8 July   Constitution reorganized administration, introduced a civil and penal code.. Capital punishment for heresy ended.

1823      Death of Pius VII. Election of Leo XII (1823–9) in the Quirinal, where the election of succeeding popes took place until King Victor Emanuel occupied the Quirinal, 1870.

Leo XIII and succeeding popes were elected in the Vatican. Consalvi retired but was recalled a short time before his death, 1824.

1824      5 May    Encyclical condemned liberty of faith and anathematized Bible societies.

1829      Election of Pope Pius VIII (1829–30). France encouraged rebellion by declaring she was ready to defend Italy from intervention by outside powers. In fact she did nothing but intercept volunteers.

1830      2 Feb    Election of Gregory XVI (1830–46) after conclave of 50 days. He immediately ordered an inquiry into the grievances of the Legations.

3 Feb    The Pope heard that rebellion had started. Bologna rose, followed by Forli, Ravenna, Imola, Ferrara and Ancona.

8 Feb    Bologna declared the temporal power of the Pope at an end.

13–23 Feb    Spoleto joined rebellion; 14 Feb, Perugia, Urbino, Pesaro; 15 Feb, Osimo, Foligno, Todi, Assisi; 17 Feb, Macerata; 18 Feb, Loreto, Recanati; 19 Feb, Tolentino; 21 Feb, Camerino, Fermo; 23 Feb, rebel leader Sercognani at Ascoli. At Rieti the Bishop, Mgr Gabriele Ferretti, repulsed the rebel army from his walls. Rebels also checked near Orvieto. Most people sought the reform of priestly government and a share in it, not a united Italy.

25 Feb    Bologna proclaimed United Provinces of Italy. Louis Napoleon, future Napoleon III, took part in skirmish against papal volunteers at San Lorenzo.

21 Mar    Austrians, answering papal appeal for help, occupied Bologna.

25 Mar    Battle of Rimini; surrender of rebels under General Zucchi.

Rebels under Sercognani surrendered near Spoleto to Archbishop Mastai Ferretti (afterwards Pope Pius IX). He made surrender easy and gave them money to get home. Among those refused amnesty was Count Pietro Ferretti, a cousin of the future Pope. Cardinal Tommaso Bernetti, Secretary of State, told the powers that preserving and handing on the papal dominions was a sacred duty for the Pope, and he could only do so with Austrian help.

1831      21 May    The Memorandum – reforms suggested by the great powers. They were rejected by the Papacy.

5 July    Bernetti's Edict, alternative to Memorandum.

15 July    Austrians evacuated Bologna. Legations at once rose in rebellion.

1832      19 Jan    Papal troops advanced, with Cardinal Albani in command as Commissary Extraordinary.

20 Jan    Rebels from Cesena, Forli, Faenza, Imola and Bologna, probably 1800 strong, concentrated on Madonna del Monte, hill

near Cesena. Rebels defeated, towns recaptured and Austrians returned to Bologna.

28 Feb   French occupied Ancona. Cardinal Bernetti started enlisting force of 13,500 regulars, best of whom were the Swiss Brigade and Roman Dragoons. For economy he added volunteers, the Centurioni, accused by liberals of being assassins.

1836   12 Jan   Cardinal Bernetti, said to be pro-French, resigned; succeeded by Cardinal Lambruschini, Genoese, very conservative, reported to be pro-Austrian.

1837   French and Austrian troops withdrew from Papal States.

1843   Abbé Gioberti's *Del Primato morale e civile degli Italiani*, suggesting a federation of Italian states with the Pope as President and King Charles Albert as defender. This was banned. Church for English had to be outside Rome, opposite Porta del Popolo. Inquisition edict against Jews included 'no Israelite shall entertain amiable relations with Christians'. Moto di Savigno rising. Felice Orsini among those arrested. In 1858 he flung bomb at Napoleon III and Empress Eugénie.

1844   Count Cesare Balbo (1789–1853) published *Delle speranze d'Italia*. He emphasized that no pope could lead a military campaign against his Austrian spiritual subjects.

1845   Cardinal Gizzi (1787–1849) refused to allow military commission seeking out liberals to enter his legation, Forli. At Ravenna Cardinal Amat, the legate, gave passports to 5 leading liberals before the commission arrived. Manifesto of Rimini, programme of reform presented by moderates. Secularization of administration among objects sought.

## SARDINIA (PIEDMONT, SAVOY, SARDINIA)

1814   The clergy recovered their lands, courts and privileges. Ten bishoprics restored. The Jesuits (reconstituted by Pope Pius VII, Sep 14) returned.
Victor Emanuel I cancelled every act of government since 1787. Even the Botanical Gardens in Turin were grubbed up as being a reminder of Napoleonic days.

1817, 1828 Concordats made by Count Barbaroux, Minister of Clerical Affairs (d. 1843).

1831   Giuseppe Mazzini (1805–72) exiled for fomenting insurrection. He made national unification a religious duty.

1833   Abbé Vicenzo Gioberti (1801–52), Doctor of Theology 1823, priest 1825, resigned court chaplaincy 1833, imprisoned and included among those exiled after a plot fomented by Mazzini's Giovina Italia.

1839 Gregory XVI re-established papal nunciatura at Turin, 'the city of the Blessed Sacrament'. First nuncio Mgr Gibbi (d. 1841); then Mgr Guzzi, cardinal 1844, Secretary of State to Pius IX 1846. Mazzini made secret pact with the Protestant 'Christian Alliance' of the United States to end Papacy.

1841 Mar Concordat on clergy convicted of crimes. Basis of clerical immunity abandoned but penalties for clergy limited. Charitable institutions of the Church in the kingdom, as listed by the government: 1727 charitable institutions, including 187 hospitals, 10 hospitals for incurables, 42 orphanages, 46 institutions for needy, 1277 institutions for distributing alms, 75 for providing dowries for poor girls, 26 for teaching children a trade.

1843 Abbé Gioberti's *Del Primato morale e civile degli Italiani*, suggesting a federation of Italian states with the Pope as President, King Charles Albert as defender. The King read it and offered Gioberti a pension, which he refused. The book was banned in other Italian states; in Piedmont purchasers had to give their name and address to the police.

1844 Count Cesare Balbo (1789–1853) published *Delle speranze d'Italia*. He emphasized that no pope could lead a military campaign against his Austrian spiritual subjects.


THE TWO SICILIES (NAPLES, SICILY)

1814 Jesuits, reconstituted by Pope Pius VII Sep 1814, back in Naples.

1818 16 Feb Concordat signed at Terracina. The dioceses were to be restored to the Church; 109 of them. Church to regain property not already sold. Many monasteries and religious orders restored. Church regained right to acquire property. The King promised that he and his successors would not acquire Church property and that it would be inviolable. Every year 12,000 ducats to be sent to Rome from the bishops' incomes. The Church regained jurisdiction over clerical discipline and the bishops the right to censure anyone on matters involving theology or canon law. The bishops were to have free correspondence with Rome and anyone could appeal to Rome. The bishops could prevent the printing and publication of books. The King was to choose bishops, the Pope to approve and instal them. Bishops were to promise obedience to the King and report to him any movement likely to disturb the peace.

1834    14 archbishops, 66 bishops, 26,800 priests, 11,730 monks, 9520 nuns.

## TUSCANY

Tuscany was more tolerant to Protestants and Jews than the rest of Italy because so many foreigners wintered at Florence and traded at Livorno (Leghorn), e.g. Byron, Shelley, the Brownings. Similarly its Roman Catholic leaders tended to be unorthodox.

1846    Leopold II established a Tuscan embassy in Rome; Tuscany previously represented by Austria.


# THE NETHERLANDS

1814    Belgium (million, mostly Catholics), Luxembourg and the Bishopric of Liège were given to Holland (2 million, mostly Protestant) by the Congress of Vienna. Belgian Catholics objected to the Fundamental Law of the United Kingdom because it proposed religious equality. The Catholic hierarchy was powerful in the south and supported by the Pope. Some Protestants resented the liberal outlook of William I.

1825    Education under state control. William I, determined to enlighten his Catholic provinces, sent Protestant inspectors to Catholic schools. Candidates for Catholic orders were forced to attend a college of philosophy at Louvain. Jesuits were banished. The King supported the schismatic Jansenist Bishop of Deventer. Pope Leo XII counselled Catholics 'to maintain an attitude of passivity'.

1829    Hatred of the Dutch united the liberals and Catholics in the south.

1830    Belgian revolt and secession.
        Catholics predominated in 2 of the provinces remaining in the Netherlands – Limburg and North Brabant.


# NORWAY

1537    Lutheran Church Order. All old bishops deposed. Evangelical superintendents consecrated by Luther's collaborator, Johann Bugenhagen, an ordained priest.
        Flight of the Roman Catholic Archbishop Olav ended Church independence.

1569      All foreigners had to subscribe to 25 articles containing the teachings of Lutheranism. For 250 years only Lutheranism allowed.

1814      First chapter of Norwegian constitution stated: 'The Evangelical Lutheran religion remains the official religion of the State. Inhabitants who profess this are obliged to bring up their children in the same . . . The King shall always profess the Evangelical Lutheran religion, vindicate and protect it.'


# PORTUGAL

Portuguese liberalism was strongly anti-clerical. The liberals believed that the country's decadence was due to the absolutist system and to the Church which supported it. They believed in regeneration rather than revolution, a recapturing of former glories. In the early years following the Napoleonic Wars the freemasons were most open to new political ideas.

1816      John VI (1816–26) resisted all pressure to allow Jesuits into Portugal.

1821      Liberal government abolished inquisition and took away Church privileges. The Patriarch refused to take the oath of allegiance and retired to the monastery of Bucaco. Those who refused to take the oath were deprived of citizenship.

1828      Reactionary coup, with the persecution of liberals and constitutionalists. The absolutist Dom Miguel was supported by the clergy, peasants and old nobility.

1829      Dom Miguel, Jesuit trained, allowed the Jesuits to return. Eight arrived from France. Their college at Coimbra was restored to them and they were established at Pombal, home of the Marquis of Pombal (1699–1780) who had banished them from Portuguese territories. Inquisition restored.

1832      War of the Two Brothers in which the Patriarch of Lisbon and some bishops supported Dom Pedro but most of the clergy supported Dom Miguel. Pope Gregory XVI supported Dom Miguel.

1834      Victory of Dom Pedro. Dom Miguel fled to Rome. Triumph of liberals and middle class. Priests stoned in the villages; convents, schools and some hospices closed, episcopal appointments of Dom Miguel annulled. Papal nuncio escorted to the frontier. Radical legislation of Mouzhinho da Silveria. Jesuits expelled again, religious orders suppressed, their property confiscated and donations of Crown lands revoked. Property transferred to the supporters of the new regime.

1840    Queen Maria da Gloria sent a representative to Rome to negotiate a concordat. The Pope presented her with the Golden Rose.

# RUSSIA

In 1700 Peter the Great abolished the patriarchate (primate) of the Russian Orthodox Church, substituting the Holy Synod. The Synod was under a government minister, the Procurator, responsible only to the Tsar. The Church was thus completely subservient to the Tsar and run as a state department. In 1764 Catherine II confiscated some church estates, curtailing the financial freedom and support that the Church had hitherto enjoyed from being an extremely wealthy landowner.

The Tsars, their wives and heirs, were required by law to be Orthodox. As the Tsar's power over the Church increased, the Church correspondingly lost political and social influence in the social and political field.

### ALEXANDER I (1801–25)

1811–12    Alexander I, under the influence of Prince Alexander Golitsyn, the Procurator, underwent a religious conversion. He now believed that he had a vocation to bring peace to Europe and to establish a pattern of life 'according to the precepts of the Holy Religion'. Friendly with Quakers, tolerant towards other denominations and towards his Moslem subjects, he stopped the Holy Synod persecuting those who did not profess the Orthodox faith. Alexander was at first friendly towards the Jesuits, who had been welcomed in Russia by Catherine II when their society was abolished in 1773 and they were expelled from Catholic countries. They were allowed to work in Russia, chiefly as teachers. This was an embarrassment to the Pope, as canonically the Jesuits were rebels.

1814    Golitsyn became alarmed at the number of Catholic converts and the Jesuits were accused of proselytizing. In Dec the Jesuits were ordered to close their schools in Moscow and St Petersburg and were exiled to the provinces, being allowed to stay there if proselytizing stopped.

141

| | |
|---|---|
| 1815 | Pact of the Holy Alliance signed between the Emperor Francis I of Austria, King William I of Prussia and Tsar Alexander I. According to the pact they were henceforth brothers of one faith which, according to Holy Scripture, looked to Jesus Christ as the only true sovereign. |
| | Castlereagh described it as 'a sublime mysticism and absurdity'. To the Holy See this fraternal agreement between rulers one of whom was Orthodox, one Protestant and one Catholic was near-syncretism. |
| 1817 | Alexander's religious enlightenment policy. The Ministry of Education united with the Ministry of Spiritual Affairs under Prince Alexander Golitsyn, Procurator and President of the newly formed Russian Bible Society. All religions, including the Russian Orthodox faith, to be treated equally. |
| 1818 | Concordat between Russia and the Holy See establishing the canonical position of Catholics in Poland. |
| 1819–21 | Alexander's policy of religious toleration was denounced by the monk, Photius, as an insult to pure Orthodoxy and as a sin against the Holy Ghost. The campaign of Photius was successful and repressive measures were introduced. Professors at the new universities were removed, textbooks on natural law, morals and logic were banned as not being based on Holy Scripture. Golitsyn was dismissed. |
| 1820 | Jesuits expelled from the Russian Empire for continuing to proselytize. |
| 1822 | Imperial decree, banning secret societies. Until this time free-masonry was flourishing in Russia. The 'Decembrists', originally freemasons, had already broken away to form their own secret society called 'the Union of Salvation' until 1818, then 'the Union of Public Welfare'. Among its discussed reforms was the improvement of clerical morals. The 'Decembrists' remained undetected until the uprising of 1825. |

NICHOLAS I (1825–55)

The reign of Nicholas saw the rise of the Slavophils, intellectuals who were strongly religious and believed in a utopian, Christian peasant kingdom. Russian Orthodoxy to them represented Christianity uncorrupted by Western influence, as against the Westerners who believed in the superiority of Western civilization and that Russia should westernize as quickly as possible.

Nicholas saw the Church as another kind of army, with himself as commander-in-chief, and expected a military discipline from it. He was as severe to those who did not kneel at the right times in the services as he was to those whose beliefs were considered to be in error. His persecution of the Catholics after the Polish rising of 1830–1 stemmed from this attitude, which was aggravated by the Holy See's refusal to allow Nicholas sovereignty in the choice of Catholic bishops.

The Tsar, who in his twofold capacity as Imperator Pontifex Maximus was accustomed to the complete submission of the Orthodox clergy, did not understand the independence of the Catholic Church; he regarded it as a slur on the principle of sovereignty; in his eyes it was a usurpation which, for his part, he wished to avoid as well as he could.                    *Ficquelmont to Metternich*, 5 Apr 41.

1830    Polish rising, powerfully supported by the Catholic clergy. Nicholas I demanded that Pope Gregory XVI should condemn all the clergy who had taken part, and the Pope did so, reminding them that they should respect 'the legitimate authority of princes'. But the conversion of Orthodox believers in Poland was forbidden, mixed marriages were declared null and void, and 200 monasteries closed.

1822    9 June  Encyclical *Superiori Anno* in which Pope Gregory directed Polish Catholics to 'obey their mighty Emperor who would show them every kindness'. This was published in Poland just as the Russian occupying forces were persecuting the Catholic Church. At the same time the Pope wrote to the Tsar denouncing the 'wicked chicanery' of the government in Poland and asking that a papal *chargé d'affaires* be sent to Poland. This letter was not published and there was no reply.

1835    Cardinal Bernetti pressed the Tsar for a reply to the Pope's protest and request. The reply was that the deplorable events in Poland were the fault of the Catholics and particularly of the clergy.

1839    Greek Uniat Church, which had been linked to the Catholic Church, united with the Russian Orthodox. Nicholas I proposed uniting the Polish Catholic Church with the Catholic Church of Russia, under one archbishop and a college of bishops. Persecution of Catholic clergy and laymen who were suspected of proselytizing.

1840    Dispute over Holy Places. Greek lamps in chapel of the Holy Sepulchre broken by Latin monks. Proposed marriage between the Grand Duchess Olga, third child of Nicholas I (Orthodox), and Archduke Stephen of Austria (Catholic) failed because of the opposition of the Catholic Church. State grants to augment clerical salaries.

1841    Dispute over Holy Places. France suggested making Jerusalem a free city.

1842    July  Gregory XVI published a denunciation of Russian persecution of Catholics in Poland and particularly of the 'fraudulency responsible for a rumour that the Holy See had betrayed the Catholic cause'.

1843    Nicholas tried again to arrange the marriage of the Grand Duchess Olga and Archduke Stephen, and sought the consent of the Pope. The Pope agreed on condition that Nicholas ceased the persecution of the Catholic Church. Nicholas denied that he was persecuting the Church, claiming he was only dealing with rebels.

1845    Visit of Nicholas to Rome. The Pope reminded Nicholas that he had taught people to render unto Caesar that which is Caesar's. 'I remind Caesar of what belongs to God.' The Pope protested against laws which prevented Catholics from practising their religion. Nicholas asserted that the Catholic clergy in Russia were undisciplined and wore religion as a mask to hide rebellion. No progress was made at the meeting. The marriage of Grand Duchess Olga was not mentioned. Austro-Russian relations were strained, as the Austrian royal family remained adamant on the religious question and refused to contemplate the marriage.

1846    Dispute over the Holy Places. Bishop of Bethlehem assaulted.
Concordat between Russia and the Holy See arranging a method of appointing Roman Catholic bishops in Russia. Nicholas I demanded that the Austrians refuse to allow a schismatic group of Russians to establish a convent in Bukovina.
First Russian Ecclesiastical Mission established in Palestine. Started as a scholarly body that assisted pilgrims.

## SPAIN

1809    Spanish clergy encouraged resistance to the French invasion and to Napoleon's brother Joseph as King. Napoleon deported suspected priests, suppressed the Inquisition, abolished monastic and mendicant orders, annulled right of asylum in churches and ended privileges of the Church. Masonic lodges were opened.

1814    Return of Ferdinand VII. All Church privileges restored, including return of religious communities and of the Inquisition (apart from liberal interlude, 1820–3).

Jesuits returned and freemasonry made a capital offence (1824). But Spanish Church was anti-Roman.

1833    The dynastic Carlist wars and chaos that followed Ferdinand's death encouraged anti-religious outbursts. Monasteries and churches were sacked. The government closed 800 monasteries and expelled the Jesuits.

# SWEDEN

The untaxed Swedish church was extremely rich before the Reformation, bishops and consistories having an income estimated at 12 times the revenue of the State. Sweden broke with Rome in 1527. The Church remained episcopal and was not officially Lutheran. Many Church estates were confiscated by the Vasteras Recess. In 1593 300 leading clergy met at Uppsala to accept the Augsburg Confession (1530). The Church became an Evangelical Lutheran national Church. The diaconate was dropped in the seventeenth century.

The eighteenth and nineteenth centuries saw a retreat from the narrow orthodox discipline imposed by the clergy. By a law of 1719 all faiths were tolerated except the Jewish, Mohammedan or pagan, but dissenters could not meet publicly. Apostasy of Lutherans was punished by exile. A Conventicle Act of 1726, which remained on the statute book until 1859, was aimed against the Pietist movement. Attendance at proscribed religious meetings was punished at the third offence by exile. In 1781 foreigners were allowed to worship according to their faith, and Jews allowed to live in Stockholm, Gothenburg and Norrköping and enjoy religious freedom.

1823    King Oscar I married a Roman Catholic, Josephine Beauharnais. Her spiritual director was Mgr Studach.

1833    Peter Wieselgren (1800–97), pastor of Vasterstad in Skoane (and later Provost of Gothenburg Cathedral), campaigned for total abstinence.

1838    Measure for relieving disabilities of Jews withdrawn after riots.

1846    Erik Jansson (1808–50) from Biskopskulla, north Sweden, who claimed to be a prophet, won many followers. He was jailed, escaped to America and founded the Bishop's Hill colony of 1200 religious emigrants near Galesburg, Illinois. He was shot dead in a dispute over the wife of a follower.

Lars Levi Laestadius (1800–61), a pastor, leader of the New Readers, with emphasis on public confession, absolution and excommunication. His followers came to indugle in wolf-like cries, convulsive movements, ecstatic embracings and faintings. Not officially registered as a sect.

C. O. Rosénius (1816–68), native of Nörrland, strongly influenced by pietist devotion. Borrowed methods of G. Scott, English Methodist minister who worked in Stockholm until forced to leave after a church riot (1842). Rosénius edited the *Pietist* and the *Mission* newspaper and gained many followers as a lay preacher in his 'Bethlehem Church', Stockholm. He remained a member of the state church.

Peter Fjellstedt (1802–81), peasant's son from Vermland, became missionary for the English CMS in South India and Turkey (1829). He returned home and became head of the Mission Institute, training school for pastors in Uppsala. Spoke 12 languages, wrote 16 and understood 30. His Bible commentaries said to have had more influence on religious thought in Sweden than any book save the Bible, Luther's Catechism and the Swedish Hymn Book.

## SWITZERLAND

| | |
|---|---|
| 1815 | Confederation divided by religious differences, 12 cantons having a Protestant (Calvinist) majority, 7 having a Roman Catholic. |
| 1841 | Existing monasteries were protected by constitution, so Catholics of Aargau rioted when 8 monasteries were threatened by liberal canton government. |
| | Two demonstrations took place in Lucerne against Jesuits, who had gained control of education there and opposed freedom of press and political equality. |
| 1845 | Ultramontane leader, Siegwart-Muller, having vainly appealed to Metternich and Roman Catholic states, formed (1845) secret armed separatist union of Roman Catholic cantons, the Sonderbund. The confederation Diet voted (1847) for dissolution of the Sonderbund, expulsion of Jesuits and revision of constitution. Sonderbund's 79,000 men defeated in brief war by Diet's 100,000 |

# TURKEY

One quarter of population of European Turkey estimated (1848) to be Moslem. Rich Christians pressured by taxes to become Moslem, poor Christians tempted by better prospects. Christian subjects of the Porte were free to exercise their religion and choose their education. Orthodox bishops, regarded as important functionaries, could settle causes among co-religionists. But there was the constant risk of massacre for political ends (see individual states).

Approximate dividing line between jurisdiction of Roman Church and Eastern Church ran north-south through Bosnia. Croats were Roman Catholic (hence loyalty to Austria-Hungary), Serbs Orthodox. Herzegovina and east Bosnia mostly Orthodox, Dalmatia and west Bosnia mostly Roman Catholic.

Armenians, Christians of the Eutyches heresy condemned by Council of Chalcedon 451, admit only one nature in Christ. Seat of their Catholicus at Etchmiadzin, near Erivan, a monastery founded 302 and claiming to be the oldest in the world. Other patriarchs at Sis in Cilicia and at Ahthamar on island of Van. The Catholicus was superior to Armenian patriarchs of Jerusalem and Constantinople, created by Sultan and consequently mis-trusted. Cypress allowed only on Turkish graves, so Armenian graves adorned with terebinth or turpentine.

Some 15,000 Armenians acknowledged the Pope (1854).

By Treaty of Kutchuk Kainarji (1774) Russia had been allowed to build and protect a Christian church in Galata (Constantinople) and Turkey promised to protect Christian religion in her territories. Catherine the Great and her successors encouraged the 10 million Christian subjects of the Porte to regard Russia as their champion.

| | |
|---|---|
| 1821 | Orthodox Patriarch Gregory of Constantinople hanged by Sultan in Greek War of Independence. Massacre of Greeks on Chios ordered. |
| 1829 | 69,000 Armenians moved to Russian territory. |

# UNITED KINGDOM

## CHURCH OF ENGLAND

### Churches, clergy, and Easter Day communicants, 1801–31

|       | Churches and chapels | Clergy | Easter Day communicants ('000) | Easter Day Communicant Density |
|-------|----------------------|--------|--------------------------------|-------------------------------|
| 1801  | 11,379               |        | 535                            | 9.9                           |
| 1811  | 11,444               | 14,531 | 550                            | 8.9                           |
| 1821  | 11,558               |        | 570                            | 7.9                           |
| 1831  | 11,883               | 14,933 | 605                            | 7.2                           |

Source: Gilbert, p. 28

### Regional variation in the average size of an Anglican parish in 1811

| Region         | Total number of parishes | Area in acres | Average size of parish in acres |
|----------------|--------------------------|---------------|---------------------------------|
| East           | 1634                     | 3,240,000     | 1980                            |
| South-east     | 1048                     | 2,594,000     | 2475                            |
| South Midlands | 1379                     | 3,558,000     | 2580                            |
| North Midlands | 1236                     | 3,517,000     | 2840                            |
| South-west     | 940                      | 2,703,000     | 2880                            |
| South          | 873                      | 2,541,000     | 2910                            |
| West Midlands  | 1253                     | 4,021,000     | 3200                            |
| Cornwall       | 205                      | 868,000       | 4230                            |
| Yorkshire      | 630                      | 3,898,000     | 6190                            |
| North          | 290                      | 3,419,000     | 11,790                          |
| North-west     | 156                      | 1,852,000     | 11,860                          |

Source: Gilbert, p. 100

## ROMAN CATHOLIC CHURCH

|      | Estimated Catholic population | Churches and chapels | Actual Mass attendants |
|------|-------------------------------|----------------------|------------------------|
| 1720 | 115,000                       |                      | 61,600                 |
| 1780 | 69,376                        |                      | 37,200                 |
| 1800 |                               |                      |                        |
| 1840 | 700,000                       | 469                  | 371,500                |

(Figures are for England and Wales only)

Source: Gilbert, op. cit.

148

Congregational, Particular Baptist, and New Connexion General Baptist Membership 1750–1838

| | Congregational | | Particular Baptist | | General Baptist New Connexion | |
|---|---|---|---|---|---|---|
| | Members | Density | Members | Density | Members | Density |
| 1750 | 15,000 | | 10,000 | | | |
| 1772 | | | | | 1221 | |
| 1780 | | | | | 1800 | |
| 1790 | 26,000 | | 17,000 | | 2843 | |
| 1800 | 35,000 | 0.65 | 24,000 | 0.45 | 3403 | |
| 1810 | | | | | 5322 | |
| 1820 | | | | | 7673 | 0.11 |
| 1830 | | | | | 10,869 | 0.13 |
| 1838 | 127,000 | 1.38 | 86,000 | 0.94 | 13,947 | 0.15 |

Total Methodist membership as a percentage of the adult English population 1801–36

| | |
|---|---|
| 1801 | 1.6 |
| 1806 | 1.9 |
| 1811 | 2.3 |
| 1816 | 2.8 |
| 1821 | 2.9 |
| 1826 | 3.3 |
| 1831 | 3.4 |
| 1836 | 4.0 |

Wesleyan and New Connexion Membership, 1767–1819

| | Wesleyan Membership | New Connexion | Combined Total |
|---|---|---|---|
| 1767 | 22,410 | | |
| 1771 | 26,119 | | |
| 1776 | 30,875 | | |
| 1781 | 37,131 | | |
| 1786 | 46,559 | | |
| 1791 | 56,605 | | |
| 1796 | 77,402 | | |
| 1801 | 87,010 | 4815 | 91,825 |

|  | *Wesleyan Membership* | *New Connexion* | *Combined Total* |
|---|---|---|---|
| 1806 | 103,549 | 5586 | 109,135 |
| 1811 | 135,863 | 7448 | 143,311 |
| 1816 | 181,631 | 8146 | 189,777 |
| 1819 | 184,998 | 9672 | 194,670 |

REVENUES FROM BISHOPRICS, 1760

| *See* | *Revenue p.a.* |
|---|---|
| Canterbury | £7000 |
| Durham | £6000 |
| Winchester | £5000 |
| York | £4500 |
| London | £4000 |
| Ely | £3400 |
| Worcester | £3000 |
| Salisbury | £3000 |
| Oxford | £500 ( +£1800) |
| Norwich | £2000 |
| Bath and Wells | £2000 |
| Bristol | £450 ( +£1150) |
| Exeter | £1500 |
| Chester | £900 ( +£600) |
| Rochester | £600 ( +£900) |
| Lincoln | £1500 |
| Lichfield and Coventry | £1400 |
| St Asaph | £1400 |
| Bangor | £1400 |
| Chichester | £1400 |
| Carlisle | £1300 |
| Hereford | £1200 |
| Peterborough | £1000 |
| Llandaff | £500 ( +£450) |
| Gloucester | £900 ( + rich Durham prebend) |
| St Davids | £900 ( + two livings) |

*Source: A List of the Archbishops, Bishops, Deans and Prebendaries in England and Wales, in His Majesty's Gift, with the Reputed Yearly Value, of Their Respective Dignities (1762).*

# 8 POPULATION

## AUSTRIA[1,2]

| | |
|---|---|
| 1786 | 11,875,000 |
| 1800 | 12,600,000 |
| 1818 | 13,381,000 |
| 1821 | 13,964,000 |
| 1824 | 14,519,000 |
| 1827 | 15,131,000 |
| 1830 | 15,588,000 |
| 1834 | 15,714,000 |
| 1837 | 16,083,000 |
| 1840 | 16,575,000 |
| 1843 | 17,073,000 |
| 1846 | 17,613,000 |

*Vienna*

| | |
|---|---|
| 1800 | 232,000 |
| 1821 | 260,224 |
| 1830 | 317,768 |
| 1834 | 326,353 |
| 1846 | 407,980 |

[1] Cisleithania, the Italian provinces, are not included.
[2] All figures are exclusive of Bosnia and Herzegovina.

## BELGIUM

| | |
|---|---|
| 1816 | 4,166,000 |
| 1831 | 4,090,000 |
| 1846 | 4,337,000[1] |

[1] In 1839 certain areas, with a population of 326,000, were ceded to the Netherlands.

*Brussels*

| | |
|---|---|
| c.1810 | 66,000[1] |
| 1846 | 124,000[1] |

[1] Exclusive of suburbs.

## DENMARK[1]

| | |
|---|---|
| 1787 | 842,000 |
| 1801 | 929,000 |
| 1834 | 1,231,000 |
| 1840 | 1,289,000 |
| 1845 | 1,357,000 |
| 1850 | 1,415,000 |

[1] The Duchies of Schleswig, Holstein and Lauenburg are not included.

## FINLAND

| | |
|---|---|
| 1780 | 664,000 |
| 1785 | 679,000 |
| 1790 | 706,000 |
| 1795 | 771,000 |
| 1800 | 833,000 |
| 1805 | 896,000 |
| 1810 | 863,000[1] |
| 1815 | 1,096,000[2] |
| 1820 | 1,178,000 |
| 1825 | 1,259,000 |
| 1830 | 1,372,000[3] |
| 1835 | 1,394,000 |
| 1840 | 1,446,000 |
| 1845 | 1,548,000 |
| 1850 | 1,637,000 |

[1] In 1809 certain parishes in the Tornie River basin, with a population of 12,000, were added.
[2] In 1811 Viipuri province, with a population of 185,000, was added.
[3] The Greek Orthodox population was included for the first time, in 1830, when it numbered 25,000.

# FRANCE

| | |
|---|---|
| 1801 | 27,349,000 |
| 1806 | 29,053,000 |
| 1821 | 30,462,000 |
| 1831 | 32,569,000 |
| 1836 | 33,541,000 |
| 1841 | 34,230,000 |
| 1846 | 35,402,000 |

*Paris*

| | |
|---|---|
| 1801 | 547,756 |
| 1811 | 622,636 |
| 1821 | 713,966 |
| 1831 | 774,338 |
| 1836 | 909,126 |
| 1841 | 935,261 |
| 1846 | 1,053,897 |

# GERMANY

| | |
|---|---|
| 1816 | 22,377,000 |
| 1828 | 26,646,000 |
| 1834 | 28,237,000 |
| 1840 | 30,382,000 |

*Berlin*

| | |
|---|---|
| 1819 | 201,138 |
| 1837 | 283,722 |
| 1840 | 328,692 |

# PRUSSIA

| | | |
|---|---|---|
| 1816 | 10,349,031 | 25.5 |
| 1834 | 13,507,999 | 25.6 |
| 1837 | 14,098,125 | 25.8 |

(*continued*

## PRUSSIA (*continued*)

| 1840 | 14,928,503 | 25.9 |
|------|------------|------|
| 1843 | 15,471,084 | 26.2 |
| 1846 | 16,112,938 | 26.7 |

## GREECE

| 1821 | 939,000 |
|------|-----------|
| 1828 | 753,000 |
| 1838 | 752,000 |
| 1843 | 915,000 |
| 1848 | 987,000 |
| 1852 | 1,002,112 |

## HUNGARY[1]

| 1787 | 7,117,000 |
|------|------------|
| 1793 | 7,141,000 |
| 1804 | 7,961,000 |
| 1817 | 8,314,000 |
| 1850 | 13,192,000[2] |

*Budapest*

| 1800 | 61,000 |
|------|----------|
| 1820 | 85,000 |
| 1831 | 104,600 |
| 1850 | 156,506 |

[1] Including Croatia-Slavonia.
[2] Civilian population only.

## ICELAND

| 1801 | 47,000 |
|------|---------|
| 1840 | 57,000 |
| 1850 | 59,000 |

154

# IRELAND

| | |
|---|---|
| 1781 | 4,048,000[1] |
| 1785 | 4,019,000[1] |
| 1788 | 4,389,000[1] |
| 1790 | 4,591,000[1] |
| 1821 | 6,802,000[2] |
| 1831 | 7,767,000[2] |
| 1841 | 8,175,000[2] |

[1] Estimated figures.
[2] Civilian population only.

# ITALY[1]

| | |
|---|---|
| c.1795 | 16,257,000 |
| c.1800 | 17,237,000 |
| c.1816 | 18,381,000 |
| c.1825 | 19,727,000 |
| 1833 | 21,212,000 |
| 1838 | 21,975,000 |
| 1844 | 22,936,000 |
| 1848 | 23,617,000 |

[1] Estimated figures.

# LUXEMBOURG

| | |
|---|---|
| 1839 | 170,000 |
| 1843 | 180,000 |
| 1846 | 186,000 |
| 1849 | 190,000 |

# THE NETHERLANDS

| | |
|---|---|
| 1795 | 1,880,463[1] |
| 1816 | 2,047,000[1] |
| 1829 | 2,613,000[2] |
| 1839 | 2,861,000 |
| 1849 | 3,057,000 |

[1] Excluding Belgian provinces.
[2] Excluding Belgian provinces, but including the part of Limburg ceded by Belgium in 1839.

# NORWAY

| | |
|---|---|
| 1801 | 883,000 |
| 1815 | 885,000 |
| 1825 | 1,051,000 |
| 1835 | 1,195,000 |
| 1845 | 1,328,000 |

# PORTUGAL

| | |
|---|---|
| 1801 | 2,932,000 |
| 1821 | 3,026,000 |
| 1835 | 3,062,000 |
| 1838 | 3,224,000 |
| 1841 | 3,737,000[1] |

*Lisbon*

| | |
|---|---|
| 1801 | 350,000 |
| 1857 | 275,286 |

[1] Including the Azores and Madeira.

# RUSSIA

| | |
|---|---|
| 1796 | 36,000,000 |
| 1811 | 41,000,000 |
| 1815 | 45,000,000 |
| 1835 | 59,000,000 |

*Population in cities*

| | |
|---|---|
| 1794 | 2,279,412 |
| 1811 | 2,850,926 |
| 1825 | 3,521,052 |

# SERBIA

| | |
|---|---|
| 1834 | 678,000 |
| 1840 | 830,000 |
| 1843 | 862,000 |
| 1846 | 915,000 |
| 1850 | 957,000 |

156

## SPAIN[1]

| | |
|---|---|
| 1787 | 10,268,000 |
| 1797 | 10,541,000 |
| 1800 | 10,836,000 |
| 1820 | 11,411,924 |
| 1857 | 15,455,000 |

*Madrid*

| | |
|---|---|
| c.1800 | 156,670 |
| 1820 | 167,607 |
| 1857 | 281,170 |

[1] Including the Canary Islands.

## SWEDEN

| | |
|---|---|
| 1780 | 2,118,000 |
| 1785 | 2,150,000 |
| 1790 | 2,188,000 |
| 1795 | 2,281,000 |
| 1800 | 2,347,000 |
| 1805 | 2,427,000 |
| 1810 | 2,396,000 |
| 1815 | 2,465,000 |
| 1820 | 2,585,000 |
| 1825 | 2,771,000 |
| 1830 | 2,888,000 |
| 1835 | 3,025,000 |
| 1840 | 3,139,000 |
| 1845 | 3,317,000 |
| 1850 | 3,471,000 |

## SWITZERLAND

| | |
|---|---|
| 1837 | 2,190,000 |
| 1850 | 2,393,000 |

# UNITED KINGDOM

*England and Wales*

| | |
|---|---|
| 1801 | 8,893,000 |
| 1811 | 10,164,000 |
| 1821 | 12,000,000 |
| 1831 | 13,897,000 |
| 1841 | 15,914,000 |

*Scotland*

| | |
|---|---|
| 1801 | 1,265,000 |
| 1811 | 1,608,000 |
| 1821 | 2,092,000 |
| 1831 | 2,364,000 |
| 1841 | 2,620,000 |

*Ireland*: *see* p. 155.

# 9 ECONOMIC DEVELOPMENT

## CHRONOLOGY OF ECONOMIC EVENTS

| | |
|---|---|
| 4 Aug 89 | Feudal system abolished in France. |
| 21 Dec 89 | *Assignats* issued in France. |
| −90 | General prohibition of coalition for employers and employees in England. Oxford–Birmingham canal opened. |
| −91 | Inflation of French currency by immense issue of *assignats*. Freedom of trade introduced in France. First general strike in Germany (Hamburg). |
| −92 | Denmark became the first state to abolish slave trade. National bankruptcy in France; maximum prices introduced. Illuminating gas used in England for the first time. |
| −93 | English law *re* free insurance companies against sickness, invalidity and old age. First legal recognition of friendly societies. Board of Agriculture established in England. |
| Mar 93 | Convention between Russia and England to interdict all trade with France in the Baltic. |
| −94 | Abolition of slavery in the French colonies. Foundation of the École Polytechnique at Paris. First telegraph Paris-Lille. Eli Whitney invents cotton gin. |
| −95 | Speenhamland Act (Poor Law): wages supplemented by doles. |
| −96 | Edward Jenner introduces smallpox vaccination. Alois Senefilder invents lithography. |
| −97 | Bank of England suspends cash payment. |
| 30 Sep 97 | Repeated bankruptcy of State in France. England begins to export iron. Maudslay invents the metal lathe. |
| 22 Oct 97 | First parachute descent (from a balloon). |
| −98 | Malthus: *Essay on The Principle of Population*. Emancipation of peasants on the left bank of the Rhine. |

England abolishes free coinage of silver. Invention of the voltaic pile.

−99  Pitt introduces income tax (abolished 1802 and 1815–42). Russo-American Company obtains monopoly of Alaska. Louis Robert invents paper machine.

1800  Robert Owen starts social reforms at New Lanark. Fichte: *The Isolated Commercial State*, advocating state socialism. Bonaparte begins road over Simplon (completed 1806).

−01  Danes occupy Hamburg and Lübeck and exclude English ships from the Elbe. Bank of France founded.

−02  First protective law against child labour in England. J. W. Ritter constructs first accumulator.

−03  Robert Fulton experiments with a steamboat on the Seine. Bonaparte begins road across Mont Cenis (completed 1810). Caledonian Canal begun.

27 Oct 04  Stein appointed Prussian Minister of Trade.

−05  Abolition of internal customs duties in Prussia. Congreve re-invents the artillery rocket. First factory to be lit by gas, in Manchester.

−06  First agricultural institute in Germany.

Apr 06  England declares blockade of French coasts.

21 Nov 06  Berlin Decree; Napoleon closes Continental ports against English imports (Continental System).

−07  Abolition of slave trade in British Empire.

7 Jan 07  England declares blockade of coasts of France and her allies (again on 11 and 25 Nov 07).

7 July 07  Russia joins Continental System.

9 July 07  Prussia joins Continental System.

28 Aug 07  Introduction of commercial law code in France.

7 Dec 07  Napoleon issues Decree of Milan against British trade.

−08  Freedom of trade established in Prussia.

9 Jan 09  United States issues Non-Intercourse Act against British commerce. Sömmering (Munich) invents electric telegraph.

26 Apr 09  England restricts blockade of Europe.

14 Oct 09  Austria joins Continental System.

−10  Founding of Krupp works at Essen.

6 Jan 10  Sweden adopts Continental System.

18 and 25 Oct 10  Decrees of Fontainebleau, to confiscate and burn English goods. The *Seehandlung* becomes Bank of Prussia.

| | |
|---|---|
| 2 Feb 11 | United States renews Non-Intercourse Act. |
| 20 Feb 11 | State bankruptcy in Austria. |
| Mar 11 | Luddites begin to destroy machines in England (−1815). |
| 1 Apr 11 | Civil Code introduced in Austria. |
| Dec 11 | Secret agreement between Russia and England, aimed at breaking Continental System. Steam power used at Leeds to convey coal on a railway. |
| 11 Mar 12 | Emancipation of Jews in Prussia. |
| 23 June 12 | England revokes Order in Council of 26 Apr 09 *re* American vessels. |
| 1 July 13 | Abolition of trade monopoly of East India Company. State bankruptcy in Denmark. |
| 25 July 14 | Stephenson uses first effective steam locomotive. Apprenticeship and Wages Act of 1563 repealed. |
| Feb 15 | Ricardo: *Essay on the Influence of a Low Price of Corn on the Profits of Stock*. Puddling process introduced in England. John Macadam appointed Surveyor-General of British roads. |
| Mar 15 | Corn Law passed. |
| −16 | Gold standard restored in Britain. |
| −17 | D. Ricardo: *Principles of Political Economy and Taxation*. W. Cobbett: *Paper against Gold: The History and Mystery of the Bank of England*. |
| 26 May 18 | English Board of Agriculture abolished. |
| −19 | Twelve-hour day for young workers in England. Adam Müller: *Necessity of a Theological Foundation of all Political Economics*. Serfdom abolished in Mecklenburg. *Savannah*, the first ship fitted with steam engine, crosses the Atlantic (26 days). |
| −20 | First iron steamship in England. Robert Malthus: *Principles of Political Economy*. |
| −21 | St Simon: *Système industriel*. |
| 1 May 21 | Bank of England resumes cash payments. |
| −22 | Fourier: *Traité de l'association domestique agricole*. |
| −23 | St Simon: *Catéchisme des industriels*. Electromotor invented. |
| −24 | Anti-combination laws repealed; workmen in England allowed to combine. |
| −25 | First steam-locomotive railway, between Stockton and Darlington. St Simon: *Nouveau Christianisme*. |
| −26 | First German gasworks at Hanover. |

161

| | |
|---|---|
| −28 | Central German customs associations of Prussia–Hesse and Bavaria–Württemberg. |
| −30 | Charles Babbage designs first computing machine. Liverpool-Manchester railway opened. |
| −31 | Revolts of silk-weavers at Lyons (also in 1834). Faraday discovers electro-magnetism. |
| −32 | First railway in mainland Europe completed, from Budweis to Linz. |
| 22 Mar 33 | German *Zollverein* established. Gauss and Weber invent telegraph. |
| July 33 | Factory inspection introduced in England. |
| −34 | New English law of inheritance sets individual before family. Robert Owen: *The Book of the New Moral World*. |
| 1 Aug 34 | Slavery terminated in British possessions. |
| −35 | Baden joins *Zollverein*. |
| 7 Dec 35 | First German railway between Nuremberg and Fürth. |
| −36 | Chartist movement (−1848). First train in London (to Greenwich). V. Considérant: *Destinée sociale*. Gold discovered in Wales at Clogan St David's. |
| −37 | First patent for electric telegraph. |
| 31 July 38 | First Irish Poor Law. |
| 24 Sep 38 | Anti-Corn-Law League founded. |
| 9 Mar 39 | First prohibition of child labour in Prussia. Louis Blanc: *L'Organisation du travail*. Photography invented by Daguerre and Fox Talbot. |
| 10 Jan 40 | Rowland Hill introduces penny postage. Proudhon: *Qu'est-ce que la propriété?* (*C'est le vol!*). First Opium War between China and Britain. |
| −41 | First law for protection of workmen in France. F. List: *National System of Political Economy*. |
| −42 | Ashley's Act forbidding child or female labour underground. Peel abolishes prohibition of imports of meat and cattle. |
| −43 | First workmen's Co-operative Societies (Pioneers of Rochdale). *The Economist* started. |
| −44 | Graham's Factory Act regulates working hours of women and children. First workmen's union in Germany. Weavers' riots in Silesia and Bohemia. |
| −45 | Friedrich Engels: *Situation of the Working Classes in England*. |
| Aug 45 | Beginning of potato disease in Ireland. First Roman Catholic journeymen's association, founded by Kolping. |

| | |
|---|---|
| —46 | Zeiss optical factory opened in Jena. Repeal of Corn Laws. Invention of gun-cotton by Schönbein. |
| —47 | Hamburg-America shipping line founded. |
| —48 | Karl Marx and Friedrich Engels issue *Communist Manifesto*. |

## MINERAL PRODUCTION

### AUSTRIA (CISLEITHANIA)

| | Coal (tonnes '000) | Iron ore (tonnes '000) | Pig iron (tonnes '000) |
|---|---|---|---|
| 1819 | 95 | | |
| 1820 | 125 | | |
| 1825 | 152 | 192 | |
| 1828 | | | 73 |
| 1830 | 214 | 235 | |
| 1835 | 251 | 280 | |
| 1840 | 473 | 429 | |
| 1841 | | | 113 |
| 1845 | 689 | 429 | 134 |
| 1848 | 884 | 687 | 146 |

### BELGIUM

| | Coal (tonnes '000) | Pig iron (tonnes '000) |
|---|---|---|
| 1831 | 2305 | 90 |
| 1835 | 2639 | 115 |
| 1840 | 3930 | 95 |
| 1845 | 4919 | 135 |
| 1848 | 4863 | 162 |

### FRANCE

| | Coal[1] (tonnes '000) | Iron ore (tonnes '000) | Pig iron (tonnes '000) | Crucible steel and wrought iron (tonnes '000) |
|---|---|---|---|---|
| 1802 | 844 | | | |
| 1811 | 774 | | | |
| 1815 | 882 | | | |

FRANCE

| | Coal[1] (tonnes '000) | Iron ore (tonnes '000) | Pig iron (tonnes '000) | Crucible steel and wrought iron (tonnes '000) |
|---|---|---|---|---|
| 1819 | | | 113 | |
| 1820 | 1094 | | | |
| 1825 | 1491 | | 199 | 144 |
| 1830 | 1863 | | 266 | 148 |
| 1835 | 2506 | 830 | 295 | 210 |
| 1840 | 3003 | 995 | 348 | 240 |
| 1845 | 4202 | 2460 | 439 | 355 |
| 1848 | 4000 | | 472 | 283 |

[1] Hard coal and lignite.

GERMANY

| | Coal | | Iron ore | Pig iron | Copper | Zinc |
|---|---|---|---|---|---|---|
| | Hard (tonnes '000) | Brown | (tonnes '000) | | (tonnes '000) | |
| 1817 | 1300 | | | | | |
| 1820 | 1300 | | | | | |
| 1822 | | | 175 | | | |
| 1823 | | | | 85 | | |
| 1825 | 1600 | | 192 | 95 | | |
| 1830 | 1800 | | 235 | 110 | | |
| 1835 | 2100 | | 280 | 155 | | |
| 1837 | | 500 | | | 32 | 51 |
| 1840 | 3200 | 700 | 429 | 190 | 30 | 53 |
| 1845 | 4400 | 1200 | 429 | 190 | 35 | 127 |
| 1848 | 4400 | 1700 | 687 | 210 | 41 | 127 |

HUNGARY

| | Coal (tonnes '000) | Pig iron (tonnes '000) |
|---|---|---|
| 1841 | | 24 |
| 1842 | 19 | |
| 1845 | 21 | 32 |

LUXEMBOURG

|  | *Pig iron*<br>*(tonnes '000)* |
|---|---|
| 1842 | 12 |
| 1845 | 13 |
| 1848 | 18 |

RUSSIA

|  | *Pig iron*[1]<br>*(tonnes '000)* |
|---|---|
| 1789 | 123 |
| 1790 | 128 |
| 1795 | 135 |
| 1800 | 160 |
| 1805 | 149 |
| 1810 | 144 |
| 1814 | 123 |
| 1820 | 135 |
| 1825 | 158 |
| 1830 | 187 |
| 1835 | 175 |
| 1840 | 189 |
| 1845 | 187 |
| 1848 | 198 |

[1]  Figures apply to the 50 provinces of European Russia (excluding Finland, Poland and the Caucasus).

SWEDEN

|  | *Iron ore*<br>*(tonnes '000)* | *Pig iron*<br>*(tonnes '000)* |
|---|---|---|
| 1836 | 236 | 107 |
| 1840 | 261 | 125 |
| 1845 | 234 | 98 |
| 1848 | 289 | 143 |

UNITED KINGDOM

| | Coal (tonnes '000) | Pig iron (tonnes '000) | Copper[1] (tonnes '000) | Tin (tonnes) | Lead (tonnes) |
|---|---|---|---|---|---|
| 1788 | | 69 | | | |
| 1789 | | | | 3500 | |
| 1790 | | | | 3200 | |
| 1795 | | | | 3500 | |
| 1796 | | 127 | 5100 | | |
| 1800 | | | 5300 | 2600 | |
| 1805 | | | 6300 | 2800 | |
| 1806 | | 248 | | | |
| 1810 | | | 5800 | 2000 | |
| 1815 | | | 6600 | 3000 | |
| 1816 | 16,200 | | | | |
| 1818 | | 330 | | | |
| 1820 | 17,700 | 374 | 7600 | 3000 | |
| 1825 | 22,300 | 591 | 8300 | 4400 | |
| 1830 | 22,800 | 688 | 11,100 | 4500 | |
| 1835 | 28,100 | 1016 | 12,500 | 4300 | |
| 1840 | 34,200 | 1419 | 11,200 | | |
| 1845 | 46,600 | 1537 | 13,100 | | 53,500 |
| 1848 | | | 13,100 | 10,300[2] | 55,800 |

[1] Figures relate only to copper sold publicly in Cornwall and Devon.
[2] Crude ore.

## AGRICULTURAL PRODUCTION

AUSTRIA

| | Wheat | Rye | Barley (hectolitres '000) | Oats | Maize | Potatoes |
|---|---|---|---|---|---|---|
| 1842 | 9399 | 23,521 | 15,996 | 28,850 | 2156 | 41,992 |
| 1845 | 9634 | 23,534 | 16,173 | 30,171 | 2677 | 40,687 |

BELGIUM

| | Wheat | Rye | Barley (hectolitres '000) | Oats | Potatoes | Sugar Beet[1] |
|---|---|---|---|---|---|---|
| 1846 | 3584 | 2055 | 1143 | 4770 | 15,292 | 78 |

[1] Tonnes '000.

## FRANCE

| | Wheat | Rye | Barley | Oats | Maize[1] | Potatoes |
|------|-------|------|--------|------|-------|----------|
| | | | (tonnes '000) | | | |
| 1815 | 2960 | 1400 | 830 | 1710 | 410 | 1630 |
| 1820 | 3330 | 1800 | 1240 | 1960 | 410 | 3090 |
| 1825 | 4580 | 1890 | 920 | 1580 | 460 | |
| 1830 | 3960 | 1910 | 1280 | 2460 | 510 | 4170 |
| 1835 | 5380 | 2340 | 1160 | 2320 | 490 | 5470 |
| 1840 | 6070 | 1970 | 1080 | 2290 | 540 | 6920 |
| 1845 | 5400 | | | | | 5920 |
| 1848 | 6600 | | | | | 6640 |

[1] Includes millet.

## GERMANY

| | Wheat | Rye | Barley | Oats | Potatoes | Sugar Beet |
|------|-------|------|--------|------|----------|-----------|
| | | | (tonnes '000) | | | |
| 1846 | 1416 | 2927 | 1533 | 2383 | 7055 | 233 |

## IRELAND

| | Wheat | Barley | Oats | Potatoes |
|------|-------|--------|------|----------|
| | | (tonnes '000) | | |
| 1847 | 624 | 297 | 1639 | 2081 |

## NETHERLANDS

| | Wheat | Rye | Barley | Oats | Potatoes |
|------|-------|------|--------|------|----------|
| | | | (hectolitres '000) | | |
| 1842 | 1051 | 2642 | 1101 | 2296 | |
| 1845 | 1168 | 2927 | 1284 | 2735 | |
| 1848 | 1749 | 3410 | 1452 | 2634 | 8217 |

## NORWAY

| | Wheat | Rye | Barley | Oats | Potatoes |
|------|-------|------|--------|------|----------|
| | | | (tonnes '000) | | |
| 1845 | 1.5 | 10 | 62 | 112 | 394 |

SWEDEN

| | Wheat | Rye | Barley | Oats | Potatoes |
|------|------|------|------|------|------|
| | | | (tonnes '000) | | |
| 1802 | 14 | 140 | 165 | 105 | 44 |
| 1805 | 14 | 158 | 157 | 100 | 56 |
| 1810 | 15 | 193 | 177 | 113 | 90 |
| 1815 | 17 | 172 | 201 | 106 | 122 |
| 1820 | 20 | 213 | 209 | 119 | 216 |
| 1825 | 31 | 286 | 234 | 139 | 404 |
| 1830 | 33 | 307 | 241 | 152 | 469 |
| 1835 | 36 | 319 | 230 | 156 | 517 |
| 1840 | 36 | 308 | 244 | 167 | 596 |
| 1845 | 44 | 353 | 273 | 199 | 676 |
| 1850 | 48 | 366 | 282 | 209 | 624 |

# INTERNATIONAL TRADE

| | Imports | Exports |
|------|------|------|

AUSTRIA/HUNGARY

| | Imports | Exports |
|------|------|------|
| | (kronen m.) | |
| 1831 | 137 | 160 |
| 1840 | 222 | 217 |
| 1845 | 244 | 226 |
| 1848 | 176 | 97 |

BELGIUM

| | Imports | Exports |
|------|------|------|
| | (francs m.) | |
| 1848 | 182 | 151 |

FINLAND

| | Imports | Exports |
|------|------|------|
| | (marks m.) | |
| 1820 | 4 | 7 |
| 1830 | 8 | 9 |
| 1840 | 13 | 13 |
| 1848 | 20 | 13 |

| FRANCE | *Imports* | *Exports* |
|---|---|---|
| | *( francs m.)* | |
| 1800 | 323 | 272 |
| 1810 | 339 | 366 |
| 1820 | 335 | 543 |
| 1830 | 489 | 453 |
| 1840 | 747 | 695 |
| 1845 | 856 | 848 |
| 1848 | 474 | 690 |

| GREECE | | |
|---|---|---|
| | *( drachmas m.)* | |
| 1849 | 21 | 13 |

| NETHERLANDS | | |
|---|---|---|
| | *( gulden m.)* | |
| 1846 | 162 | 118 |
| 1848 | 181 | 124 |

| RUSSIA | | |
|---|---|---|
| | *( paper roubles m.)* | |
| 1820 | 245 | 223 |
| 1830 | 198 | 272 |
| 1840 | 78 | 85 |
| 1845 | 83 | 92 |
| 1848 | 91 | 88 |

| SPAIN | | |
|---|---|---|
| | *( pesetas m.)* | |
| 1845 | 144 | 105 |
| 1848 | 135 | 117 |

| SWEDEN | | |
|---|---|---|
| | *( kroner m.)* | |
| 1840 | 27 | 31 |
| 1845 | 26 | 37 |
| 1848 | 35 | 32 |

| UNITED KINGDOM | Imports | Exports |
|---|---|---|
| | *(£m)* | |
| 1800 | 30,570 | 38,120 |
| 1810 | 41,136 | 45,869 |
| 1820 | 36,514 | 51,733 |
| 1830 | 46,245 | 66,735 |
| 1840 | 62,004 | 97,402 |
| 1845 | 85,281 | 131,564 |
| 1850 | 95,252 | 175,126 |

# 10 THE EXPANSION OF EUROPE: COLONIES AND DEPENDENCIES

The colonies and dependencies are arranged in alphabetical order of the European 'mother-country' – Denmark, France, Britain, the Netherlands, Portugal, Russia, Spain and Sweden.

Details of Governors, Residents and Administrators of the colonies and dependencies are listed in: Cook, C. and Keith, B., *British Historical Facts, 1830–1900* (London: Macmillan, 1975) and Henige, D. P., *Colonial Governors from the Fifteenth Century to Present* (Madison: University of Wisconsin Press, 1970).

## DENMARK

*Danish Gold Coast.* Denmark abolished the slave trade by 1803, on which it depended for its prosperity in the trading centres. In 1850 Britain purchased all the fortifications and integrated them into the Gold Coast.

*Danish West Indies.* The Danish West India Company began the settlement of St Thomas in 1672, and in 1683 claimed St John also, colonizing the island in 1717. In 1733 St John was abandoned after a slave rebellion and, in the same year, Denmark bought St Croix from the French. This island was the seat of the Governor-General from 1756 to 1871, while the other two islands retained a separate but subordinate administration. By this time the group had been made a Danish royal colony (in 1754) and Charlotte Amalie a free port (in 1755). From 1801 to 1802, and again from 1807 to 1815, the Danish West Indies, like almost all overseas European colonies, were occupied by the British, but they were restored in 1815. A serious slave rebellion in 1848 resulted in the abolition of slavery in that year, causing a general decline in economic activity.

*Tranquebar.* Tranquebar was the chief settlement of the Danish East India Company from 1620; the 3 mainland posts of Tranquebar were sold to Britain in 1845, following the British occupation of 1808–15, while the Nicobar Islands were gradually abandoned after 1848 and were finally ceded to Britain in 1869.

# FRANCE

*Algeria.* An unpaid debt dating from the 1790s, owed by France to the Bey of Algiers, caused an incident in 1827 which led to a French invasion of Algeria in 1830, following a naval blockade. Algiers itself was taken in the first year of the war, and in 1837 Constantine capitulated. However, the opposition of the Berber leader, Abd Al-kadir, meant that the French were unable to gain control of the near interior until 1847. Dispensing with the form of a protectorate, the French deposed the Bey and from the first ruled the area directly. Until 1879 Algeria was a military province, but after that date it had a civil government and a quasi-colonial relationship with the metropolis. French colonization and development in the territory was greater than that in any other of their overseas possessions.

*Cochin China.* French interest in the region culminated in the occupation of the area around the Mekong River delta, beginning in 1858, and in the following year Saigon was taken. As a result of the French occupation, Annam ceded the eastern province of Cochin China, which included Saigon, Mytho and Bienhoa, to France in 1863, and the western province, which included Chaudoc, Hatien and Vinhlong, in 1867. Cochin China was administered as a colony, unlike the other parts of Indochina which were French protectorates, and it joined the Union of Indochina in 1887.

*French Guiana.* The first French attempts at colonization from 1604 onwards failed, and the colonists were ousted by the Dutch who were, in turn, evicted by the French in 1664. By about 1700 the French had a more secure grip on the territory, and, although a further attempt at colonization (1763–5) was abortive, French Guiana grew in population and prosperity. From 1794 to 1805 it received a large number of deportees from France, and after 1852 became France's principal penal colony. It was occupied by Britain in 1803 and by Portuguese from Brazil in 1809, but was restored to France in 1817, from which time it flourished until the final abolition of slavery in 1848 brought ruin to the plantations. In the same year the inhabitants of French Guiana were granted full French citizenship and the right to vote.

172

*French India.* The French established their territorial limits in India in 1816, after which French India, known as the *Établissements français dans l'Inde,* consisted of Pondichéry, Karikal, and Yanaon (Yanam) on the Coromandel coast, Mahé on the Malabar coast, and Chandernagore in Bengal. Pondichéry had been acquired by France in 1674, and had been captured in 1761, 1778 and 1793 by the British in the course of the Anglo-French power struggle in India, being the principal settlement in French India. Karikal was acquired in 1739, while Yanaon was established as a trading post in 1750. Although the latter was occupied by the British in 1793 it was restored to France in 1817.

Mahé, important as the only French possession on the west coast of India, was occupied by the French *c.* 1725. In 1761, and again in 1779, it was captured by the British, but was restored to France finally in 1817.

The settlement of Chandernagore was begun by France in 1673, and under Dupleix became of considerable commercial importance. Taken in 1757 and 1794 by the British, it was finally returned to France in 1815.

*French Polynesia.* Tahiti was made a French protectorate in 1842 at the request of its ruler, and 2 years later the Gambier group, to which French missionaries had been sent in 1834, was similarly granted French protection. Eventually Tahiti was annexed, although this was later rescinded in 1847 by the French government, the protectorate only being continued, and the colony was finally ceded to France in 1880. Other islands were acquired from 1842 onwards; the Tuamotus were claimed as dependencies of Tahiti within the protectorate of France in 1847, becoming part of the colony in 1880, the Marquesas were ceded to the French in 1842, while Rimatara and Rurutu were placed under the French protectorate in 1889 and annexed in 1900.

*Gabon.* By the late eighteenth century the French had gained a dominant position in the region, which was an important centre of the slave trade until this was abolished in 1815. The French signed treaties with the African rulers of the Ogooué estuary in 1839 and 1841, and Christian missions were established there between 1842 and 1844, while additional treaties were signed with other neighbouring native leaders from 1842 to 1862. Libreville was founded by the French in 1849 as a settlement for freed slaves.

French settlements on the Gabon coast were subject to Senegal in 1843.

*Guadeloupe.* Taken over by the French as a trading post in 1626, Guadeloupe remained in French hands until 1759 when it was occupied by the British until 1763. Restored to France in 1763, it was occupied a second time by the British in 1794, allied with French Royalists, and was later again under British control during the periods 1810–14 and 1815–16, after which it was finally restored to France.

*Ivory Coast.* By 1843 a French military mission had established protectorates at Grand-Bassau and Assinie in the coastal zone, and posts were set up there and later at nearby Dabou. These establishments, like those in Gabon, were under the general authority of the commandant of the naval division of the west coast of Africa.

*Louisiana.* The territory was first claimed for France in 1682, and serious colonization began in 1699, New Orleans being established in 1718. In 1731 it became a French crown colony, but it was later ceded, together with New Orleans, to Spain by a secret treaty of 1762. Louisiana then remained in Spanish hands until 1800 when it was restored to France, who sold the territory (Louisiana Purchase) in 1803 to the United States of America.

*Madagascar.* A French colony at Fort Dauphin was maintained from 1643 to 1674 as a way-station on voyages to the East Indies and India. During the eighteenth century the Mascareigne Islands to the east were colonized by the French with the help of Malagasy slaves. In 1750 the island of Ste Marie was ceded to the French, and in 1841 the island of Nosy Bé. Two attempts at fortified settlement during this period failed, one at Fort Dauphin, the other at Antongil Bay, but French trading settlements prospered, particularly the one at Tamatave.

In 1817 a native ruler, Radama I, allied himself with the British on Mauritius and captured Tamatave, and from that time launched annual expeditions against the coastal populations, eventually conquering almost the entire east coast, together with large areas of the rest of the island. The French retained only the island of Ste Marie.

*Martinique.* The island was first occupied by the French in 1635 when a settlement was founded at Fort Saint-Pierre by Pierre d'Esnambuc. The following year his nephew, Jacques Dyel du Parquet, bought the island from the *Compagnie des Isles d'Amérique* and developed it into a very prosperous colony. In 1658 the French king, Louis XV, resumed sovereignty over Martinique, and in 1674 it was made part of the French crown domain, being administered according to the *Pacte Colonial.* It was not until 1787, under Louis XVI, that the island was granted the right to establish a Colonial Assembly.

There were British occupations in 1762–3, 1794–1802 and 1809–14, after which the island was finally restored to France.

Slave uprisings occurred in 1789, 1815 and 1822, and the abolition of slavery in 1848 created a considerable labour shortage. In the same year universal suffrage was proclaimed, although it was later abolished by Napoleon III.

*Mayotte.* Mayotte, one of the Comoro Islands, was ceded to France by its ruler, Andriantsuli, in 1841 and became a French protectorate from 1843 while attached to Réunion.

*Nosy Bé.* Nosy Bé, an island off the north-west coast of Madagascar, was ceded to France by its Sakalava ruler in 1840. It was used as a naval station almost exclusively, although some settlement was attempted. Until 1843 it was under Réunion, then under Mayotte until 1878, when it was made a separate colony.

*Réunion.* The island was uninhabited until settled by the French in *c.* 1642 as a penal colony. In 1665 it became a post of the French East India Company, when the name of the island was Bourbon. From 1806–10 the name was changed to Bonaparte but reverted to Bourbon in 1810 when the island was occupied by the British, and remained so called until 1848. After 1815 the British retained Île de France and the Seychelles, and Réunion became the only French possession in the Indian Ocean.

*Sainte Marie de Madagascar.* Sainte Marie was ceded to the French by its Malagasy ruler in 1750, but it remained unoccupied until 1819. Until 1843 it was under Bourbon. From 1843 to 1853 it was subject to Mayotte, and from 1853 to 1877 it was a separate colony. In 1878 it was returned to Réunion's jurisdiction where it remained until 1896 when, like France's other small colonies on Madagascar, it became part of Madagascar.

*Saint Pierre and Miquelon.* First settled by Basques, but probably the islands were colonized by France in 1604. In 1713 they were taken by the British but restored to France in 1763; twice retaken by Britain, they were finally returned to the French in 1814 with the provision that they be unfortified.

*Senegal.* The French established a post at the mouth of the River Senegal in 1638 and in 1659 founded St Louis on an island there. With the capture of Gorée from the Dutch in 1677 they gained an important naval base in West Africa, and French influence was extended into the interior. During the Seven Years War (1756–63) Britain captured all the French posts in Senegal, returning only Gorée in 1763. France retook her possessions between 1775 and 1783, although she was compelled to surrender Gorée to Britain under the Treaty of Paris (1783). In 1809 she lost them again but recovered them finally in 1817. At this time the French presence was limited to St Louis, Gorée and Rufisque, and there was little contact with the interior during the first half of the nineteenth century.

*Wallis Islands.* The islands were governed as a French protectorate from 1842, being administered by the High Commissioner of New Caledonia.

# GREAT BRITAIN

*Aden.* The British established themselves in 1839, when they seized the town from the Sultan of Lahej in an almost bloodless *coup.*

*Afghanistan.* In 1809 the British concluded a treaty of friendship with the Shah to counter the threat of a Russian attack on India. British interest in Afghanistan continued, and in 1839 a British client ruler, Shah Sujah, was installed. By 1841, however, the country was in revolt, and the British expeditionary force was blockaded in Kabul, making a retreat to India necessary. The retreat was unsuccessful, the vast majority of the British troops being massacred, and Shah Sujah was deposed. Attempts by the British in 1842 to regain their influence met with little success, and Afghanistan was evacuated.

*Ajmer and Merwara.* Ajmer and Merwara were ceded to the British by the Sindhia ruler of Gwalior in 1818, and between 1832 and 1871 were part of the North-West Frontier Provinces.

*Andaman and Nicobar Islands.* The Andaman Islands had been used as a penal colony by the British in India from 1789 to 1796, when the colony was abandoned. In 1858 the penal colony was re-established.

*Assam.* In 1786 the Assamese sought the help of the British against Burma. Peace was restored, but a Burmese invasion of Assam in 1817 prompted further intervention by the British. Subsequently Britain concluded the Treaty of Yandabo with Burma in 1826 by which Assam, Arakan and the coast of Tenasserim were ceded to Britain, and the territory of Assam was administered as part of Bengal until 1919.

*Assiniboia.* The region of Assiniboia, which was the official name of the Red River Settlement, was formed in 1811 by a grant from the Hudson's Bay Company, and until 1836 was governed by Lord Selkirk and his heirs. Thereafter, having been re-acquired by the Hudson's Bay Company, the territory was created the 'District of Assiniboia', and was administered by a local governor and council who were appointed by the Company, until it was absorbed into the newly created province of Manitoba in 1870.

176

*Australia.* Britain's interest in Australia dated from the late seventeenth century with the voyages of William Dampier. He was succeeded by Capt. James Cook who landed in several places during 1770, notably at Botany Bay and Possession Island, where he claimed the land, giving it the name New South Wales. His voyages led to settlements from which further exploration was carried out. In 1798 Tasmania was circumnavigated by Flinders and Bass, and in 1802 Port Phillip was discovered. In 1801 Flinders completed the charting of Australia, and the name was changed from New Holland to Australia in 1817.

New South Wales was colonized by the British in 1788, and many convicts were deported there, the first settlement being founded at Port Jackson. An out-station was founded at Norfolk Island in the same year, but abandoned in 1813. It was revived in 1825 to provide a prison for law-breakers from the mainland.

In 1829 an area around Sydney was designated the Nineteen Counties, and settlement in the region was encouraged.

South Tasmania was settled in 1803. The settlements were united in 1812 and were supervised by Sydney. Other penal out-stations were established, Newcastle in 1804 and Moreton Bay in 1824. During the mid-1820s the British extended their possession over the entire continent.

The government was authoritarian: all the governors were military officers, and there were no representative bodies until the Judicature Acts of 1823 and 1828 by which executive and legislative councils were established. These councils comprised the chief government officers and an equal number of private individuals, who were appointed by nomination. Supreme courts of justice were set up in New South Wales in 1814 and in Tasmania in 1824.

Further exploration, in particular the passage of the Blue Mountains in 1813, led to the formation of more states: 4 of the eventual 6 were formed between 1829 and 1859. In 1837 the first colonists of South Australia founded Adelaide, Melbourne was created in 1835, and in 1851 the name Victoria was granted to the Port Phillip District. Queensland came into being in 1859.

All the colonies with the exception of Western Australia eventually gained responsible self-government, led by New South Wales in 1842.

*Bahama Islands.* The first British settlers arrived early in the seventeenth century from Bermuda, but the first systematic colonization was undertaken by the Eleutheran Adventurers in 1648.

In 1776 the islands were taken by America, and in 1781 by Spain, but they were restored to Britain as a Crown colony under the Treaty of Paris (1783). The Bahamas became a refuge for many loyalists after the American Civil War and gained considerable prosperity, but with the emancipation of slaves in 1833 the plantations declined.

*Bahrain.* In 1805 the British intervened to restore peace and suppress piracy, and in 1820 a treaty was concluded. It was not until 1861, however, that Bahrain became a British protectorate.

*Barbados.* In 1605 the British landed in Barbados but it was 1627 before settlement took place. It became a Crown colony in 1662 but was governed by the Governor of the Windward Islands from 1833 to 1885, not becoming a separate colony until 1885.

*Bay Islands.* The British Crown claimed the islands in 1841 and in 1852 they became a Crown colony. Unrest was caused in 1848 by the garrisoning of the islands by the British, but the situation was improved by the Clayton-Bulwer Treaty (1850) and eventual cession of the colony to Honduras in 1859.

*Bengal.* The first settlement in Bengal by Britain was made in 1642 by the British East India Company. Having ousted the Dutch and French, and conquered the native rulers, the Company was able to establish the nucleus of a presidency at Fort William in 1700. The British victories of Plassey (1757) and Buxar (1764) terminated Moslem control of Bengal and added most of the Ganges plain, including Agra province, to the British-controlled territory. Bengal was granted the administration of the presidencies of Bombay and Madras in 1774, and acquired Orissa in 1803 and Assam in 1826, while Agra was detached in 1833. Calcutta (Fort William) became the capital of India in 1833.

The term 'Bengal' was used during the nineteenth century to denote the area of British control in North India and included the Punjab.

*Bermuda.* The islands were uninhabited until the English Admiral Sir George Somers was shipwrecked there in 1609. Then, in 1612, they were included in the Virginia Company's third charter and received 60 settlers, remaining under company administration until they were acquired by the British Crown in 1684. However, Bermuda never became solely a Crown colony: government was the joint responsibility of the Virginia Company and the Sovereign. In 1767 Bermuda was made a base for the British fleet. The capital was moved in 1815 from St George Town (founded 1612) to Hamilton.

*British Columbia.* Capt. Cook visited the territory in 1778. Spain laid claims to the area but in 1790 relinquished it to the British under the Nootka Convention. In 1805 the first trading post was established at McLeod Lake, and many additional posts followed the absorption of the North-West Company into the Hudson's Bay Company in 1821. The territory was not completely defined until 1903, although the Washington (Oregon) Treaty of

1846 fixed the southern boundary at the 49th parallel, with a deviation to include Vancouver Island. This island was granted to the Hudson's Bay Company and in 1849 became a Crown colony. The mainland colony of British Columbia was not established until after the gold rush of 1858, and until then was known as New Caledonia. Although a separate colony, it was governed by the Governor of Vancouver Island.

*British Guiana.* During the early seventeenth century the English founded colonies in the area, but in 1667 was forced to cede them to the Dutch by the Treaty of Breda. Between 1796 and 1802 the British again held the colonies of Essequibo, Berbice and Demerara, but they did not finally gain possession of them until 1815. In 1831 the 3 colonies were united as British Guiana.

*British Honduras.* The colony was founded in the early seventeenth century by British buccaneers, but possession was disputed with Spain until the Battle of St George's Cay in 1798 after which the British settlers were unchallenged until 1821, when the area was claimed by Guatemala. This claim was abrogated in 1859.

*British Kaffraria.* British Kaffraria became a Crown colony in 1847 and was annexed to the Cape Colony in 1866.

*British Virgin Islands.* The British Virgin Islands have been in British possession since 1666, when they were acquired from the Dutch.

*Burma.* Arakan and Tenasserim were annexed in 1824–6 following the First Anglo-Burmese War and, after a second war, Pegu was annexed in 1852–3. In 1862 the 3 provinces were united to form Lower Burma. In 1885 Upper Burma was annexed and the whole territory called Burma.

*Canada.* John Cabot reached the east coast of Canada in 1497, but France established the first Canadian settlements. Britain attacked Port Royal in 1614 and captured Quebec and Champlain in 1629, but Quebec was restored to the French in 1632. By the Peace of Utrecht (1713) Britain gained Acadia, the Hudson Bay area and Newfoundland, and in 1759 retook Quebec, followed in 1760 by Montreal.

In 1763 Britain acquired all France's North American possessions, except Louisiana, by the Treaty of Paris. From then until 1791 Canada was under British rule, during which time the province of New Brunswick was founded (1784).

In 1791 the British government decided to attempt to assimilate the French population of Quebec by the Canada Constitutional Act. At this time Canada

179

was divided into two separate provinces, Upper and Lower Canada, the latter comprising a large proportion of French. By this Act both provinces were given the same constitution.

Following the war with America in 1812 the boundary line between the United States and Canada in the Great Lakes area was finally settled, although the rest of the boundary was disputed until 1846.

Agitation by constitutional reformers resulted in a general uprising in 1837, and consequently the Earl of Durham, who was sent to Canada in 1838, urged that 'responsible government' be granted: this was not realized, however, until 1848. Before that the British government allowed the union of the two provinces to form the single province of Canada (1841); self-government was granted first to Nova Scotia , then to Canada, in 1848. The eastern provinces of Nova Scotia, Prince Edward Island, Cape Breton, New Brunswick and Newfoundland were governed as separate colonies until the granting of autonomy.

By the Treaty of Oregon (1846) the United States–Canadian boundary was permanently fixed at the 49th parallel, and Vancouver Island was allotted to Britain.

*Cape Colony.* The Dutch first settled the area in 1652 with the founding of Cape Town, and although the British captured the colony in 1795 it was restored in 1803. In 1806 it was again seized by Britain and Cape Colony was established. The Cape settlement was finally ceded to the British in 1814, becoming the Colony of the Cape of Good Hope, and in 1820 a large number of settlers arrived from England and founded Albany and Port Elizabeth. The Dutch Boers founded the Orange Free State and Transvaal (1836–8). In 1835 the Governor of Cape Colony annexed Kaffraria, and Natal was established in 1843. Parliamentary government was introduced in 1852.

*Cayman Islands.* In 1670 the Cayman Islands were ceded by Spain to Britain but not settled until 1734. Until 1900 they were locally governed by justices of the peace.

*Ceylon.* In 1795 the British took Trincomali in Ceylon from the Dutch, who surrendered the island in 1796. The British initially viewed the occupation as temporary and administered the island from Madras, but once they became aware of its strategic importance they decided to retain it; in 1802 their possession of Ceylon was confirmed by the Treaty of Amiens and it became a Crown colony. In 1815 the inland kingdom of Kandy was conquered and Britain was able to annex the entire island.

*Dominica.* The Earl of Carlisle was granted the island in 1627, but initial

180

attempts to occupy it were thwarted by the native Caribs. Attempted settlement by the French was prevented by the British in 1759, and the Treaty of Paris (1763) formally ceded the island to Britain but it was 1815 before Dominica passed to the British, and in 1833 was included in the Leeward Islands colony as a presidency.

*Falkland Islands.* The islands were probably discovered by the Englishman John Davis in 1592, but they were first settled by the French. The British took possession in 1765, and a colony was established the following year, only to be lost to Spain. It was not until 1832 that Britain was able to reclaim the islands which by then were in the hands of Argentina: the British needed the territory in order to protect whalers in the area. The Falkland Islands remained a Crown colony, although Argentina never abandoned its claim.

*The Gambia.* In 1588 the British won trading rights in the area from Portugal, but were unable to establish settlements until the early seventeenth century. In 1816 St Mary's Island was purchased from a local chieftain and a small fortified settlement, Banjul, was founded. The Gambia was made part of Sierra Leone in 1821, but from 1843–66 was a separate colony, after which it was returned to the administration of Sierra Leone.

*Gibraltar.* The British have been in possession of the island since 1704: it was occupied during the Spanish War of Succession and officially ceded by Spain to Britain in 1713 by the Treaty of Utrecht.

*Gold Coast.* In 1821 the Crown assumed direct control for the settlements along the Gold Coast, placing them under the control of Sierra Leone. In 1850 the nearby Danish settlements were purchased, and the combined colony ceased to remain under Sierra Leone.

*Grenada.* Grenada was captured by the British in 1762 and ceded in 1763, retaken by the French in 1779, and restored to Britain in 1783.

*Heligoland.* Heligoland was seized from Denmark by Great Britain in 1807 and formally ceded (in 1814). The island remained a colony of Great Britain until 1890, when it was ceded to Germany in return for Zanzibar.

*Hong Kong.* The island was seized by the British in 1841 during the First Chinese War. China was forced to cede the island, which was made a Crown colony, by the Treaty of Nankin in 1842: she also opened Canton, Amoy, Foochow, Ningpo and Shanghai to British trade as 'treaty ports'. The Kowloon Peninsula was ceded to Great Britain in 1860.

*Hudson's Bay Company.* Formed in 1670 the Company was granted the territory which became known as Rupert's Land. Its initial settlements were lost to the French but restored in 1713, and the conquest of Canada by Britain prompted the Company to build fur-trading posts inland, the first such post being Cumberland House, established in 1774. In 1808 the Earl of Selkirk gained control of the company and encouraged colonization, but prosperity was hindered by the rivalry of the North-West Company. The situation improved, however, when the two companies were united in 1821. American immigration began to cause a decline in trade after 1834, and in 1846 when Oregon Country was divided between the United States and Great Britain the Company's influence was considerably diminished, so that it was compelled to sell all its lands to the Dominion of Canada in 1870.

*India.* The British East India Company established a number of trading posts: Surat (1613), Bombay (1661) and Calcutta (1691), but the beginning of the British Raj in India dates from 1757. Opposition from the Sultan of Mysore was finally suppressed in 1799. In 1801 the Carnatic was annexed, followed by the outlying territories of Oudh and Tanjore.

In 1803 a protectorate was established over Poona and the Maratta princes were defeated so that, by 1805, the only remaining opposition was in the north-west. By 1818 most of India was under British rule. Control over Sind was established in 1843 and the Punjab in 1849. The Indian Mutiny of 1857 led to the British Crown taking over the administration of India from the East India Company.

*Ionian Islands.* The islands of Cephalonia, Cerigo, Corfu, Ithaca, Leucas, Paxos and Zante were occupied by Venice until 1797, when they were ceded to France. In 1799 Russia occupied the islands and created in 1800 the Septinsular Republic under its protection. Surrendered to France by the Treaty of Tilsit, they were occupied in 1809 by Great Britain and in 1815 Britain established a protectorate over the islands. Finally, in 1864, they were ceded to Greece.

*Jamaica.* Jamaica was seized by the British in 1655 and ceded by Spain in 1670. Representative government was abrogated in 1866 and only partly restored in 1884.

*Labuan.* In 1846 Labuan was ceded to Britain by the Sultan of Brunei, and became a Crown colony in 1848.

*Leeward Islands.* The first British settlement was on St Kitts in 1623, when Sir Thomas Warner was appointed Governor-General of the whole group. By

1632 the neighbouring islands were also colonized, but France and Spain disputed British possession and the islands changed hands frequently until they were finally granted to Britain in 1815. In 1833 Dominica was added to the Leeward Islands.

*Malta.* The island was captured from the Knights Hospitallers by the French in 1798, but in 1800 it was taken by a British fleet. By the Treaty of Paris (1814) Britain formally annexed the island as a British colony.

*Mauritius.* Britain seized the island in 1810, and it was ceded as a British colony in 1814.

*Montserrat.* Montserrat became a British colony in 1632. Captured by the French in 1644, it was restored in 1668, only to be retaken in 1782. It was restored to Britain the following year.

*Natal.* The first permanent European settlement was established by the British at Durban in 1824. In 1837 a number of Boers arrived in the province and, defeating the Zulus, created a republic (1838–9), but in 1843 Britain annexed the colony and most of the Boers left. The following year it became a province of Cape Colony; it did not become a separate Crown colony until 1856.

*New Brunswick.* British control of the region was confirmed by the Treaty of Utrecht (1713–14), and it became a colony in its own right in 1784 when it was separated from Nova Scotia. Responsible government was granted in 1849.

*Newfoundland.* The island was claimed for Britain in 1583 and first settled in 1610. Not until 1763, however, were Newfoundland and Labrador finally granted to Britain, although in 1783 the French regained the west coast.

Labrador was included in the government of Newfoundland from 1763; in 1832 representative government was introduced, followed by a parliamentary system in 1855.

*New Munster/New Ulster.* In 1848 New Zealand was divided administratively into New Munster, which included part of North Island, and New Ulster, which included the remainder of North Island and all of South Island. This experiment proved unsuccessful and in 1853 the two provinces were abolished.

*New South Wales.* Claimed by the British in 1770, New South Wales originally included the whole continent (except Western Australia), together with New Zealand. Tasmania was detached in 1825, South Australia in 1836,

183

New Zealand in 1841, Victoria in 1851, Queensland in 1859, and Northern Australia (which was placed under South Australia) in 1863. Sydney, its capital and the first Australian settlement, was founded in 1788. Representative government was granted in 1842.

*New Zealand.* Attempts at settlement in 1826 failed and in 1837 the New Zealand Association was formed. In 1841 New Zealand became a Crown colony. Beginning in 1843 a series of wars with the Maoris expanded the area of the colony until it included the entire area of both islands. From 1848 to 1853 New Zealand was briefly divided into New Munster and New Ulster (*qq.v.*).

*Niue.* Niue was discovered by Capt. James Cook in 1774.

*Norfolk Island.* Norfolk Island was discovered by Cook in 1774 and was used as a convict settlement by New South Wales, 1788–1844, and by Tasmania, 1844–56 (except during 1853). In 1856 administration of the island reverted to New South Wales.

*Northern Australia.* The first settlement took place in 1824 but was abandoned in 1829. More permanent settlement occurred after 1838.

*Nova Scotia.* Throughout the seventeenth century the British and French struggled for colonial rights in the region known as Acadia, which included Nova Scotia, New Brunswick and Prince Edward Island. Finally Great Britain received the Nova Scotia peninsula under the Peace of Utrecht (1713–14), although Cape Breton Island remained in French hands. In 1763 Prince Edward Island was joined to Nova Scotia, but was separated once more in 1769. Further settlements were established after *c.* 1784 with the immigration of United Empire loyalists. Cape Breton was attached to Nova Scotia in 1820.

The colony became, in 1848, the first to be granted responsible government, and in 1867 became one of the 4 original members of the Canadian Confederation.

*Orange River Colony.* In 1848 the area north of the Orange River occupied by the Boers was annexed by the Governor of Cape Colony. This annexation proved abortive and British sovereignty was transferred, under the Bloemfontein Convention of 1854, to the Boers, who established the Orange Free State.

*Pitcairn Island.* Pitcairn Island was discovered in 1767, and in 1790 it was settled by mutineers from the *Bounty*.

184

*Prince Edward Island.* Prince Edward Island was occupied by the French until its seizure by the British in 1758. From 1763–9 it was part of Nova Scotia, and was then created a separate colony.

*Punjab.* As a result of the First Sikh War the eastern part of the Punjab was annexed to British India in 1846, and the remainder was annexed in 1849.

*Queensland.* The first settlement in Queensland was a penal colony established from New South Wales in 1824, and free settlement was established in 1842. In 1859 it became a separate colony.

*Saint Helena.* St Helena was first taken by the British East India Company in 1633 and, although lost to the Dutch in 1673, was recovered in the same year. The island was administered by the East India Company until 1834, except for the period of Napoleon's exile there from 1815 to 1821, when it was directly administered by the Crown.

*Saint Kitts/Nevis/Anguilla.* St Kitts (St Christopher) was settled by the British in 1624 and was partly occupied by the French until 1713, when the islands were ceded to Britain. Nevis was first settled in 1628. Further troubles ensued, and Britain only gained undisputed possession in 1783.

*Saint Lucia.* The island was settled by the French in 1660, but the British disputed their possession, and it was finally ceded to Britain in 1803. In 1848 it was attached to the Windward Islands.

*Saint Vincent.* The island was first colonized by the British in 1762; although taken by the French in 1779 it was restored in 1783. The Carib Indians were deported in 1797.

*Sarawak.* Sarawak in northern Borneo was ceded to James Brooke by the Sultan of Brunei in 1841. Thereafter, it was ruled by Brooke.

*Seychelles Islands.* In 1794 the Seychelles were captured by the British, but they were treated as a French colony until 1810, when they were annexed and attached to Mauritius. They were formally ceded by France in 1814 by the Treaty of Paris.

*Sierra Leone.* British slave traders became prominent from the beginning of the seventeenth century, but in 1772 slavery was abolished in Britain and efforts were made to resettle freed slaves in the region, culminating in the founding of Freetown in 1792 on the Sierra Leone Peninsula.

185

The British government took over Freetown from the Sierra Leone Company in 1808, and it became a naval base for anti-slavery patrols. In the same year Sierra Leone became a Crown colony. From 1821 to 1827 and 1843 to 1850 the British possessions on the Gold Coast were administered by the Governor of Sierra Leone.

*Singapore.* Singapore was purchased by the British East India Company in 1819 from the Sultan of Johore. In 1826 it was joined with Penang and Malacca, acquired from the Dutch in 1825, to form the Straits Settlements. In 1836 it succeeded George Town (Penang) as the capital.

*South Australia.* The area of South Australia was under New South Wales until its creation in 1836, following the introduction of the South Australian Colonization Act in 1834. Convicts were not accepted as settlers as they were in Western Australia.

*Straits Settlements.* In 1786 the Sultan of Kedah ceded the island of Penang to the British East India Company. From 1791 the British paid annual sums to the Sultan in return for the territory, to which the mainland province of Wellesby was added in 1800. Singapore was founded by the British in 1819, followed in 1824 by the acquisition of Malacca from the Dutch. In 1826 Penang, Singapore and Malacca were brought under a joint administration and became known as the Straits Settlements. Until 1867 the colony was part of British India, and it then became a separate Crown colony.

*Tasmania.* Tasmania was discovered in 1642 by Tasman and named Van Diemen's Land. Great Britain annexed it to New South Wales in 1803 for use as an auxiliary penal colony. It was separated from New South Wales in 1825 and made a colony in its own right. In 1853 the island was renamed Tasmania.

*Tobago.* The British had colonized the island in 1616 but had been driven out by the native Carib Indians. It was then held by the Dutch and French, and the British finally regained it from the latter in 1803.

*Trinidad.* In 1797 Trinidad was seized from Spain by Britain, and the occupation was confirmed under the Treaty of Amiens in 1802. In 1888 the neighbouring island of Tobago was added to Trinidad, and the Crown colony was then called Trinidad and Tobago.

*Turks and Caicos Islands.* Occupied by Britain in 1766, the Turks Islands were annexed to the Bahamas in 1804 and the Caicos Islands were administered by the Bahamas from 1799. In 1848 the Turks and Caicos Islands were constituted a presidency under the Governor of Jamaica.

*Victoria.* Attempts at colonization on the site of Melbourne were made in 1803 and 1826, but the first permanent settlement in Victoria was at Portland in 1834 by free settlers from Tasmania; this was followed by the re-establishment of Melbourne in 1835. The region became part of the colony of New South Wales in 1836 and established as a separate colony, Victoria, in 1851.

*Western Australia.* A penal colony was established at Albany in 1826, followed in 1829 by the first colonial settlement, which was given the name 'Swan River Settlement'. Until 1831 Western Australia was governed by New South Wales, and in 1890 was granted responsible government.

*Windward Islands.* The islands were first colonized by the British and French in the early 17th century, with the result that there was a continuous struggle for supremacy until 1815, when the islands were ceded to Great Britain. Comprising St Lucia, St Vincent, Tobago, Grenada and the Grenadines, they were constituted a British colony in 1855.


# NETHERLANDS

*Curaçao.* The island, together with Aruba and Bonaire, was captured from Spain by the Dutch in 1634 and, although occupied by Britain during the Napoleonic Wars, Curaçao was restored in 1816. From 1828 to 1845 it was subordinated to the Government-General of the Dutch West Indies, with headquarters in Surinam. The colony, with St Eustatius, St Martin and Saba, became known as the Netherlands Antilles in 1845.

*Gold Coast.* Trading posts were established from at least the early seventeenth century. In 1867 the eastern posts were sold to Britain, and in 1872 the remaining posts were also sold for cash or for concessions in Sumatra.

*Netherlands Antilles.* In 1845 the colony of Curaçao with its dependencies of Aruba and Bonaire, and the colony of St Eustatius and its dependencies of St Martin and Saba, were united, with the seat of the government on Curaçao. They were then termed the Netherlands Antilles.

*Netherlands East Indies.* Occupation of the territory of Indonesia was begun in 1596, but the Dutch did not gain complete control until they finally ousted the

British in 1623. The Dutch East India Company then extended its influence throughout the area, but its holdings were taken over by the Dutch government in 1798 and became known as the Netherlands (or Dutch) East Indies. From 1811 to 1815 the British occupied Java and most of the other islands, but by an agreement of 1824 the Dutch were left with a free hand in the East Indies.

*Saint Eustatius.* Occupied by the Dutch in 1632, from 1828 to 1845 St Eustatius and its dependencies were part of the Government-General of the Dutch West Indies. Upon the dissolution of the Government-General in 1845 St Eustatius was attached to Curaçao and ceased to exist as a separate colony.

*Surinam.* By the Treaty of Breda (1667) the territory was granted to the Dutch by Britain in return for New Netherlands, although it was re-occupied by the British from 1799 to 1802 and in 1804. It was finally ceded to the Netherlands in 1815. It was the only Dutch possession in Guiana to be returned after the Napoleonic Wars.

## PORTUGAL

*Angola.* Angola was discovered by Diogo Cao in 1482, and Portuguese colonization began in 1575 with the founding of Luanda. It was under Portuguese control from 1491 but remained nominally independent until 1883.

*Cape Verde Islands.* Settlement of the Cape Verde Islands began in 1462.

*Macao.* Macao was leased from China in 1557, and a trading post was established. In 1849 Portugal proclaimed its sovereignty over Macao and ceased paying an annual rent to China. The Chinese confirmed the separation in 1887.

*Mozambique.* The region was visited by Vasco da Gama in 1498, but the Portuguese did not begin to settle until 1505, when Sofala was founded. During the sixteenth century they extended their influence inland, establishing trading posts along the Zambesi. Until 1752 Mozambique was ruled as part of Goa (India); subsequently the territory received separate administration. Invasion by South African peoples during the 1820s and 1830s weakened the Portuguese hold quite considerably, but by the early twentieth century their position was once again secure.

*Portuguese Guinea.* This was probably discovered in 1446 and settled in the sixteenth century. It was administered as part of the Cape Verde Islands until 1879.

*Portuguese India.* Portuguese India consisted of 3 enclaves: Goa, seized in 1510; Diu, occupied in 1535; and Damão, occupied in 1538. About 1760 the seat of government was transferred from Goa to Pangim.

*Sảb Tomé and Principe.* Discovered in 1470. The São Tomé settlement was established in 1483, and the islands were proclaimed a Portuguese colony in 1522. Captured by the Dutch in 1641, they were restored to Portugal in 1740 and were of considerable importance as supply stations until the establishment of plantations during the eighteenth century.

*Timor.* The island was first settled *c.* 1520 by the Portuguese, but the western end was occupied by the Dutch in 1618. It came under British rule 1811–16. The Dutch-Portuguese border was settled in 1859. Until 1844 Timor was under Portuguese India and from then until 1896 under Macao.

# RUSSIA

*Abkhazia.* In 1810 the area of Sukhumi was annexed by Russia from Turkey, and the Russians established a protectorate over all Abkhazia. The entire region was not formally annexed by Russia until 1864.

*Armenia.* The territory was acquired from Turkey in 1828.

*Azerbaijan.* The region, known as Albania, was disputed between Turkey and Persia until it was ceded to Russia by Persia in 1813 (Treaty of Gulistan) and 1828 (Treaty of Turkmanchai). Elizavetpol had been taken in 1804, and Baku was annexed in 1806.

*Bessarabia.* The annexation of Georgia (completed 1810) gave rise to the Russo-Turkish war (1806–12). At the Treaty of Bucharest Russia was granted Bessarabia, additional areas on the east coast of the Black Sea, and extensive rights in Moldavia and Wallachia on the Danube. Under the Treaty of Adrianople (1829) these Danubian principalities were guaranteed autonomy under a Russian protectorate.

*Crimea.* In 1783 the Crimea was annexed by Russia from Turkey. In 1787 the

Turks issued an ultimatum on the evacuation of the area, and the second Turkish War (1787–92) resulted. By the Treaty of Jassy (1792) Russia acquired Ochakov fortress and the Black Sea shore as far as the Dniester River. Turkey recognized Russia's annexation of the Crimea.

*Daghestan.* The region of Daghestan was ceded to Russia by Persia by the Treaty of Gulistan (1813).

*Finland.* Finland was invaded in 1713, and in 1721 under the Treaty of Nystad Sweden ceded the province of Vyborg to Russia. In 1809 Finland was finally given to the Russians under the Treaty of Hamina: as a grand duchy it retained some autonomy, being governed by a Russian governor-general and the Finnish Senate. The Governor-General was the personal representative of the Tsar. In 1811 Russia returned to Finland the territory taken from it in 1721 and 1743.

*Georgia.* Held by Persia and Turkey, east Georgia (Kartlia and Kakhetia) and west Georgia were acquired by Russia, the former in 1800–1 and the latter between 1803 and 1810. Kars was annexed in 1829.

*Ossetia.* From the early eighteenth century the region was strongly influenced by Russia, and by 1806 the Russians had annexed the entire territory.

*Poland.* By the partition of 1772 Russia had gained Latgale and Byelorussia east of the Dvina and Dnepr rivers. Russia again invaded Poland in 1792, and by 1793, after a second partition, only central Poland remained independent – and even this was under some Russian control.

A third partition in 1795 enabled Russia to annex Courland and Lithuania. Boundary changes in Russia's favour were also made at the Congress of Vienna (1815).

*Russian America (Alaska).* The coasts of Alaska were explored in 1741 by Bering. Various Russian trading companies were established after 1784, when Grigori Shelekhov founded the first permanent settlement (on Kodiak Island). The Russian–American Company were granted a monopoly in 1799, and prospered under the direction of Aleksandr Baranov, who founded Sitka as his capital in 1799. In 1812 he established a colony in north California.

In 1821 the Tsar claimed the 51st parallel as the territory's southern boundary, but this was disputed by Britain and the United States, and the boundary was fixed at 54° 40′ N in 1824. Subsequently, Russian influence in Alaska declined, and it was sold to the United States for $7.2 million in 1867.

# SPAIN

*California.* In 1822 California became part of the Republic of Mexico. Alta California fell into the hands of the United States in 1846, while Baja California continued to be a state of Mexico.

*Ceuta and Melilla.* Ceuta was acquired from Portugal in 1580; Melilla had been held since 1496. Governed separately until 1847. With the formation of the Spanish zone of Morocco in 1913 they lost their administrative identity.

*Cuba.* Spain began the conquest of Cuba in 1511 as a convenient base from which to launch exploratory expeditions to the Americas. With the exception of a brief British occupation (1762–3), the island remained a Spanish possession until it was occupied by the United States in 1898.

*Guam.* The island was discovered by Magellan in 1521 and belonged to Spain from 1668 until 1898, when it was ceded to the United States in the Spanish–American War.

*Philippine Islands.* Spain began a systematic conquest of the islands in 1564 and had gained a secure hold by 1571. The British gained possession of the Philippines in 1762 but restored them in 1764, after which the islands remained in Spanish hands until ceded to the United States following the Battle of Manila Bay in 1898.

*Puerto Rico.* A settlement was established by the Spanish in 1521, and the island quickly became one of the most important possessions of the Spanish Empire, being subjected to frequent attacks by the British, French and Dutch. Britain held the territory for 5 months in 1598. Uprisings against Spanish rule in the 1820s culminated in the Lares rebellion of 1868, and in 1898 some autonomy was granted to the island, only a short time before its cession to the United States by the Treaty of Paris (1898).

*Spanish Guinea.* Ceded to Spain by Portugal in 1777, the territory was abandoned by 1781 because of yellow fever. The islands were leased to Britain from 1827 to 1843, and in 1844 Spain re-acquired Fernando Po and began to establish settlements. The Spanish started to administer the area in 1855.

# SWEDEN

*Saint Bathélemy.* This was a neutral port during the French Revolution and

191

became prosperous. After the Revolution it became an economic liability to Sweden, which had bought it from France in 1784, and the Swedish government attempted to sell it to the United States in 1845, 1868 and 1870. France re-purchased the island in 1878 and incorporated it as a dependency of Guadeloupe.

# INDEX

Most of the chapters in this book run in alphabetical sequence and for this reason we have not attempted to produce a completely detailed index. The main aim has been to allow the reader to locate the country or event by page for any major subject included in this publication.